CRUTCHLESS

Crutchless

AND FIVE LIFE LESSONS
from NO ONE IMPORTANT

Daniel J. Wellington

Copyright © 2025 by Daniel J. Wellington

All rights reserved. This book or any portion thereof may not be reproduced or used in any manner whatsoever without the express written permission of the publisher except in the case of brief quotations embodied in a book review.

Dedicated to JoAnn, my greatest love and the person who makes everything make sense. I am lost without you. And to Connor, Kathryn, Ryan, Josephine, and Geaton, pure absolute love and my greatest joy in life. And to my brother John, a real-life hero.

And to any child or former child who was ever told they weren't good enough.

'Hank'—the inspiration for the front cover and an inspiration for my life. I found Hank triumphantly alone in a clearing. It was a tree that at its core was rotting and sick from top to bottom. Yet, even full of disease, the tree fought back, not only surviving, but thriving year after year. As I manage through my own cancer, I pass by Hank often and think of our similarities. I remind myself that all is possible, and to never live as a victim.

Contents

Foreword 9
Introduction 11
Author's Note 13
1. Mom and Dad 19
2. Baltimore 25
3. New Arrival 35
4. Home Sweet Home 41
5. The Characters and More 57
6. Virgo, Gemini, Cancer...and God 69
7. Painting and Vertigo 94
8. Being an American Arbutan, and
   Some Guidance from the Universe 108
9. Lock and Key and Oceans 1000 118
10. Crime Lord 128
11. New Beginnings 139
12. Compassion and Understanding for Mom and Dad ... 150
13. Learning to Fly, a True Hero Revealed 159
14. Dog Gone Nightmare 175
15. Fight Club 180
16. An Unexpected Flashback 197
17. The Middle of Things 205
18. What Happened with Mom and Dad? 233
Lessons Learned from All of This 253
Epilogue 292
Acknowledgements 296
Appendix 298
Letters to Mom and Dad 311

Foreword
by Dr. Tomek Wyczesany, PhD

The book in front of you is a true story of exploration of the human predicament from the perspective of an extraordinary man who calls himself ordinary. Even though it's a single-person account, it is surprising how universal it feels, how familiar it sounds, and how relevant it is in times when we are so uncertain of who we are and where we are heading. Even though Daniel's story is still unfolding, in my opinion, it's the ultimate hero's journey. As the reader, you will follow Daniel on his trials and challenges that pushed him to grow, learn, and evolve to arrive at newfound wisdom and renewal. In the process, the story may reveal something about yourself, as happened to me.

I met Daniel when he was already accomplished personally and professionally. I did not know what he had to go through to get where he is now. My role was simply to introduce him to mindfulness, to help him be more present, and perhaps, to better deal with his diagnosis. Our sessions very quickly went off topic, and I had the privilege to hear some of the stories included in this book. Later this developed into a friendship, in which mindfulness is a common theme. However, mindfulness comes much later in Daniel's life. More significant to the book is the intimate journey through Daniel's childhood, in which the figures of his parents play the crucial role. They become unwitting architects of his suffering, trying to crush his emerging sense of self beneath the weight of their own unresolved conflicts. In spite of constant trials and tribulations, what we witness is a remarkable transformation, a journey of resilience in which Daniel transcends his upbringing to forge his own destiny. Central to the story is the theme of overcoming the trauma that serves not only as the inspiration for this autobiography but gives hope for others grappling with their own demons.

But Daniel's book is more than a chronicle of trauma. It is a testament to the enduring resilience of the human spirit and the transformative power of faith, family, and love. Within these pages, we find echoes of the American Dream: a belief in the inherent promise of opportunity and the relentless pursuit of a better life, deep-seated patriotism, a reverence for the ideals upon which his nation was founded, and a commitment to upholding those values in the face of adversity. And at the heart of Daniel's journey lies a profound spiritual awakening—a journey of faith and self-discovery that transcends the boundaries of religion to embrace a universal spirituality rooted in mindfulness and presence. And just like that we arrive at the present moment through the labyrinth of the past and the aspirations of the future.

For me, Daniel's story resonates on a deeply personal level, evoking memories of my own journey through childhood and adolescence. It surely reminds me of struggle but also gives me the courage to face and overcome adversity. My past does not define me and my future is mine to shape.

Introduction

One day in 2003, I was feeling particularly happy, which isn't something that came easily to me. The sun was shining, and the sky was blue. With a little grin on my face, it occurred to me that, despite a troubled past, my life had turned out really good, and on some levels, even *great*. For possibly the first time in my life, I gave myself permission to "be" better and allow for the self-framing of my past without feeling anger or self-pity.

The feeling was not a complete transformation, but being able to see over the wall of my previously miserable life was refreshing. After years of pinning my identity on my trials and tribulations, the Universe had granted me a moment for a spontaneous reconciliation. My achievement of some hard-earned dreams that revealed my ability to reach my goals likely triggered this moment of peace.

Any success I experienced was influenced by the grace and support of my first wife, Ann-Marie. She only knew how to be kind, generous, and loving. While I lacked these qualities, I had been blessed to have chosen an exceptional person with whom to spend my life.

Things were looking up, and I afforded myself a momentary opportunity to be OK with enjoying the present without being stuck in the past.

The moment didn't stay with me long, but I knew what I was feeling inside was genuinely real. At least momentarily, I could see that there was great value in *all* of my life experiences, both bad and good. I felt good knowing I had gotten myself to that point despite dealing with some difficult things.

After processing these feelings, the thought of writing a book came to mind. Initially, I thought I could use a book as a tool to put a hard stop at the end of a sentence in my life. I wondered, *If I clear out some heavy baggage, what opportunities will be waiting on the other side?*

As the idea expanded, I thought that maybe making the effort wasn't about discovering a better, lighter me, but instead, through my vulnerability, I might offer some therapeutic value to others. While the clouds were clearing a bit, I was still struggling to understand and gain perspective on who I was, where I came from, what happiness can be, and how to be a decent human being. Perhaps stringing all my experiences together on paper would help me understand myself better. Essentially, I envisioned a map showing me where I had been, and I hoped it might subtly point the way to where I needed to go next on life's journey.

I admit I did have some apprehension that diving into my history might unwind me and send me some place dark. But I also began to realize that maybe someone might read my words and find hope and humor. A good laugh has always been a friend to me, though I admit laughter hasn't always come easily.

So I wrote this book for me, for anyone else who might be messed up like me, and for anyone who cares about living a *Crutchless* life—a life without being married to your past or stuck waiting for help—where you are not looking for someone to blame for troubles from yesterday. I want this book to offer hard evidence that, through it all, I managed to find success, happiness, and deep love in my life without using the crutches of victimhood and excuses. I also want my children to be able to learn something about the crazy man who is their father. Maybe somewhere in these pages, they will answer some of their own questions about their lives and who they are becoming. I hope they will come away knowing there is always an opportunity for a rich, fulfilling life no matter who you are or where you come from.

This is my story. I hope that anyone struggling with or dealing with darkness in their lives might see from my words that there is always opportunity to create lasting, meaningful change for themselves and for future generations. Humor, willpower, hope, music, and refusing to live as a victim all have proven to be powerfully effective tools enabling me to lead my life toward a better place and beyond. I believe those qualities can do the same for you. I also hope you might see some proof that God (or whatever you might call your higher power, if anything at all) is with each of us and will be until we draw our last breath. Without blaming or making our histories our identity, we can all become *Crutchless* and live rich, fulfilling lives.

Author's Note

One of the many gifts in my life is the wide landscape of music I have been exposed to. I originally wanted to include specific songs and lyrics in this book, but there would need to be too many permissions gained and money spent, so I opted out. Music has always spoken to me and served as a therapeutic tool in a very personal way, and I have a deep appreciation and respect for musicians, singers, writers, producers, music video creators, and anyone in or around the music business. I have always tied good and bad memories to specific songs. Some people, like my wife, can remember a neighbor's best friend's birthday party from twenty years ago and tell me who was there and the flavor of the cake—this is not my strength. However, if I hear a song from thirty years ago that resonated with me in some way back then, I can tell you exactly where I was when I first heard it, who was with me, and why the song made such a strong imprint. Some people enjoy the instruments, while others are focused on the lyrics. For me, the therapeutic part occurs when the music and lyrics are written in just the right intertwined combination to grab my attention, as if demanding that I hear and digest the artist's message. Over and over, I have listened carefully to these storytellers to gain perspective about my own life and to help me make decisions. These writers and singers have always been my free, on-demand therapists.

My turning to music for help was a bit like when a person loses one of their senses. For these individuals, their body and mind compensate by developing advanced abilities through their remaining senses. Losing or not having an active support system is not the same as being without one of my senses, but without one, I was driven to find ways to compensate in order to bring support into my life. Identifying role models to emulate, analyzing music, and even studying and copying things I learned on television were all components I found useful in building my own support system. Because I lived in a volatile and dangerous environment without love, affection, or guidance, I was in desperate need of help and was willing to take it where I could find it. These resources for finding support, while unconventional, were readily available in the environment in which I lived.

As a parent, I now know that basic childcare skills provide the needed building blocks for gaining a sense of safety and trust that every child should receive. It doesn't take an advanced degree in psychology to understand the damage done to children born into circumstances where that support is not only unavailable, but where even baseline care has been replaced with dysfunction and violence. The Universe was kind to me in that it graciously offered these substitute support systems as tools to provide some answers while helping me work my way through the darkness. While I did not fully understand these gifts from the Universe at the time, I did my best to frame what I was witnessing in a way that would at least keep hope alive within me. When I had no one to speak with or to serve as a role model, these writers and singers *never* failed to be my always-available advisors and therapists. The words they sang and the passion they shared not only entertained me but offered the community, optimism, raw will, and direction I so deeply needed.

Of course, the power of music to strongly influence the listener is not a new concept, as even in music's earliest forms, civilizations have used it in their traditions to enhance all forms of life experience. Music can lead to the mind making positive shifts and can induce the release of positive-impacting biochemicals that can change a disposition right there on the spot. If you ever doubt that fact, think of the almost involuntary response of your feet as you tap out the rhythm to a new favorite song and smile. I don't know how the Universe worked music into the grand plan, but I have no doubt it is another gift meant to help us all. If you believe that, then it's probably not a stretch to believe that when a listener connects with lyrics and the artist's total offering, the result may even be lifesaving. While that connection may not be a complete substitute for qualified therapy, it was the only kind available to me, and I absorbed it for all it was worth. Of course, therapy was not thought of in the 1970s and 80s the way it is today, though even if it had been, my parents would never have identified it as something I needed. So music lifted me up and kept me patched together when I needed it most.

Anna Nalick's song "Breathe (2 AM)" offers a good example. I had been journaling long before 2005, when this song was originally released, but when I heard it for the first time, Nalick's lyrics regarding life struggle made me stop and think not only about what I was trying to do in my own life, but how I was going about doing it. The song also told me that if this singer and writer had experienced something in her life that made her write these lyrics, then there was at least one other person in the world who knew what I was thinking, which meant I was not alone. This was "community" to me. Nalick's song was released well into my adulthood, but I was still leaning hard on music to guide me. This has not changed; even today I am digesting new music and letting it teach and inspire me.

"Breathe (2 AM)" also made me understand an important reason why I was writing so diligently in my journals. As her lyrics imply, my ability to get the detail of difficult events on paper gave me very effective short-term relief and therapy. Modern therapists often suggest journaling to their clients, so back in the early '80s, my high school creative writing teacher, Mrs. Hickman, might have been considered ahead of her time in helping me to embrace this tool. My objective in journaling through most of my life was to detail as much as possible, including the emotions I was experiencing. At that time in my life, fear and struggle were primary emotional anchors. My writing entries helped me to understand why that was the case, while nudging me to see beyond my current reality.

Never knowing that they were on my therapy team, songwriters like Anna Nalick and my teacher Mrs. Hickman, were unyielding in their efforts to help me get through the day. While they will never know that by sharing their experiences and gifts they made my life measurably better, their contributions nonetheless were immense. Getting my life experience all down on paper effectively allowed me to take the sharp edge off of painful life conditions out of my head. From there, I could put the troubles in a mental box I could then put on a high shelf away from everyday life and continue to push through. On most days, that was enough.

This is my story. I hope that anyone struggling with or dealing with darkness in their lives might see from my words that there is always an opportunity to create lasting, meaningful change for themselves and for future generations. Humor, willpower, hope, music, and refusing to live as a victim all have proven to be powerfully effective tools enabling me to lead my life toward a better place. I believe those qualities can do the same for most. I also hope that you might see some proof that God (or whatever you might call your higher power, if anything at all) is with each of us and will be until we draw our last breath. Without blaming or making our histories our identity, we can all become *Crutchless*.

Daniel J. Wellington

- Please be advised that there are examples of child and animal abuse that might be triggering to some.

- Also, I use 'God', 'Universe' and 'Higher Power' as equal interchangeable terms throughout. However, my use of these words are not anchored in any religion and there is no effort or desire to change the minds of those that don't believe. For more insight about how I came to have a relationship with God late in life, please see the appendix.

The beginning...

1

Mom and Dad

In 1963, Brian Wilson of the Beach Boys wrote a song called "In My Room." When I heard it for the first time in 1982, I couldn't help but notice some similarities between Mr. Wilson and myself. He suffered from agoraphobia and his song was an attempt to explain what living with that condition was like for him. While I did not suffer from this ailment myself, I deeply understood how a room could become a sanctuary.

Like Wilson, I shared a room with a younger brother. Even with a roommate, I still considered our bedroom to be my sanctuary, albeit a vulnerable one. Family members had kicked in the door to our bedroom many times, so there was no door jamb left for the lock to catch. I knew that any moment of safety could be disrupted unexpectedly by an angry, perhaps violently incensed, parent.

Still, even with an unlockable, destroyed door frame and a constant fear of the unknown, I could relate to Wilson's perceived feelings of safety and solitude in my only semi-private space. More importantly, I empathized with his sad disposition, as he managed through his fears to try to find answers in his life. The lyrics are few and simple, and what they say about his experience made me feel that Wilson could have been writing about *my* experience. While I did not understand it at the time, I know now that this was one of those moments when my higher power was helping me. Wilson's creativity and vulnerability were a gift to me from the Universe to help me sort things out in my own life and cling to hope.

Which leads me back to 1967, the year I was born. I often think about how my mother and father might have been living in those days. They both experienced tough upbringings, and I'm sure my mother and father were, for good reason, more worried about their personal survival than the important events of the time, whether the Vietnam War, the Civil Rights Movement, or the Space Race.

While I cannot say I ever got to know my parents on a deeply personal level, I do know they had innate survival instincts and were hard workers. They definitely wanted better for themselves than what they were born into. I am equally certain that, despite the difficult, often violent environment in which they raised us, our lives have turned out much better than theirs did.

My father experienced no shortage of real evil in his young life. His daily dose of hard-life tales easily explained how he became the type of man we came to know. While some parents shelter their children from their past trauma, he shared his experiences constantly, and there were lots of them.

With my father, it was never a matter of the glass being half full or half empty. His glass was cracked and leaking all of the time, with the contents washing over and eroding any hope of normalcy for our family. And sadly, his pain only seemed to deepen with each passing year.

Given his negative outlook and fits of rage, his presence was oppressive to everyone in our family, including my mother, who also bore the brunt of his verbal attacks. While I understood and appreciated that my father was a survivor and gave us much more than what he was given, it wasn't until much later that I would understand just how much he made out of so little. However, I never respected him in his role as a father, and he gave me plenty of reasons not to. Although I learned a great deal from him, he wasn't a pleasant man on most days. Some days I liked him, and there were some good moments, but mostly, if truth be told, I lived in fear of him.

As for my mother, she grew up with her own share of sad stories. However, unlike my father, she rarely shared them with us. Perhaps she felt my father shared enough stories and the dark cloud he kept over our family offered no room for the introduction of anyone else's misery. Where my father was outwardly mad at the world, my mother internalized everything and fought her demons from inside her mind. She was an immensely private woman, and, as our lives progressed, she only became more introverted. While her approach may not have been the healthiest for her, she nonetheless was strong.

In fact, while both of my parents contributed to me having the type of focus that would allow me to take important life-building steps, I give my mother credit for gifting me the important "stick-to-it-iveness" I have called upon regularly throughout my life. Most days, she was hard as nails.

Still, on rare occasions, she could show a sweetness that was so needed and appreciated I felt like an angel had touched me. The infrequency made the moments potent, and I carry them with me to this day.

Perhaps not surprisingly, no one said "I love you" in our home, but since we had no expectations of ever hearing those words, my brothers and I never missed it. To us, hearing "I love you" said between family members was something out of a television fantasy, not much different than watching Wonder Woman fly in her invisible jet.

Other kind words and physical gestures of affection were also foreign to my parents. I suspect this was because they were raised that way themselves. What my father and mother did share was a strong work ethic, and they both preached to me that, no matter the adversity, anything could be accomplished with hard work, commitment, and discipline. At the same time, their utter lack of parental support on my life journey made me realize I needed to accomplish my goals and dreams myself. Their role was merely to let me know that any dependence on them for navigating life was wasted energy. While I didn't know it until later, in many important ways, their lack of ambiguity on this point was beneficial to the successes in my life.

While neither parent actively helped me to achieve anything, my mother did provide a template for how to succeed through her own striving. She had a no-nonsense attitude about most things and *never* bragged about her achievements. This made sense because, in our household, there was only room for my father's ego. In fact, that may be why he discouraged her from going to college by telling her, "You're not smart enough and, besides, you need to be at home with the children."

He further enforced his position by refusing to offer any financial support toward her degree, claiming it would get in the way of her duties at home. In response, however, this determined woman used her tips from waiting tables at a local diner to pay for tuition and eventually earn a college degree on her own.

The example she set was nothing short of heroic. She took classes in the evening after she put my brother John and I to bed, and then studied deep into the early morning hours. It was not unusual for me or John to wander downstairs in the middle of the night and see a solitary light on at the kitchen table. There we would find our mother, with books and papers spread out before her, studying with great determination.

Her years of hard work and resilience in the face of adversity paid off. She earned a degree from the University of Maryland, graduating near the top of her class. She never discussed her efforts with us, though. If I hadn't seen her studying at the kitchen table with my own two eyes, I would never have known how hard she worked or that she was working to earn a degree at all!

In fact, the only way we had any idea she had received her degree was because her sisters in Pittsburgh threw her a surprise party, which we all attended. A picture from the occasion shows my mother appearing to be full of anguish and anxiety the moment she realized the party was not for her sister, as she had been led to believe, but instead was to celebrate her graduation from college. She literally hated that people made a fuss over this great accomplishment and couldn't wait to leave.

Obtaining a college degree was an admirable, solo-driven accomplishment no one in her family had ever attempted. While I was only twelve years old at the time she graduated, the achievement, the ridicule she endured from my father throughout her journey, and her unyielding determination to finish found a permanent place in my mind. Perhaps more importantly, her avoidance of fanfare and complete lack of need for any outside affirmation made me realize that if she could do great things without support—or even the need for support—then maybe I could, too.

I am sure all of this history strongly suggests that the union of my mother and father was something of a tragedy. I knew it from as early as the age of five. I can remember thinking on the matter, and even in my young and immature mind, I could not understand how these two beings could have consciously made the decision to get married and have children. Their coupling offers a stark example of the horrible things that can come of two people falling in love. If it ever even was love. Perhaps it was desperation on both their parts.

So much that went on in my childhood was painful and frightening. When I look back on my earliest journal entries, they are filled with sadness and anger. I often cursed my parents' very existence and wished they would either leave forever or I could go somewhere—*anywhere*—far away from them. In the decades since, maturity and life experience have given me some perspective on these days, and I now view things in a healthier light. I can even genuinely give thanks to them for having given me life and genuinely mean these words, whereas as a child I many times wished I had never been born.

My father once told me that holding onto anger and resentment was like drinking poison and expecting the other person to die from it. While I know he borrowed the quote from elsewhere, and that he had been completely unable to follow the advice himself, it made sense to me at the time he said it, and in time, I was able to let go of my anger and resentment toward them. I realized I was only hurting my own life by being chained down by my hatred of and anger toward these two flawed people.

In time, I even learned to forgive them. It was a great gift I gave to myself to both finally understand that forgiveness was the answer and that applying it could lift some of the darkness I carried with me. The results were not instantaneous but getting the bulk of bad feelings behind me allowed for some partial peace and a higher quality of life. I finally realized that putting so much emotional capital into resenting them significantly limited my ability to find happiness. Embracing forgiveness allowed me to be in the room with them for brief periods without searching for a reason to leave. It wasn't perfect, and I would never be able to speak of them in words resembling a Hallmark greeting card, but letting go and forgiving made a huge difference in my life.

I now wish I had forgiven them much sooner, if only for the benefit it had on my own mental well-being. As a child of the '70s and '80s, I learned from television sitcoms that forgiveness could be a magical cure-all for grudges and pain, but as great as the idea sounded in concept, it had no place in my young life. How could I forgive these people who seemed to make it their business to make my life harder?

After all, my parents had never seemed remorseful for anything they had ever done, even though their actions could have landed either of them in jail, even back then. Furthermore, they had no idea or interest in how I felt, nor would they likely have cared if they had known. We were all in survival mode, and so forgiveness would have to wait until I was wise enough to learn its value.

Despite the dysfunction in the Wellington family, things did get done and we endured. The clearer hindsight that came decades later has allowed me to finally repackage my life experience in terms that are not completely overrun with negative emotions. As I now see it, my parents, having emerged out of their own incredibly miserable upbringings, were doing the best they could at the time and trying hard to carve a piece out of this world for themselves.

No, they were not planning for their kids' education or family vacations or making sure their little Danny got the therapy he needed. And no, their lives were not about their children or creating a rich family experience for us. And still no, they had no intentional goals of giving their children safe or inspired lives. All their hard work was geared toward finding the best life for *themselves*, and if our childhoods were improved in the process, fine.

While I have forgiven them, the fact remains that my brothers and I were long-term, expensive nuisances that were byproducts of some moments of pleasure my parents shared together. I suspect it was my father's need for physical gratification, and not any sort of true love, that led to my mother getting pregnant six times, albeit with three miscarriages. Incredibly enough, at least half of those pregnancies occurred when they were either separated or divorced. It seems the man had insatiable needs, and the cost did not matter in those moments.

2

Baltimore

Richard Marx wrote and sang many memorable power ballads in the '80s. I gave those tunes many a listen as I gazed off in the distance and dreamed of girls I had crushes on, girls who almost always did not feel the same way about me. However, one special Marx tune had a far different message than those of his usual heart-tuggers, and that was 1989's "Satisfied." The message that was shown in the "Satisfied" video, along with Marx's crisp guitar licks, always lifted me up when I needed a push forward.

Marx exclaims to the world, "I won't give up until I'm satisfied" (if you grew up an MTV kid like me, you might be singing along by now). Like Marx, I wanted that moment of truth and a chance to untie my hands and release myself to the world. He gave me permission to envision myself far away from where I was at the time, which was deep in my college studies. While I was studying hard for the first time in my life, I had no idea where I was going.

At the time, I had no notion of what "satisfied" meant to me personally, but I was smart enough to know I didn't want to just float along on the river of life. No, I wanted big things for myself to offset where I had come from, and in the absence of any role models or mentors, my intuition had to step up again. That persistent voice from deep inside told me there would be no absolutes, but if I did the work, the rest would come. Paying attention to that intuition changed my life, and playing "Satisfied" repeatedly gave me moments of real power and inspiration, something I could find nowhere else in my life. I believe this wonderful connectivity, in this case between Richard Marx and me, exists among every living thing, but it's up to each of us, through intention and intuition, to know where to pay attention. Looking back, I can see that another helpful gift had been dropped in my lap, and luckily, those licks and lyrics were powerful enough to grab my attention and keep me moving forward.

That river of my life traces back to Pittsburgh's North Side, where my father was living. My brother John Robert Jr. was born in Pittsburgh on May 29, 1964. Shortly after his birth, my father made the decision to move his young family to Baltimore. He believed the best job opportunities were there and accepted a job as a low-level computer programmer within the federal government. In fact, he would spend his entire work life in the service and safety of the government. Like everything else, he preached about how his way was the *right* way, and to him, being neatly tucked into the government payroll, with its secure stream of benefits and promotions, was a no-brainer.

When my father took that first job in Baltimore, the rest of the family, which at that time consisted of my mother and my one-year-old brother John, stayed in Pittsburgh. My father decided it would be best for him to go alone and get settled. After that, he promised he would arrange for my mother and John to join him.

To put it mildly, he took his time with the settling process, and he hardly stayed in close touch. In the late '60s, the only means of communication available to everyone were letters and phone calls. Since it was expensive to talk to someone hundreds of miles away, my mother rarely spoke directly with my dad on the phone. While he did write her letters, which we found after she passed, they were few and far between. They were also dry, unemotional, and full of complaints about his difficult life, but were quite lean on any compassion for my mother and brother and their struggle to manage things on their own without him. As he saw it, his exploration of Baltimore, finding a place for his family to live, and starting a new job was a gigantic, difficult, mountain-moving undertaking. The letters were also void of any romance, emotion, or sincere desire to be reunited with his family.

All told, given his infrequent calls and his self-centered, unempathetic letters, my mother must have felt very alone in Pittsburgh. Reading the letters many years later, and being a father myself, I cannot understand how he could be without his wife and new first son for such a long period and obviously not miss them. Yet, as was always the case in my father's tragic and painful life, he made himself front and center.

My father was nothing if not complex. His innate ability to survive and to think ahead meant he was always exploring his options. This skill set had served him well as a virtually homeless youth running the streets of Pittsburgh, and it never left him. Unfortunately, a darker side of his survival skills took hold of him while he lived in Baltimore alone. Even as he was supposedly planning for John and Mom to join him at the earliest possible moment, my father actually was spending significant time and effort inquiring about other available government positions. I learned about his concentrated search for faraway employment after my mother had passed. Employment-related correspondence from multiple agencies, reflecting their interest in talking further, were found amongst my mother's personal belongings. Apparently, she had decided to hold on to these for her and John's own protection and not pass them on to my father.

While I will never know for certain why my father would even consider a position on the opposite side of the country and overseas when he had a young wife and an infant son in Pittsburgh or why he eventually would resume having children with a woman he seemed intent on leaving, I suppose I should be thankful my mother never told him she not only knew about his efforts, but had purposely obstructed his plan. Had she confronted him about the letters I found all those years later, he might very well have left her then and there, in which case, I would never have been born!

Having stalled long enough, and with his secret plan dashed, my father moved forward with bringing my mother and brother to Baltimore to live, and they arrived sometime in 1966. By this time, my father had secured a home just inside the Baltimore city line on Wilkens Avenue, a major street leading from Baltimore County into the city. The house at 1319 Wilkens was a white asbestos-shingle home with green shutters, and it stood out like a mansion in a sea of rowhomes. It was a grand old home with a dirt-floor basement, dark mahogany staircases, an attic, and a large yard with two or three large pear trees, a small pond, and blackberry bushes.

John at this point was around two years old, and he'd had it tough from day one. My father had been angry that his first born arrived with crossed eyes and irrationally found a way to blame it on my mother, who worked tirelessly to get John help for his eyes and to soothe my father's abusive attitude about his condition.

While John's eyes were the focus of much discussion and turmoil, the truth is my father seemed to take issue with most everything John did. I suspect that all of the pressure he put on John reflected the fact that his very birth itself had been a great burden to dear old dad. I know now this was the truth, given his lack of engagement with our family and his schemes to abandon us. Even while my mother was in Pittsburgh anxiously waiting for my father to come and collect her and John for their move to Baltimore, his single mention of John in the many letters he wrote to her proves to me that John was not a priority in his thoughts. Sadly, that fact is confirmed by a note I discovered on one of my mother's aging, yellowed calendars in her personal effects. Next to John's birthdate on the calendar in 1964, she wrote, "John Jr. born. Where was John Sr.?"

Did he not even show up for his birth? I will never know for certain. It is terribly sad for me to think that an infant would enter this world only to be greeted by a father who didn't want him, and would treat him so poorly and unlovingly.

Luckily for John, my mother tried her best in these early years, and she was deeply relieved as a mother and a wife when doctors eventually operated successfully to repair his eyes. However, the surgery could not repair the ongoing damage caused by my father's abuse, and, of course, Dad found plenty more reasons to find fault with his young son once the easy and obvious target of John's eyes was gone. His negative disposition toward his first son would robustly continue and set up a lifetime of bad blood between the two.

The abuse only grew worse over time, and no matter what effort my brother made to be a better son, he could never earn our father's affection. As the abuse escalated, it became obvious to me that John had been made the black sheep of the family long before he ever had a chance to earn the title.

Although John may have suffered the most abuse at the hands of our father, he was hardly alone. My father started to physically assault me when I was three or four, at least that's as far back as I can remember. It doesn't take much physical pain to drive home a cease-and-desist message to a toddler, so when I received a swift hand to the back of the head or a hard slap on my backside, one that would send me across the room, I course-corrected quickly. But as I grew older, my offenses grew more evil to my father, and he concluded that light physical punishment was no longer effective. There were many serious beatings from both my mother and father, but my father's disciplinary measures were the most severe, lengthier, and more frequent. We always needed to stay clear of our parents, but once physical abuse became the best option for my father, he became the man we hoped would never come back from wherever he frequently disappeared to...ever. By today's standards, for his actions, he would have been locked away in prison for many years.

The psychological abuse was also heavy, as my father made it clear throughout our lives that he did not just regret having children, but he deeply *resented* it. As an adult, I struggle to understand how a grown man, blessed with free will, could openly express his hatred of the idea of his own children. While he undoubtedly heard horrible comments from his own mother, that hardly excuses his abusiveness. While he never went so far as to say he specifically hated us as individuals, he would wrap his acidic proclamations in a cloak of generality, as if to somehow soften the message to us.

Stranger still, I became not just accustomed to hearing his venomous words, but I also accepted them as our norm. I bought into his pitch that he was "just being honest" when he said he hated having children. He would even say, "It's not you guys, it could be any children," and while twisted, this made me feel better. He basically used the classic breakup line, "It's not you, it's me," only he was applying it to his parenting.

Regardless, my father's distaste for John was especially difficult to understand because John was a sweet toddler and by no means a child who acted out. Looking back, what I remember most is how sad John felt *all* the time and how desperate he was to earn our father's love, which simply was not possible. John's birth represented an anchor in our father's life that held him in place, when what he desperately wanted was to leave. With each look at his firstborn child, our father was reminded of his dreams of unimpeded flight he'd never achieve, and that only added fuel to the darkness already in his heart.

Mixed in with his regular disclosures about his disappointing life, my father found it necessary to develop a series of pet names for us boys. He rarely used our actual names when speaking to us, and his nicknames were not always original for each of us. He would simply put a number behind whatever name he used so we knew who he was referring to at the moment. No matter where we were in my mother's house, which was always as far away from him as possible, if my father called out, we stopped and intently listened. There were many names, but the ones that really stuck were, "Slagheap," "Buns," "Rope-a-dope," and the good, old fashioned, frequently used "Shitbag" and "Asshole." As the middle child, the words "Number 2" would always come behind whatever name he used to call me. (John was Number 1, David was Number 3.) If he was looking for me in the house, he would yell out, "Asshole number 2, come on dooooooowwwwwwwn" (he liked to mimic the contestant announcer Rod Roddy from *The Price Is Right*). Using these names didn't always mean he was angry about something, he would use these names all the time. If he was in a good mood, he would sometimes allow for our protests. In response, he would often snicker and seem pleased with himself at the name itself and that it had successfully landed as intended. This was just good, clean, American fun in our home. This only encouraged him to find ways to insert it wherever he could. He liked that he could get under our skin, and that the names were bothersome to us. He might have hated being a father, but he seemed to enjoy this sick type of abuse. Like when he would sit on us and tickle or rub his beard stubble on our faces until we literally cried, his thinking must have been that us simply breathing oxygen and being his financial responsibility was more than sufficient rationale to warrant this behavior. It was *quid pro quo* for the stress of us being born and the sentence of having to provide for us. He was comfortable doling out huge servings of emotional abuse to us because it was important that we participate in his misery; it was just fair play to him and deserved by the people who'd ruined his life. He would laugh out loud, and I mean for real laughing out loud, at how clever and fitting the names were, dismissing our concerns completely. I sensed that what he felt was pride in his creativity. Also, when we had the courage to complain (almost always when he was in a "calm" mood), he would inform us that if he didn't have these names to call us, he would end up killing one of us. It is a puzzling, almost curious thing to hear your father say something like that, but because he was so violent, I believed he was sincere. This made me thankful for the gifts of the names and the beatings as they seemed a better option than dying.

Some time between me being three and six, my parents split up for the first time. While I could pretend the separation was dramatic and painful, that wasn't the case. In fact, I don't remember my father leaving. I just knew he wasn't sleeping regularly at the house anymore, although he did visit frequently. Naturally, I do not remember exactly what I was thinking at three or four years old, but I do know that at some point, I was happy our father was not living with us full time.

I know that my birth came only because he viewed my mother as an undrainable, open-legged resource who was put on this Earth to satisfy his impulses and listen to his complaints, not someone with whom to share love or intentionally build a family with. To him, sex with my mother, even when separated or divorced, was a perk my father felt was owed him, even long after he had left the home. As far as uninvolved, abusive fathers go, he had a sweet deal. There was no requirement that he live there with us, no requirement to act as a husband or father, and beyond the small check he sent every month, no requirement that he support the family in order to maintain his controlling status and keep the benefits. Seen from this perspective,

I can understand why he kept coming back to the well, even if his behavior lacked any dignity whatsoever.

And come back to the well he did, over and over again. My brother David was born in early December of 1970, a few years after my birth. He was a beautiful baby and the kindest of the three of us. From as far back as I can remember, David attracted attention, and women cooed over him wherever we went. He was the quietest and seemingly most content child straight out of the womb.

He had a knack for being able to stoically tune out everything around him, even when violence played out right before his eyes. David knew instinctively how to avoid the danger and confrontation that filled the house. Where John and I bore the brunt of my parents' heavy rule, David somehow managed to navigate the minefields by keeping quiet and mastering avoidance techniques.

No matter what he witnessed, his demeanor never changed from that of a happy, smiling, yet private, kid. His mission seemed to be about just surviving the day. He was not big on sharing any emotions or thoughts. David was a pro at maintaining his cool in any situation and could do so for long periods of time.

Of course, all that suppression and quiet, happy avoidance was like a pressurized time bomb, and if you pushed David too far, he would explode, and nobody did well on the receiving end of one of his outbursts. Only these rare reactions to being pushed too hard suggested there was much more to him than I knew.

When David was an infant, John and I—though mostly John—were tasked with cleaning David's cloth diapers. My father always gave a great chuckle at watching seven-year-old John head down to our basement to scrub the solids and urine out of the soft cotton. I also remember John as a five-year-old being responsible for cleaning *my* diapers when we lived on Wilkens Avenue. He'd scrub the diapers in the sink with my father providing instruction over his shoulder. As John worked with disgust painted on his face, my father would giggle, and I would do the same. It wasn't that I thought it was funny, it was just a rare moment to share a laugh with a man who rarely broke a smile. Eventually, I guess I laughed too hard, because my father began to send me down to the basement on these diaper-cleaning missions to serve as John's assistant. As I stood on a can of paint "assisting," I quickly realized exactly why John was always so grossed out. The rats didn't mind, though. In fact, they sometimes ate through the spent diapers my mother had left in the basement before we could clean them, which of course angered my father because of the expense.

One of the most humorous memories I have of my brother David came during his potty training phase. David was a late bloomer when it came to using the toilet. It wasn't so much that he didn't know how, he just preferred to shit his pants rather than be bothered with sitting on the commode. Urinating in the potty was a breeze for this kid, and there was rarely a time he would wet his pants, but when it came to solids, he loved the feel of the cotton diapers when he did his business. This preference did not endear him to me or John, since we were forced to clean those diapers, and eventually, his underwear.

However, there was some rewarding levity in reference to his bowel movements, because each incident drove our father crazy. Like a seismograph pinging to the extreme, David's face had a telltale look that an eruption was about to occur. John and I knew the look instantly, but somehow my parents never seemed to pick up on it. As a baby, "the look" was like that of most babies in the midst of a bowel movement, but by the time he was a young boy, David's face would turn shades of crimson and purple, and his breathing would almost completely stop as he pushed right there in his seat. Humor was in short supply in our house, and David's contortions were hilarious, but John and I had to use every ounce of willpower we had to contain ourselves. If we laughed, David would be interrupted in mid-process, and we would be robbed of the enjoyment of watching our father's guaranteed reaction as the smell of fresh shit reached out to greet him from across the dinner table.

David's "accidents" inevitably took place when our father was talking at the dinner table about great topics of self-importance like his long work hours, making the mortgage payment, and the worthlessness of his freeloading kids and wife. Unbeknownst to our father, as he was complaining, David would be working hard in his chair to complete the impossible task of having a bowel movement at the table without attracting any attention. It was the slow and focused concentration of a snake shedding its skin. It was quite a procedure to watch David evacuate his bowels while leaning forward and feigning interest in my father's dissertation. When the task was complete, David would return to his meal, oblivious and unconcerned at the fallout that was only moments away.

Suddenly, in mid-sentence, my father would catch the scent we had already detected at our lower elevation and greater proximity to ground zero. He would well up in anger and frustration and bark at David for the violation of his airspace and the interruption to his monologue. He would say, "David, did you shit your fucking pants again?" while David would just stare at him with his apologetic, sweet, perfect smile.

Seeing our smiles and barely contained laughter, our father would get even more angry, and we would be lucky to escape with just a tongue-lashing. But whatever the punishment, it always was worth it, because the enjoyment we both felt in watching David's silent attack on my father was immeasurable.

In a way, it is hard to understand why we gained so much pleasure in all of this madness, since, after all, we were the ones who would have to clean up the resulting mess. Even so, with so little joy in our house, we cherished the rare opportunity to have a well-suppressed laugh at our father's expense and for the most part get away with it. Call it a subtle rebellion, since our father attempted to control every area of our lives. Yet no matter how hard he tried, there was no discipline or sharp words that could control David's bowels.

As the baby, David lived on the low end of the abuse hierarchy. Maybe this was because by then our father's feet were almost out the door, and he could no longer be bothered with terrorizing another child into compliance. By watching John and I try, David had already understood that challenging my mother and father in any way yielded few rewards and mostly stiff retribution, so he did little to rock the boat, and for whatever reason, from the start, he also seemed to get the least amount of attention from my parents. In our home, the less attention, the better, so he kept quiet, and aside from the diaper incidents, went mostly unnoticed, which was a solid strategy in our house.

As young kids, my brothers and I were close in that we had a shared objective—navigating around my parents' outbursts while trying to live our version of kids' lives. It was a dysfunctional form of comradery based primarily on survival, not love or friendship. It was difficult trying to be the television-advertised brand of "normal" when living in a live minefield, but in our own ways, we each did our best.

Meanwhile, I was not any sort of "normal" to kids who knew me growing up during these years. I was often disheveled and dirty, had zero social skills, and the slightest perceived provocation revealed to anyone that I was very insecure. I'm sure most kids found me to be strange and an easy target. Growing up in the '70s and '80s in Arbutus, Maryland, I was at the bottom of the social food chain. Along with being bullied and abused at home, being bullied in middle school and my early years of high school was an everyday adventure. Life was made much harder by the fact that bullying back then was pretty much seen as a normal rite of passage for kids. Any complaints about bullying were addressed the same by parents and teachers alike. While the bullies might receive a slap on the wrist for their actions, victims like myself were told to suck it up and avoid their antagonists. Naturally, this wide acceptance of bullying almost ensured that it would be prevalent. In fact, the docile response from adults sent the message that being an asshole was a sign of strength and that the weak were meant to be treated harshly.

I don't think of my brothers and I as fitting in anywhere. My inability to connect impacted me for most of my childhood and well into adulthood. As we grew older, my brothers and I grew further apart and siloed ourselves. With our parents' regularly proactive messaging that they would not be there for us, each of us tried to find some meaning and direction in life outside of the home. We were three kids scrapping it out in separate theatres of operation.

While we were alone in our pursuits, John protected me from the bullies, which was about as big a gift as anyone could ever give me at the time. I know that at his core, he could not stand the idea of someone hurting me, even though at times he didn't mind giving me a solid asskicking himself. I also believe John welcomed the opportunity to release some of his own pent-up rage whenever the opportunity presented itself. While at the time I interpreted his defense of me as valiant and heroic, it was also a pressure release for John.

John would also run interference for me against my mother at times, which resulted in different outcomes, both good and bad. He was rarely successful in getting her to calm down, but I was grateful for the few times he did successfully divert her attention from whatever I had done at the time. I, in turn, protected and provided for David whenever I could. If I was stealing food from the local convenience store or taking clothes off of someone's clothesline for myself, I would be sure to get some for him, too. And if someone picked on him, I was always quick to sort the matter out definitively.

All told, we were a family in name only. There was no closeness between Mom and Dad and us kids in any conventional sense. My parents didn't even try to fake it, as they were themselves in survival-and-build mode, seeking to achieve their own goals above all. Developing a trusting and loving family unit was never on their radar, and they were unapologetic about this fact. However, my brothers and I shared an organically created connection to defend each other when we could. Though we might be getting abused at home, the thought of someone doing that to one of us outside our home filled us with fury. It was a sad, strange way to build a bond, but God was working for us even when we didn't know it. Somewhere in our pre-existing wiring, we knew to protect each other from the harsh world. In that sense alone, my brothers and I were "family."

3

New Arrival

The *Blizzard of Oz* album, Ozzy Osbourne's solo debut after he broke away from Black Sabbath, was a gem of a disc full of great songs that John had purchased for his collection. I listened to it on his record player any time I could. As I rocked out to Ozzy's songs, as always, I listened carefully to the messages found in the lyrics. Ozzy, like other artists, helped me to know I was not alone. To me, Ozzy and his band, including young guitar virtuoso Randy Rhoads, were new friends openly sharing their experiences and providing me with lessons on how to live my own life. I could relate to these rockers because they seemed to understand my pain and to understand *me*. Their relatability provided another example of community, and with that, I discovered another gift from the dark rockers.

The signature song "Crazy Train" offered me a funny way of looking at my own life. Ozzy sang about mental wounds not healing and how they were hurting him badly, or "driving him insane," as he put it. I could relate to his tormented lyrics, as I searched in my youth for ways to deal with the demons in my life. I was afraid of what was going on in my head, and the lyrics gave me an awareness that normal people, even rock stars, struggle to find their way out of holes. I had some fear I might be on the crazy train he was describing, but fortunately, the song's more important message told me I needed to do everything I could to keep myself on the rails and move forward. Gifts sometimes come in the form of unpleasant, hard-to-hear lessons. The seriousness of Ozzy's message made me take note that things could get worse, but that it was my job to keep them from going too far "off the rails." Another message was being sent that I was not alone and that there were people out there like me, and there is nobody quite like Ozzy as a mentor!

My crazy train started its journey on May 29, 1967. It was a Monday, when at around 2:30 in the morning, my father and mother piled into their 1959 Ford Falcon and made their way to Baltimore General, the hospital where I would be born later that day. I don't know the real facts around the day of my birth, but I feel like I have earned the right to use some creative license. When mixing fantasy with what I know about the people that were my parents, I think that the picture I'll paint is close enough to reality, while also providing a bit of comic relief.

Dad was likely cursing to himself the entire way about the inconvenience of it all. He had worked a full day and here he was, in the middle of the night, driving through the empty streets of Baltimore. He was thinking to himself, *Couldn't she wait just four more days until the weekend?* He was irritated that despite his coaching and aggressive attempts to push for a Friday evening birth, Mom's failure to comply meant he had no choice but to use up two vacation days for my arrival.

He complained about the cost along the way, as he had done for several months up to this point. The way he rambled on, one would think that my mother's pregnancy had occurred by divine intervention, with my father as just an innocent bystander. Secretly, he thought to himself that, with my expected arrival, he was digging an even bigger hole for himself. In between complaints, he thought hard about those positions on the West Coast and in Europe that he had applied for. A voice in his head wondered, *I was fully qualified for those positions, why didn't they at least respond? I know mail takes time, especially international mail, but this is ridiculous! Probably just a matter of time before I get some news and can depart this mess I am in. How will I sell her on the idea of me taking a job overseas, especially with a newborn? Damn, why did I get her pregnant again? I don't even want to be married! I wish they'd respond to me! Ugh, Hell, the first kid she gave me is cross-eyed. What will this one be like? I'm fucked.*

The grunting and panting of my mother in the passenger seat were barely noticeable to him over the sounds of his incessant bitching, both in his head and streaming from his mouth. As was normal, focusing on himself was as far as his thoughts could go, even in a moment that was supposed to be as wonderful as the birth of a child, and even with Mom having painful contractions.

In between contractions, Jana Ann, my mother, didn't have much to say about his complaints. By this time, she had years of experience in quietly tolerating his banter. With the pain I was giving her from the inside, and the pain from the driver on the outside, it was incredible that she could still find the strength to smile. While she was financially dependent on this man seated next to her, she certainly did not depend on him for emotional or intellectual support, and after many months of raising John on her own in Pittsburgh while he "found his way," she still couldn't even depend on this man for the basics, like spending the night in their home on Wilkens. He was clear with her that it was important to him that he had his freedoms.

As evidenced by the intercepted mail, given all of the applications he had submitted, she knew it was likely he would eventually leave her, but she wasn't going to make it easy for him. Like many women of the time, she had learned to placate him. While her irritation with his conduct was real, she kept it deftly buried under the surface. After the birth of John, my father complained regularly about...well...*everything*. Although "everything" seems way too general, no other word fits, because truly nothing was off-limits.

He mostly complained about the cost and inconvenience of kids and marriage, and how he would be forced to work even *harder* to support the growing family. Because he was the provider, he gave himself unfettered permission to be miserable about everything. It never crossed his mind that his own actions were the reason he was in that spot in the first place. After all, all the time that he was complaining, he was having sex with my mother, and not even staying the night on most evenings. His part-time status didn't seem to matter to him, as he left us so often it became part of our "normal." My mother had gotten pregnant six times by my father, so as smart as he was, and as little as he seemed to want children, you would have thought that spending a couple dollars on a box of condoms would have made sense.

Thinking of the pressure my mother must have been under makes me sad for her. When she announced her pregnancy with me to him, his disdain and bitterness for his personal situation, and by association our family, only grew. Most likely, he saw his dream to abandon us slipping away. Two more miscarriages had come and gone and still his complaining never yielded to any thought of birth control. Despite all the belittling comments and threats of keeping our family to a minimum, he would climb onto her whenever the urge presented itself. After all, he perceived unlimited intercourse with her as a small price to pay for his misery.

Their ritual reminds me of an event I once witnessed at the San Diego Zoo. It was an odd scene that made the kind of memory that has no practical use, but because of its visual impact, stayed with me forever. A male monkey, after howling and seemingly berating a female with loud screams and chest pounding while sitting on a branch high in the trees, simply swung down from his limb, bent her over, and aggressively penetrated her from behind. The entire event lasted less than thirty seconds and ended with the male carelessly ejaculating in every direction for all to see as he disengaged from the female. With that, he returned to his position in the fake tree and resumed his verbal outbursts. This life in the cage, complete with the fake surroundings, the dominance of the male, the sex, the lack of gratitude or compassion after, and their mutual roles seemed a lot like the life my mother and father shared.

My mother's well-rehearsed smile for my father was most likely interpreted by him not as a gesture signifying her quiet and patient tolerance of him, but as a dumb blonde, "nothing between the ears" look. I have seen "the look" many times in their wedding and couples pictures. If I were not her son and didn't know how smart she was, I may have been fooled, but I came to learn this look, was more accurately, her "Don't rock the boat, Jana, my time will come" look.

My father continued to complain the entire way on the drive to the hospital. My mother looked over at the belligerent driver, her partner in life, and as each contraction passed, she grinned. The smile on her face must have seemed poorly timed and out of place to him. Perhaps she used the combination of her extreme pain and his endless stream of complaints as the perfect opportunity to fantasize about punching him hard in the face. Perhaps she thought of how his head would look with her arm coming out of the back of his skull as his mouth swallowed her arm all the way up to her elbow. I am sure these images would have been much more satisfying than the breathing techniques that had been encouraged in her birthing book. While she was rarely brave enough to directly challenge the man, she had developed coping mechanisms, and as his complaining continued, every exhale brought calm and tranquility to her face. Her smiles fed his anger, but she didn't seem to care. Whatever he felt, I was on the way, and there was nothing he could do to stop that.

Hours later, and without complication, Daniel James Wellington made his entry into the world. No fanfare other than that I shared the same birthday as John F. Kennedy, Will Ferrell, and my older brother John. Two days later, Jana Ann and John Robert took me home to their rental on Wilkens Avenue. With that, the challenging but ultimately adventurous trip that has been my life was underway.

By all outside appearances, we were your average upper-lower class, barely white-collar Baltimore family. Yet in many ways, we were a family in name only. We shared little except for our own private desires to be somewhere other than where fate had brought us. While a life of insecurity and sometimes unfettered insanity may not be the dream life for a child, at least I had been granted life. Laughter was rare, but that made the funny moments that much more important.

An example of an opportunity for laughter occurred when my mother was feeling mischievous one hot summer day. My father was cleaning his white Ford convertible in the driveway. He was almost finished polishing the yards of chrome trim as my mother coached John and me along in our first—and last—covert prank. In our kitchen, she used a saucepan to fill a large, plastic laundry hamper with water. Next, the three of us managed to get the hamper up two flights of stairs to a small window in our attic. At the ages of only seven and four, this was quite a job for me and John.

Unbeknownst to us, there was something very funny about to happen. While we had no idea of my mother's plan, to see her giggle the way she did, we would have carried that hamper to Memorial Park and back. We were delighted to be included in her joy.

When we reached the attic, she quietly pried a small window open, and we all looked down at my father proudly glowing over his sparkling clean car. The pieces came together quickly, and my brother and I didn't know whether to laugh or panic as we watched my mother wrestle the hamper to the windowsill. Without warning, she happily poured the heavy tub of water on my father and his gleaming vehicle below. Laughter was so infrequent in their marriage that I could not understand why she would take such a risk. Even at my young age, I knew that my father seldom found humor or lightheartedness in *anything*, especially if it was at his expense.

We sat on the floor hidden from his view below the windowsill and giggled until we were in stitches. My mother's genuine, ongoing laughter encouraged us to continue with our fun. The three of us were a happy family for just a few moments, as we laughed even harder. My father was a serious man, and I was sure he would never find humor in this prank, but I cannot remember any other occasion where we laughed so hard or for so long. This was a payback moment for my mother, and I was happy that she had taken the initiative.

When we could wring no more silliness out of the event, we started our descent to the kitchen, where we could hear my father drying off angrily. John's smile was ear to ear as he trailed our group in a distant third. Reading John's face, it appeared that his satisfaction seemed to be twice what I felt that day. Though he was only seven, John took pleasure in seeing our usually condescending and dismissive father as nothing more than a powerless wet mop. Seeing my father as something other than a tyrant, momentarily stripped of his authoritarian power, showed me that he was human and vulnerable, too. Looking back, the event also represented a beautiful proof of the power of laughter and its ability to transform a situation, if only for a brief moment in time. Seeing the good in a potentially volatile moment was another gift, one that would stay with me for life.

4
Home Sweet Home

In 1984, the Cars, a rock band that still ranks highly on my list of all-time-greats bands, had soared to the top of the charts with their *Heartbeat City* album. The now-classic album is filled with hits, but it was the song "Drive" that inspired me most, if in a backwards way.

"Drive" is a slow song that some might describe as depressing, but for me, it offered a realistic view into my life. When I listened to the questions in the Ric Ocasek-penned lyrics that Benjamin Orr sings so beautifully, wondering who exactly is hearing his troubles, I realized that I, too, had no one who cared about my questions or needs.

I benefited from the song because it helped me to understand that others were trying to make it in this world with no support but were explaining to me the value of figuring things out on their own. Through the poignant lyrics, I deduced that feeling like a victim would only drag me down. I resolved that I would do whatever work was necessary to answer my own questions and meet my own needs. Symbolically speaking, I decided that rather than worry about who was going to drive me home, to paraphrase Ocasek's lyrics, I was going to figure out how to drive myself home.

Even as a youngster, it was obvious no one else in my family was going to pick me up. Our five-member pod was a group of make-it-on-your-own outcasts who were more like roommates than family. We each existed on our own islands with little regard or concern for one another. I had been conditioned to understand and accept that I should not depend on my parents for support. I also knew that even if they did do something for us, it was actually to help them get something they wanted.

It wasn't difficult to see there was a lot wrong with my family. I always felt alone, even with family members in the room, and it should come as no surprise that I often felt sorry for myself. Even in my solitude, I always felt better being away from my roommates.

Yet once I tossed aside my self-pity, I found my absolute aloneness in the world could be a *strength*. Knowing there would be no one coming to my rescue or offering a helping hand gave birth to an early sense of resilience and determination to get somewhere better without any help.

While I could have allowed my circumstances to lead to a place of defeat, blame, or victimhood, I instead held tightly to what I took away from "Drive." I could not "go on thinking nothing's wrong," but I could and would get started on the important work I needed to do. Each time I heard the song, it fueled my conviction to find a way out.

When we lived on Wilkens, the yard of our home became somewhat of a sanctuary amidst the chaos. The yard featured a large collection of mature azaleas that in the height of spring would burst with a canopy of beautiful, large pink, crimson, and white blooms. One of my great joys during that time of year was to climb to the center of the bushes, deep in the sprawling azalea patch, and lie on my back. Once comfortable, I would look up at the sun making its way through the cover of the shrubs and find comfort in the warmth it showered on me. This near-sacred place, where I lay face up, smelling the dirt and the beautifully scented flowers mixed with rays of sun cutting through the blossom umbrella, would be a frequent place of safety for me. I would find great joy getting lost in the tunnels of interconnecting branches, grabbing at and disturbing the path of the dust particles dancing in and out of the beams on thick, humid air.

In fact, our entire yard was something of an oasis on our otherwise gritty city street. The expansive blackberry patch and pear trees in our backyard provided pounds of snacks in lean times, and we looked forward to this bounty in the years we lived there. And as much as I loved the azalea patch, my all-time favorite spot in the yard was a small, man-made pond in the middle of a clearing, surrounded by several large trees and four or five thick evergreen bushes. By late spring, the pond was completely hidden from both the outside world and the insanity of our home. Behind the dense evergreens lay a half-ring of thick, thorny blackberry bushes. The cover guaranteed there could be no surprise visitors from the house to interrupt whatever secret but harmless activities John and I were doing.

The pond was a refuge for us. When things got rough, we would meet there to hang out and shed the worries of the day. Within minutes, our childhood imaginations would take over, and we would make up some new game to take our mind off our troubles. The pond offered up the best medicine for the sadness we often found in our home. As dirty as the water was, we floated many stick and leaf boats on its surface, and, against our mother's wishes, we also caught and played with the mosquito larvae and gooey frogspawn in the spring, splashed around in the cloudy water in the summer, and shoe skated on the ice in the winter. The pond was our private piece of paradise and such a welcome gift amidst all of Baltimore's concrete, railway tracks, and traffic.

Indoors, 1319 Wilkens Avenue had some great qualities. The grandness of the place made me feel like a king. That we rented the biggest stand-alone house on our street in a sea of rowhouses also made me feel important. I can still see the beautiful open foyer that showed the way to a dark, tall, mahogany-colored staircase and railing. As a toddler, the space seemed boundless, and John and I quickly discovered the many hiding places that are typical of old houses.

My favorite room in the house was the attic. It had its own staircase where each step creaked more loudly as you climbed. There were several windows, which filled the room with bright sun more fully than any other place in the house. I often sat alone in the middle of the cavernous room basking in the warmth of the sunlight on my face. As with the azalea bushes, in these private moments, I would give hours of attention to chasing dust particles in the sunbeams. I disrupted their natural course by waving my hands through the air, attempting to catch the larger bits. The boxes of Mom and Dad's old things were also stored there. These were strictly off limits to us, but of course, that only made us more curious about the contents.

There were many other moments of joy despite the turmoil of my childhood. We lived immediately across from Loudon Park Cemetery, which stretched in all directions as far as I could see. Much of the land had yet to be sown with the bodies of the departed, so there were long swaths of lush green fescue that called to me to run barefoot through the blades of grass. While we were not permitted to enter the cemetery, it was the most grass I had ever seen in one place.

One of my greatest joys at home was running to the front porch every time a heavy rainstorm came rolling through. I trace my fondness for the smell of clean, refreshing rain to those moments sitting on that porch. Feeling the rush of cool, fresh air greeting my face was another of those simple gifts that always found a way into my life. If thunder and

The attic was a sanctuary for me at our home on Wilkens Avenue in Baltimore. I always enjoyed watching the sunlight come through the window and playing with the dust particles. This is the same window where my mother, John and I dumped a hamper of water on my father far down below.

lightning were part of the storm, the unobstructed view over the graveyard would set the stage for a spectacular light and sound show.

Looking out over the graveyard, watching the lightning zigzag through the sky and waiting for the thunder to roll loudly, was better than any movie. The hard rain beating down on that uninsulated sheet-metal roof added a stereo effect that made me think I was in the middle of the storm. I can recall imagining the dead people buried there jumping in their graves as the thunder clapped. I would watch the big drops fall and puddle at my feet and, despite my mother's protests, would run out into the water to play as it coursed down the street gutter on Wilkens.

On that same porch, our family would eat blue crabs once a year if we could afford them. My father would bring home a bushel of the smalls, and I would watch my mother picking crabs and drinking wine for hours. Dad would cook them in a big pot and we would watch in delight as the crabs tried to escape while Shep, our dog, learned the hard way that these creatures were well equipped to defend themselves. Crabs were her favorite, so even bad behavior was largely ignored on crab day!

We were too young to qualify for picking an entire crab ourselves, since they cost real money and we could not be trusted with such a large investment. So we would station ourselves next to either side of my mother and wait for her to throw us some crab meat. Like baby birds being fed by their mother, we couldn't eat the scraps fast enough and immediately wanted more.

Years later, as a parent myself, I learned what it was like to feed a nest of children waiting on a meal from the relatively meager yield of these spider-like sea creatures. I also remembered my mother's solution to our pestering. She would tolerate our pleading for scraps only until the hot dogs and hamburgers arrived off the grill for us to eat. While a hot dog or hamburger was not a close substitute for delectable Old Bay-seasoned flesh, it did fill us up, which was the intent. After gorging ourselves on the processed meat alternatives and my mother's pickle-packed, egg-yolk-rich potato salad, we would be more full and less demanding of her cherished crabs.

Her respite was short-lived, though. Soon enough, we would begin to hover once again at her side, waiting for a morsel or a shell she hadn't fully cleaned. When that was not enough, we would begin to eye the exoskeleton scraps she left piled high at the center of the table. Like gulls to a trash heap, we zealously set about picking clean the already well-picked shells. We delightfully searched for *any* scrap of meat we could find, while at the same time banging the mallets on the shells and table.

Even when we were done with a discarded crab, my father would inspect each carcass to be certain there was no waste. He hated waste of any type, and the expensive crustaceans were no exception. Even in their almost fully-picked status, the crabs were a precious gift not to be squandered.

My mother was always the last one sitting during our crab feasts. Contrary to the Maryland tradition of having beer with crabs, my mom would typically combine the seafood with a light rosé, which she would generously pour over ice from a gallon bottle. She was never a big talker, but when crabs were on the table, she barely said a word. She might occasionally point a finger or slap one of us in the back of the head when we were out of line and bothering her, but her only mission on those days was to sit and finish *every* crab.

The first time I ever drank beer was on one of those hot summer crab days. When we were very young, my father would allow us to sip off of his bottle. I remember the sudsy, warm, hoppy taste of the brew on my tongue. Although I never enjoyed the taste back then, I do remember liking the way it made me feel. In hindsight, it probably wasn't the best idea to share alcohol with a six-year-old, especially given the history of alcoholism that runs deep in our family, but it certainly seemed harmless enough, and untold numbers of fathers have done the same with their own kids, so I can't judge him too harshly in those instances.

Those idyllic, hot summer days spent sitting outside under our tin-roof porch were not without their share of urban grit. The air would be filled with smells of the city, and exhaust would blow in from the heavy traffic on Wilkens Avenue, mixing with the smell of just-dug, deep, fresh, moist dirt upended for the next tenant at the cemetery.

Meanwhile, the dark gray, lead-heavy paint on the porch would warm in the direct sun, emitting a smell that could not have been healthy to be breathing, but I enjoyed it and attached the scent to the good memory of those crab days. Sizzling hotdogs and hamburgers would intertwine with the smell of Old Bay and vinegar-laced steam, making me salivate. As if that weren't enough, from the west came smells of deep-fried chicken and burgers cooking immediately next door at Gino's Restaurant, a fast-food joint started by Gino Marchetti, a Baltimore Colts legend.

While nothing could top crab day, we did love Gino's, and on special occasions, Mom would send us next door to buy a bag of Gino Giants and fries. We savored every bite of the delicious sloppy burgers and tasty fries. If we were well-behaved, a thick chocolate shake might follow.

As much as we loved Gino's food, the rats that lived in our yard and basement loved it even more. They lived like kings, eating the mountains of unmanaged waste that spilled over from the Gino's dumpsters. With this never-ending, year-round smorgasbord available to the vermin, they had little incentive to take up residence any further away than our big, inviting lawn and home. In fact, because our basement floor had a network of rat tunnels, we speculated that at least one of them must have been an expressway right to the dumpster goodies.

The thought of the rats and all of the food they were eating brought to mind the rat named Templeton from E.B. White's classic children's novel *Charlotte's Web*. While the rats in my basement were not as personable as Templeton, they certainly looked as fat and happy as he did following his feast at the state fair! Sometimes they seemed barely able to fit into their tunnels. Gino's had been very good to them.

From time to time, my brother and I would hear something crawling in the walls of our bedroom. Our mother would respond to our cries for help by running to the rescue with one of her large hardback textbooks in hand. She would wait a moment or two to isolate the location of the vermin, and then, with full force, slam the hardcover book to the wall. The sound was extremely loud, and whatever was living there responded accordingly, scurrying frantically up, down, and sideways within the walls looking for a place away from the immediate threat.

While the rats were only an occasional nuisance in the bedroom area, my mother was obsessed over the non-stop presence of the mice and roaches that thrived in our home. They were *everywhere* and in *everything*. Their favorite time to roam was in the evening, when my mother would be alone in the kitchen studying. I was often awakened by the sound of her swatting at these pests with her broom. She had little regard for any household items that might stand between her and her prey. As she swung away determinedly, all the while fully voicing her frustration, pots, pans, and plastic bowls would be dancing around the kitchen counters and floors.

Sometimes I would creep down the creaky stairs to watch her hunting the pests. She would handle the broom like a character out of a *Tom & Jerry* cartoon. As she swatted and swung, her face red, the strands of her hair flying about as her neat, hair-sprayed beehive unwound, I could not help but feel some levity in the moment. To her, though, this was no joke. This was war—a very sad and lonely war.

In just one of many examples, I remember as a toddler being delighted to be asked to reach into a tight spot behind the stove in order to grab a sprung mousetrap and its victim. I was so proud of the opportunity to help and to show her the bloody, often decapitated animal. Full of anticipation, I hoped to gain her approval and see her pride and joy at notching a win. Instead, what I saw was her tears, as she looked up from re-baiting a trap to see a herd of baby roaches streaming out of an electric socket as if to mock her efforts. My mother was a hard woman, but in these moments, I learned she could be rattled, and it hurt me to see her both cursing and crying simultaneously. It was likely the first time I would understand that beyond being my mother, she was also human.

Despite how accustomed we had become to our unwanted housemates, we never grew comfortable with cereal boxes eaten through by mice or roaches crawling out of everything. All sorts of bugs infested our pantries, and the powerfully potent sour smell of their excrement and urine was part of our kitchen experience. It was useful in a practical sense to expect the worst every time we opened anything that wasn't canned. Setting the bar low and carefully surveying what we were about to eat was a necessity prior to any meal that wasn't cooked. We were not the kind of family that had the means or desire to throw away food the pests had tainted, so my mother would make a symbolic effort to cut away or separate the affected parts of our meals. As this was standard practice, we had no problem eating whatever was left over. Like having a free range father, this simply was part of our "normal." In fact, we even came to feel fortunate that the rats mostly stayed in the basement, because it was easier for them to scrounge the unlimited supply of food waste from the fast food restaurant's dumpster located less than twenty feet from our front door than it would have been to scavenge in our kitchen.

One of our favorite things about the house turned out to be our landlord, Mr. Buchheister. He was a kind elderly man with a small, two-level, all-brick commercial building located at the end of our driveway in the backyard. John and I were delighted to learn he was a candy maker and used his space to make wonderful homemade candy to sell at the market year-round.

Every day, my brother and I would argue to see who would hand the day's mail to Mr. Buchheister. The rule was that the winner handed over the mail, while the loser, who was almost always me, would lag a few feet behind. Each day, Mr. Buchheister would answer with a big smile on his face, as the smells of fresh hard candy and taffy, items that he would sell at the famous Lexington Market in Baltimore, wafted out to greet us.

Inevitably, he would invite us in to see what he was making, occasionally allowing us to stir the contents of one of the large gas-fired copper vats. Although his famous peanut brittle was our favorite, *everything* he made was delicious. What I think made Mr. Buchheister's candy so tasty was the fact that we were eating it in his magical little building, only minutes after he had made it, and so every visit and every piece was part of a wonderful adventure. That modest little thirty-by-twenty brick building was our private, scaled-down Wonka factory, that was also free of any of the pain we were experiencing in the main house located only seventy five yards away. While we did not completely understand it at the time, John and I desperately needed those brief, daily escapes into that magical place, and we also needed Mr. Buchheister's steady, dependable kindness. Everything else in our world was marred by volatility.

Around that same time, I began school, attending Violetville Elementary for my first full-time educational experience. My brother and I walked to this city school every day, and we stayed at Violetville until John finished fifth grade and I completed second grade. It was a little over a mile walk to the school, but the distance was made much shorter when we began crossing the high-speed railroad tracks. Of course, we had been strictly forbidden to take this shortcut, but I was in my brother's charge, and I went where he told me. My mother had put all her trust in John, probably because she had to work and had no other choice, but naturally, she had her doubts about her eldest son's trustworthiness. As a further deterrent, she regularly reminded us of two brothers who had been killed a couple of summers earlier on these same high-speed railroad tracks. While I'm not sure if the story she told was real or fictional, it didn't matter, because John was going to cross the tracks anyhow, and he knew that, scared or not, I would follow him.

Along with smoking, John had picked up some of my parents' "encouragement tactics," so even though he was only in fifth grade, when he threatened to hurt me, I took him at his word. He wanted me to consider him as much of a threat as I did them, and believe me, I did. His repeated threats to beat me, along with my fear of walking to school by myself, ensured that I was a dependable and compliant tag-a-long on the dangerous venture across the tracks. I was too young to process the fact that his threats were not nearly as dangerous as the threat of being slaughtered by the high-speed commuter trains. It's quite disturbing to me to think that, as a six-year-old, I had to make and live with such frightening decisions, but at that time, John was thinking about his own needs, not mine.

When the cigarettes he lifted from my mother and father were not enough, John used my lunch money to buy cigarettes 'for his mother' from a local small store. Of course, this was legal at the time, and he was never questioned because of course a nine year old would not be a smoker. If I protested at all, he bullied me into submission.

In fact, the whole reason he liked the train track route was not so

Passing the blackberry bushes along the way to Mr. Buchheister's candy factory found in our back yard. Bringing the mail to him daily, John and I could always depend on warm candies and a kind smile. My favorite was his peanut brittle.

much because it offered a short-cut, but because we rarely saw another soul there. This allowed him to easily sneak in a smoke or two along the way. His favorite spot for a cigarette was under the bridge span where no one could see us. Because of his habit, our commute would often be stalled, making us frequently late to school.

John only made good on his threat to make me walk home from school alone one time. While I do not recall the exact circumstances, I can still see him walking away as I sat there crying and panicking. Although he was too young to fully understand the potential danger in which he was leaving me, he definitely was old enough to challenge my failure to comply and issue me a consequence.

After he disappeared, I sat alone crying for some time. I was in a panic, but then had to make the decision to head in the direction of where I thought home was. Finally, with no other alternative, I started walking, and it wasn't long before I found myself lost. I was only six or seven at the time and about as frightened as I had ever been.

Eventually, two older girls, about eleven or twelve, happened by and saw me crying, and to my great relief, they promised to walk me home. Their only condition was that they first wanted to make a stop at the local corner store, the very same one where John liked to shop. I was fine with that, happy to have their company, and excited when they promised to buy me a popsicle to help me stop crying. As we walked, though, I realized I was getting farther and farther away from what I thought was the right way home. With each step, I was becoming more and more dependent on these two girls I didn't even know.

We finally reached the store, and the girls kept their promise to buy me a popsicle, so things were looking up. We sat for some time to eat our frozen treats, and although I had no real concept of time, as we finished licking our fingers, I could see the sun was beginning to set. The girls must have sensed the passing of time, too, because they explained they could no longer walk me home and left me on the stoop of the corner store.

I felt the panic rising inside of me. I was lost and afraid, and my mind filled with uncontrollable dread. Now further from home than before, as tears fell down my face, I began walking in the direction I thought pointed me home. After covering a few blocks while experiencing skin-crawling anxiety, I sat down next to the only thing I recognized: a high chain-link fence next to the train tracks. Unfortunately, I had no idea where to find the hole in the fence John and I always passed through to cross the tracks.

I sat in place and cried hard for a short while, wishing desperately that my brother was with me. For some reason, my intuition (and what

I now know was my higher power) told me I needed to get moving. The sun was sinking in the sky, and I knew I was not in a great area to be stuck after sunset. Still scared, I mustered up the will to begin my journey home. I brushed off my pants, drew an imaginary arrow toward the direction where I thought home might be, and began walking in that direction. Off in the distance, I could see the bridge where John and I would stop so he could smoke. I felt some relief that I could now use this landmark to plot a general course towards home. I decided to follow the fence until I could find the hole to pass through, knowing that if I could find it, the rest of the way home would be doable. Along the way, buildings and abandoned cars were making the path seem more familiar, and my confidence began to grow.

Finally, when I reached a familiar, abandoned, stripped-down Chevy wagon, I knew the hole in the fence was only about twenty feet away from the vehicle. I passed through the hole and stumbled down the loose-gravel embankment, rocks cascading down with me. The hill was steep, so I had to trot down the hill, and sure enough, I lost my footing at the bottom, landing feet up, ass down at the muddy base of the hill. I sat there for a while, my pants torn, my arm with a nasty scratch, and studied my next obstacle, a smaller hill that would lead up to the first set of train tracks.

I was temporarily paralyzed with fear at the thought of climbing the slope and crossing the tracks alone without my brother's trusted play-calling, but the sun was now really setting, and the darker sky brought my fear to full boil. I clawed my way up the next hill, just as a deafening metallic ringing of the tracks called out. The awful high-frequency racket was immediately followed by a silver commuter train passing at full speed. I retreated to the base of the hill, whimpering at the thought of standing on that plateau again, but I knew that if I didn't go soon, it would be completely dark.

For whatever reason, in my young mind, the fear of being obliterated by a train came in a distant second to having to spend the entire night asleep on the gravel inside the railyard, so I mentally prepared myself to move forward again. Soon the sky was filled again with the high-pitched sound of metal vibrating uncontrollably and quick, violent overhead snaps and pops of electricity as another train flew by in the opposite direction on a different track. It was dark enough to see the sparks generated from the cables above the trains which added to my fear.

If I had been ten or fifteen years older, I would have realized it was rush hour and the Baltimore-Washington commuter trains were running very regularly, meaning I was about to attempt my crossing at the riskiest period in the day. In hindsight, it was for the best that I did *not* have this information because I had no choice but to make it home. I peered over the crest of the hill at the shiny sets of tracks that lay before me, knowing full well I would need to make several separate dashes to get across each set of tracks.

I sat by the first set of tracks I would need to cross and watched as two trains passed by in opposite directions again. The setting sun continued to feed my anxiety, pushing me to execute my plan. By this time, it didn't even matter to me that two boys had been killed in this very spot, because I knew if they had to do it all over again, they would never have elected to sleep by the tracks. With that, I stood up and looked far down the tracks in search of the headlights of any train that might be coming in either direction.

It was difficult to distinguish between distant house lights located close to the tracks and the lights of high-speed locomotives bounding through the cool night air. That was a major challenge since I knew the time between accurately spotting a train light and the arrival of the train to my location was only seconds, so I also listened closely for the telltale ringing of the tracks, signaling that a train was approaching. The closer it got, the louder and higher the speed of the vibrational tone, the greater the chance of a bad outcome. Even with what I thought to be careful planning, I was too young to fully understand the implications of a miscalculation. All I understood was that it was go time!

I stuffed my notebook under my arm with purpose, dug my toes into the stones, and prepared for the perfect moment to leap up the hill and across the first set of tracks. With a lump in my throat and my heart racing, I got myself into what I thought would be a proper dashing position. I peered hard into the setting sun in the direction I thought the train would come, crying and shaking with fear. On the count of three, I would cross.

"One... Two... Three."

No movement at all. My feet clearly were not listening to my mind.

Again, "One... Two... Three."

Again, nothing.

With the sun quickly disappearing, I counted again out loud, "One... Two... Three."

This time my legs listened, and I started to claw on all fours up the hill to the first set of tracks. Being overwhelmed with fear mixed with the difficult job of sprinting up a large-grade loose rock embankment made fast movement almost impossible. Here again, I was stumbling on the dirty, white stones as they gave way under my feet, but I made it to the top of the plateau and ran through the debris of liquor bottles and garbage.

Only ten more feet and I would be across the first set of tracks! Though the coming night air was cold, I could feel sweat running down my back and tears beginning to cloud my view. With a few more feet to go before I crossed the tracks, I suddenly felt myself slowing down when I should have been speeding up. With fear taking over, I dropped to my knees three feet from the tracks and took a long look in the quiet night down the track again. With no oncoming lights, I found a burst of courage and made my move.

Incredibly enough, as I crossed over the first rail of the first set, arriving at a dangerous position between tracks, I heard my name being called by a familiar voice. A woman's voice kept calling to me, each time more loud and more frantic, until finally she was screaming at me to get off the tracks. I was happy to comply, only I didn't know in which direction to go. Did this guardian angel want me to cross the next set of tracks, which would take me closer to home? Or did she want me to go back in the direction of the hole in the fence near the old Chevy?

I stood between the rails, looking in both directions as darkness crept closer, hoping the voice would call out again with clear instructions. When I was blessed with the angel's voice again, I was relieved I could isolate her voice as coming from the direction of the old Chevy. The voice carried fear that seemed as great as my own, but I knew I needed to run back to her, regardless of the fact that I'd be going in the wrong direction.

Before I could begin, I dropped my notebook on the tar-covered timber in the center of the track, the rings springing open and the papers and pencils went tumbling out. Should I leave everything there or attempt to gather my school things? Thinking of how my parents would react to losing my school things, I knelt down and hastily closed the metal-ringed binder, stuffing what I could back into the notebook. Then, with a quick look down the tracks in the direction in which the last train had come, I darted back over the rail and trotted down the small hill to the stone embankment.

Within seconds, the rails I had just crossed shimmered in the dusk and I turned to see a train passing at the speed of a bullet in the opposite direction of where I had just been looking. The train, void of any headlight, sped by with another group of professionals leaving the city to wherever it was they were going. Knowing I had been looking in the wrong direction, it occurred to me that I had just barely avoided certain death.

Clear of danger, I wondered who the voice calling me belonged to, and I hoped whomever she might be, she would be able to get me home.

I soon realized the woman's voice was that of my sometimes babysitter, Vicky. My mother had sent her to look for me while she stayed home with my brothers. As a young local girl, she had crossed the tracks in her own youth and knew where to look first. I had never been so happy to see her before.

As we walked home hand-in-hand at a very quick pace, she chided me furiously, with me crying hysterically the entire way. She tried to explain the sequence of events—the barreling train, the danger, and how sad my mother would have been had I died. Before long, I had returned to my second-grade mentality and could not understand what all the fuss was about. Sure, I was still scared at having been lost and abandoned by John. But surely the adults would understand that spending the night by the tracks was not the best option. I was going home and that was all that mattered to me.

When we walked in the door, my mother was forced to console both Vicky and me. By this point, my sadness and tears were largely ceremonial. The crisis had passed, and I was on to the next concern, namely that of being severely punished for my actions. I hoped that if I could convince my mother I was sorry for my mistake and still full of fear, I might get off more easily.

As for Vicky, I sensed her tears and sadness were different from mine. While I knew she had some genuine concern for me, I could tell there was more to her sadness. As she stammered and sobbed through the replaying of the event to my mother, I realized she was coming to accept the fact that she had almost witnessed her first death. And as only a teenager could, she freely admitted that while she had rescued me that day, her voice causing me to pause between the rails could have gotten me killed.

She was still quite shaken when her mother arrived an hour or so later to pick her up. Vicky moved away later that summer, and I never saw her again. I wish I had been mature enough to thank her for saving my life, but as I process these events today, I have a strong feeling that something was guiding me and Vicky that night, and that something wanted me to survive and live a lot longer. I had been granted yet another gift.

Me attempting to cross the high-speed train tracks on my own at a young age. Fortunately, another angel was looking out for me and the story ended well.

5

The Characters and More

"Here I Go Again" by Whitesnake is undoubtedly one of the most powerful hair-band rock ballads of the late '80s. I'm risking being a bit cliché by including this song among my life-savers, but it was so motivating and powerful to me that I can't dismiss its influence. This song has to have had a positive influence on anyone lucky enough to have heard it, either then *or* now! When I watched Mr. David Coverdale passionately sing his classic, I internalized his message that anything was possible and that I could find a life on my own. With Whitesnake as my guide, I could look far away from the reality of my life, and make up my mind to not waste any more time.

By the end of each listen to that hard-driving song, I would be reminded I could overcome any obstacle. Here was another person just like me, searching for answers, dealing with being alone, and using songs of yesterday to guide him. Now that was something I could relate to!

Even today, when I hear "Here I Go Again," I am reminded that nothing is impossible. The adrenaline still pumps through my veins, and, like a team of horses, I find the strength to push forward. After all these years, I now pick up on his reminder that our time here is limited and we can't wait for others to make our fate.

My mother learned about making her own fate early in life. She grew up poor on Pittsburgh's North Side, one of four daughters. Her father was abusive to her mother and her sisters, and, like my father, he came and went as he pleased. My mother rarely spoke of her father, but she did once tell us he would stay out all night, come home to sleep off his hangover, and then, after eating, would extract what little money her mother and sisters had stowed away before heading out again to the local bars. As his alcoholism intensified and the girls grew older, the abuse became more intense and more frequent.

Eventually, Marge, my grandmother, could no longer tolerate the man, so she took what she could grab and moved with her girls to the other side of town. Sometime later, she met a nice man named Henry "Hank" Small, an Air Force bomber pilot and World War II veteran. Marge and Henry married shortly thereafter, and even though the girls were now grown, times became better for all. While Henry was also a heavy drinker, he was a good drunk, making it a better situation both for my grandmother and my mother.

My mother was dealt some difficult hands in her young life, but things looked up temporarily when she met and eventually married my father, a man who would, in fact, change her life for the better. While the future he offered was hardly that of a Prince Charming, he did represent a ticket out of the world she had known up to that point.

My father was a good-looking man and naturally tough, a product of his environment and upbringing. He was born to two alcoholics in Pittsburgh. His father was a part-time window washer who was rarely around. Nonetheless, my father spoke of him with reverence, love, and affection. He described his mother as violent and condescending.

My grandmother Bertha had six children in all, but the State of Pennsylvania made her give up the first four to foster care. My father only knew one of his half-brothers, a man named Walt. This came only after my father retired and decided to search for unknown blood relatives by using one of the now popular ancestry tracking services. Dad and Walt grew somewhat close later in life, and it was in the course of building that relationship that my father discovered he had two more half-brothers and one half-sister. Uncle Walt, a recluse who lived only in the kitchen of his home, was quite introverted, and a bit eccentric, too. After he passed away in the same kitchen, we learned he had hidden much of his wealth in his stove in the form of gold bars and coins. So it was no wonder to us why he stayed in his kitchen safeguarding his riches!

Given her failure to properly care for her first four children, my grandmother's decision to have my father and his brother, my Uncle Jim, defied all logic. My father often described her as hating children (a theme that was already familiar to me), and she often spoke the mantra that *all* children belonged in "public homes," which to her meant any establishment that would pay for, house, and raise them. Naturally, she often threatened my father and his brother with just such a fate, and not surprisingly, that rhetoric eventually turned to reality, because she surrendered both of them to military schools and religious-backed institutions for most of their childhood.

Their last home growing up was a military school where they boarded for several years. While my grandfather was never up for the "Father of the Year" award, he did keep his promise to visit them every Sunday, and, despite his failure to be an active part of his sons' upbringing, my father considered him to be a good man. After hearing the many stories of misdeeds and neglect in his childhood, I was surprised my father thought so highly of the man, but perhaps this was because the bar had been set so low. My grandfather died penniless and was buried in an unmarked grave somewhere near Pittsburgh.

Maybe a year later, I met my grandmother. My father forced the visit upon my brother and me. We drove to Pittsburgh's North Side, where she lived in a tiny apartment in the projects. When I walked into the projects where she lived, I felt as if I was walking up to an abandoned house on a dark Halloween night. As soon as I laid eyes on the building, my greatest wish was that the visit would be quick so we could safely get back to the car and head home.

I remember walking into the apartment building, the acrid smell of urine and rotting trash rising up to greet us, mixed with the voices and yells of other tenants all around us. Although I was very young, I immediately understood this was not a happy place. I remember fighting back tears of fear, even horror, as we approached her door at the end of a hallway close to a shared bathroom. After my father's loud knocking and several minutes of waiting for my grandmother to noisily shuffle to the door, she finally opened the door. My eyes were glued to the floor, and I only could glimpse up for a second or two at a time at the woman who appeared and clumsily offered an awkward hug and kiss.

We wandered slowly and cautiously into the two-room apartment, as the sour smell of thick smoke and wine greeted us. The place was sparsely furnished, and an old black and white television droned on with gray, white, and black lines rolling through the projected images. An ancient, noisy refrigerator in the corner only added to the clamor. Opposite the refrigerator, by a dirty window, was an old tweed chair worn through where forearms had rested for decades; the chair's wood frame was showing through in several places. This image, combined with the view of a seat cushion retaining the sharp impression of only one person's backside, told me it was well-used. It was also one of the only items in the room not covered with a heavy coat of dust.

A fresh cloud of blue smoke cleared, and for the first time, I saw in full detail the old, broken inhabitant who was my grandmother. Even in greeting us, she couldn't set down her cigarette with the long ash hanging from it. The ash fell to the floor as she moved, though she had no concern for the mess she was leaving behind in her slow wake. I imagine she must have been nervous herself, having never met her grandchildren before.

My father and his mother were not close, which he was not shy about communicating to us, and now, seeing them together in person, it was clear he held her in disdain and disrespect. My impression was that the visit was either an extraordinarily generous gift of rare human contact for her or a lesson for us children to digest. I imagine now that it probably was some combination of both. Either way, tension filled the room. In short order, she had made her way back to the chair, where she promptly turned and freefall dumped herself onto the threadbare cushion. Her face was yellowed, no doubt from a lifetime of smoking and poor health. Her teeth were gone, and wrinkles were cut deep into her face.

As gifts for his mother, my father had brought a gallon of cheap red wine and a carton of non-filter Chesterfield 100s. She was grateful for his gesture, and it was obvious my father knew his mother well, as there could not have been two more perfectly suited gifts for her.

The lifestyle of the old woman I was witnessing in front of my eyes, coupled with the mean things my father had continually said about her, told me everything I needed to know about why things were as they were between them. Bertha was never going to leave this place for some place nicer, and my father didn't care. He set the cheap wine down at the foot of the old chair. The timing was right, as his mother had nearly finished the quart of wine that already lay at her feet.

After he presented her with the gifts, my father forced us to cross the room and give her a squeeze and to kiss her cheek, something we didn't even do in our own family. She stopped pulling on her cigarette just long enough to accept the hugs, which we gave sullenly and in silent protest. Like every child forced to give affection to an unknown relative, the entire display was fake and forced, and all parties awkwardly and instinctively knew it. The insincerity of our gestures was reinforced by the fact that my father would not or could not embrace his own mother during the visit.

Curiously, though, after my hug was done, she grabbed me firmly by my shoulders to take an extended and direct look into my eyes. Our long gaze rewarded me with the opportunity to spend some quality time studying her facial features. I noticed quickly the lack of teeth in her head. I had never seen anyone up close without teeth, but given her diet of wine, bread, and cigarettes, she had little use for them. Her eyes and skin were yellowed like the nicotine-stained walls of her two-room cell. Her body was small, and her spine was curled, causing her to be hunched over permanently. She seemed very fragile to the touch, with no hint of muscle structure. A thin housecoat hung on her bony, naked frame like a sheet over furniture. I didn't know whether the foul smell that was especially intense while in her grasp was coming from the room or from her.

She asked a few things about me, but I could see in her eyes there was more she wanted to say. I couldn't stand to be that close to anyone, let alone a dirty, smelly, crusty stranger who was groping me. The interaction ended within seconds, and then I witnessed the woman's eyes darting around the room at our faces as the frames of her life seemed to play out before her. With that, our father forced us to awkwardly huddle around her as she replayed silently in her mind some memories of the many hard years that had passed. I would have gladly thrown myself out the window rather than being forced to sit there in this extremely uncomfortable setting.

Broken adult children have a way of using their own children as a tool to force their parents to reconcile with and pay the emotional price for their sins. I believe my grandmother paid heavily that day. If she had not known so previously, in that visit, it must have become clear her life was close to over, and that no amount of effort was going to free her from this fate. She was going to die alone in that apartment and that would be the end of her story.

I also believe that in presenting us to her, my father wanted her to see that he would never forgive her for her sins. While she was ostensibly being given the gift of meeting her grandchildren, this act of revenge was likely the true purpose. To throw John and me in her face in the last days of her life must have been a poison dart with a message that said, "Here I am with my children—your grandchildren. I didn't abandon them (well, at least not yet, anyway). They are clean, in school, and happy, *and* they will never be a part of your life."

Receiving this message, she must have known there was no sense in challenging him or attempting to explain herself. She was alone and helpless and would never be a part of our family, which unbeknownst to her was broken and dysfunctional. Even though his presentation about our reality was, in fact, a lie, I am certain he inflicted the kind of pain he had intended.

There were no faked attempts of affection by him, and it was clear he was just putting in his time. It would have been foolish to badger my father about leaving because he ruled with a strict hand. Despite our obvious discomfort and fear of this woman, requesting to leave would have come with a heavy penalty—either in real time or on the long ride back to Baltimore—so my brother and I sat against the wall, below the purple smoke cloud, and half-listened as my grandmother and father exchanged empty conversation.

When forced to pay attention, John and I stared only at our father, as we feared what eye contact with Bertha might do to us. We studied him closely, waiting for any indication that a departure was forthcoming. The key was to act like we didn't care if we left or stayed. He eventually gave us the nod and with a simple, unemotional wave goodbye, we were in our jackets, flinging the door open, and darting out into the hallway. We ran down the hallway of the tenement building and out the front door. The sight and smell of trash piled high, abandoned cars, and dilapidated buildings never looked so good. We were back on the sidewalk of a place and in a city we did not know, and all I could feel was relief. The entire event from start to finish remains one of the most bizarre and fearful moments of my life.

I know how much I love my children and how much I can't wait to meet my grandchildren. I'm sure that us coming to visit and then leaving forever was enough to drive the point home of just how badly she had failed her son and her other five children. I hope this act of hostility gave my father some closure. He deserved much better than what his parents, particularly his mother, gave him.

And yet, rather than shed his demons when he began his own family, he created his own brand of misery for all of us, as did my mother in her own ways. They both came into their marriage without any good modeling in terms of what a healthy relationship could or should be, and, particularly for my mother, once that ring went on her finger, things grew grim.

Unfortunately, her childhood struggles and disappointments, along with baby making and marital challenges, led her to a dark, quiet place. She used this place to become silently resolute that she would survive whatever would come at her. What we saw from the outside was a mostly immovable force that could be as tough and inflexible as forged steel. I fantasized, even as young as ten or so, about ways that I could bring her happiness.

Years later, as a teenager, I could sense in her deepening silence that she longed for something better, and I felt sad for her. I will detail later in these pages some unfortunate happenings, but no matter how her behavior might be viewed, I know, even without her saying it, that she wanted to be and to give more to my brothers and me.

I believe she tried to be a good wife, too, particularly in the beginning. By the time I was born in 1967, my parents had fallen into the then still-traditional version of marriage and to the outside world probably seemed pretty normal, at least at a first glance. My father worked by day in his government job. My mother would have dinner ready by 5:30 every night and slippers by the door when her husband came home. She listened to what he told her, cleaned our home, and was careful to make sure his needs were met. While the '60s offered some hope that the rigid housewife construct of earlier decades was changing, she understood that life with my father was still a carefully choreographed set of predetermined traditional dances, a cultural construct that nicely suited his needs.

I believe she was cognizant of the role she assumed in the household and the oppression that went with it. Society, along with my father's expectations, mandated that she be a good wife and mother while dismissing any personal held ambitions outside of marriage and childcare. While she could see pathways to opportunities, they were, for her, out of reach because of her station in life as a housewife and mother. As much as she might have wanted to leave my father, her freedom would have come with huge risks and problems. So, she remained trapped within her own life.

On the outside, she obeyed. On the inside, she patiently waited, taking infant steps toward independence wherever and whenever she could. She knew that no matter how well she played the role of dutiful wife and mother, her husband was not happy and that one day, the life she was living, already sad, would take a turn for the worse when he deserted her. Through the letters from his prospective employers that she had intercepted, she at least had been tipped off to his secret motivations, and if and when he eventually acted on them, she intended to be ready.

My mother knew she was behind the proverbial eight ball. She had no money, no education, no skills, no friends, and no geographically close family to whom she could confide. Of course, even if her family had been living next door, she would not have confided in them, so they wouldn't have been much help. So, she pursued the hard-earned University of Maryland degree, even as my father mocked her efforts. In addition to her own tenuous future, she had her pride to consider, and I believe that was a big consideration for her. She was the first in her family to graduate from college and even though she was introverted, she wanted her family in Pittsburgh to believe she had greatly improved her station in life. In our visits, I could see how proud her sisters were of her. She would never brag, but an occasional lightness about her in their company told me that she was also proud of herself.

At the same time, she was a realist. She could not blame her husband for being who he was: an abused child grown to be an abusive husband, living in a male-dominated environment that seemed to accept his abusive and controlling behavior as normal. Besides, she needed this man to provide for her and her children for as long as possible. Despite his many flaws, I believe she loved him and spent the best part of her life waiting for him to love and want her in return, as he had promised he would. Add to that the fact that he had provided her with the only stability she had ever known in her life, imperfect as it may have been. Perhaps that's why she mustered the strength to endure both the endless routine and the fruitless efforts to live up to his expectations.

I believe at some point she wanted to be a good mother. Although she never dripped with gooey love or affection, she claimed her parenting was an improvement from what she had received as a child, and when I consider her words today, I believe her. Of course, whenever she complained about the hardships of her youth when I was a kid—which she did far less frequently than my father—her words went in one of my ears and out the other. Decades later, and with five children of my own, when I consider what my mother and father experienced at the hands of their own parents, I can better appreciate their experiences, and have grown to understand they truly did provide more to us than what they had received from their parents. For that, I am grateful.

Bertha ended up dying only a year after that one and only time I met her. Hers was the first funeral I ever attended. With a purposeful nudge, my father forced me to approach the casket alone and stare at the gray shell of the body that lay there. I was creeped out as any youngster would be, but my primary concern was to minimize the length of this special one-on-one experience with Grandma and to do so without the possibility of my father getting angry at me. She looked and smelled awful, or maybe it was the awful stale chemical smell of the funeral home or the smell of embalming fluids.

I'm not sure why he insisted I see her corpse. Maybe it was because he thought that this was how he would make a man out of his son. I also think he simply enjoyed the power of us having to listen to every order he barked, even one that demanded I participate in this absurdly uncomfortable and disturbing event for a person whom he'd repeatedly told us he despised.

Although it felt like at least an hour, I'm sure it was less than a minute before I left her side, thankful to move to the farthest point across the room from her resting box. I fell into whatever background I could find to disappear, wishing, as always, that I was somewhere else other than with him. As I recall the scene, I know there were not many people there, which wasn't surprising, but most of them were actively smoking. Because of that, a bluish cloud hung above us all, illuminated by rays of light trying to reach us from the outside. Once again, I put my attention on the dust particles—my friends—that were dancing within. The heavy flower-patterned curtains, with their sheer white liner, seemed to drink in the smoke around them. Yellowed ceilings and walls, thick with decades of nicotine exposure, seemed to fit this crowd and my grandmother perfectly.

The sparsely attended service in the grimy funeral home seemed to suit the life my grandmother had led. At that moment, young as I was, I felt some sympathy for her and wondered what had happened between the day she was born and this moment in the coffin. When had her life gone so wrong? When I combined all the bad my father had said about her with the image of her guzzling wine while sitting in that awful piss-rotted chair, smoking like it was a full-time job, I didn't have to be a psychotherapist to theorize she'd made a few bad decisions along the way. While I did not yet understand how badly her own parents had treated her, nor the ramifications their treatment of her must have had on her own self-esteem and on her life as an adult, the fact remained that she had been unable to break the generational cycle when she herself became a parent.

My father must have been satisfied that this chapter had closed for him, in the same way that I felt some relief when he passed. I feel sadness knowing how powerless she was to change her fate. Certainly the cards had been stacked against her from day one. Given the long line of drinkers, smokers, and criminals who came before her, it would have been incredibly difficult to fight off the destructive hands of generational influence. But it would not have been impossible. I'm sure that like most young girls, she had dreams. Maybe she had wanted to be a dancer, or a police officer, or a teacher. Somewhere along the way, though, she lost whatever will she had possessed and caved in to those who would encourage her to continue the long campaign of dysfunction feeding dysfunction.

I can relate to Bertha's struggle to some degree, as I have felt the same quiet hands of history nudging me in the wrong direction at times. I know from experience what those influences look like, along with their relentless call to take the easy, destructive route to nowhere good. My higher power was with me when I made some bad decisions—plenty of them, as a matter of fact—but I know now that the lessons learned in those trials were part of becoming who I am, and I am thankful that most times I quickly returned to the right path. Fortunately, I am wired to work hard, learn from my mistakes, and find success while immersed in challenging circumstances. This wiring, a gift that at times I viewed as a curse, drove me to finding a better life for myself. I knew that a better life didn't involve being in jail or letting life pass me by the way Bertha had done. Yes, I flirted with trouble, but I always had a silent hand keeping me from going too far off the rails on my own crazy train. It was exhausting at times to keep pressing forward with rewards hard won and far and few. Stubborn will was necessary, but my drive never allowed me to build the important life skills of being present and grateful for what I already possessed. Those valuable lessons would not be learned by me until much later, such that today, living in peace and happiness are so important to my very existence. I know now that learning to be present and grateful represents the most important work I will ever do in this life.

Today, I give *all* the credit for whatever success I have had in my life to my higher power. When I was younger, I felt God didn't exist in any form and if it did, it was not in the business of granting wishes to me or anyone else. To me, God was like Santa Claus, a joyful idea I believed to be a myth. Never in the first forty-plus years of my life did I credit God for anything I accomplished. I believed my hard work and the fruit that came from that effort belonged only to me. I took great pride in giving myself the credit for my achievements and used that pride to motivate me further.

While grinding it out and getting some wins along the way helped me to build some self-confidence and maintain my drive, I realize now that I lived a shallow life focused only on what lay ahead. Because my parents had trained me to be okay with being alone, feeling like I was on my own island for most of my life did not bother me. In fact, it *strengthened* me, because I took pride in not having to depend on anyone for anything. No expectations meant no disappointment. No people in my life meant no hurt. And I had been hurt enough. After all, if I couldn't trust the people who brought me into this world, how could I trust anyone outside my front door?

While I see now that I was selfish and self-aggrandizing at that point in my life, it was necessary then for my survival. I had always known I *needed* to prop myself up and create a base of experience to build on, and my wiring told me that waiting for others to help me would never get me to a healthy or happy place. That siloing mentality was useful for operating in my environment, but, in hindsight, it greatly restricted not only my ability to see the good in the world, but my ability to build friendships and trust.

I believe we all possess the needed wiring to achieve great things, where "great" is relative to each person. *Great* could mean becoming the next president or a professional athlete, but sometimes *great* can simply mean getting through a day without hunger or tears. *Great* could also mean gaining admission into the local community college after four years of blowing academics off in high school, and then leaving that college in two years with a 3.65 GPA. That was me. While I know that my GPA at Catonsville Community College is not the stuff of legend, to me, it represented my hard pivot toward taking my education seriously and owning my life. That associate's degree symbolized another critically earned brick in the foundation of building a life for myself.

I wonder why Bertha didn't build a life for herself? And why don't so many of us, including those born with seemingly every possible advantage and those born with nothing? If we all possess this wiring somewhere within us, why doesn't everyone pull themselves out of whatever brand of misery that holds them back? Obviously, I can only theorize, but I believe those who do build a life for themselves possess a willingness to pay attention to a *calling*, combined with an unwillingness to look away from the hard work necessary to fulfill that calling. It is in this hard work that change can be brought to light and where back muscles are strengthened, allowing us to raise our heads a little higher.

God suited each of us perfectly to not only survive, but to improve and grow. A quick romp through the annals of humankind proves that fairly easily. For me, when I was attending Catonsville Community College, I didn't know what my specific calling might be, but I could see a pinpoint of light in the distance, and I kept moving toward it, never relenting.

That light still calls me to this day, and never gets much bigger. I don't think the smallness of it means I have made no progress. Rather, my feeling is that the smallness means there still remains so much more for me to do, and that I must embrace whatever obstacles emerge and continue to move toward the light of opportunity.

For most that choose to ignore their intuition or are too afraid to take on the mountain, a rotting, piss-soaked chair like Bertha's is likely not their destiny. Yet from what I have witnessed in my life and from experience, many never reach their full potential because of their unwillingness either to listen to their higher power or to understand what it is telling them. Of course, the biggest obstacle to achieving any step toward a better self usually is an aversion to doing the necessary work required in all of its forms to fully respond to that voice.

Sometimes it's tough to see the enormity of the mountain that must be climbed and even tougher to willingly accept that it's a climb that will be full of failure and pain, to get to the relatively few but important wins. Looking at the height and girth of the mountains in my life, I knew I would have to exert great effort to get over them. Accepting that working through challenges was what must be done if I wanted a better life was a critical component of most of the successes I've experienced. It is hard to see the individual rocks that must be moved one by one, day by day, *every* day, when you are lost in the shadow of the mountain and the daily grind of life that continues, regardless of your ambitions. Yet I accepted the challenge, because managing my life successfully was critically important to me, especially since I had children depending on me.

In my mind, there was more to it for me. I didn't just want good things in my day-to-day life, it was also always part of my plan that I made *permanent* generational change that would exorcise the demons that had haunted those who came before me. This was a lofty objective, and one that made relaxing and enjoying life mostly impossible for me. I paid a high quality-of-life price for this focus, but I knew it was the right path for me.

Too many people in my own family did not fully understand or embrace their potential, and that rippled to my brothers and me, leaving us to have to search within for the motivation to make generational change.

6

Virgo, Gemini, Cancer...and God

In 1981, MTV (Music Television) was founded and began to release music videos, primarily from pop artists. Back then, MTV had no commercials, and I remember being glued to the screen, watching Martha Quinn and Mark Goodman announce new videos and talk about new music on the horizon. To be able to hear and connect with a great song I was hearing on the radio, and then be able to also *see* the visual presentation of the piece, was about as good as it could possibly get for me. Even Cinemax's (a.k.a. skin-a-max's) rolling bars of two-second screen freezes of enticing late-night images was less important.

God built me not just to love the sound of the music and lyrics, but also to connect deeply with certain songs to help me get through life and provide some answers. When MTV started playing videos with their video jockeys (VJs) interviewing artists and talking about the songs and the meaning behind them, that became the most inspiring influence in my life. I could tell with Quinn especially that she cared about the music and the songs and what they meant. I would hear a song on the radio and hoped they would create a video to go with it.

Along with the interviews, the videos themselves provided me with the visual stimuli to dial into what the artist was thinking about when they wrote the lyrics and to see, not just hear, their passion as they performed their craft. Lyrics, musical composition, VJs, and music videos all combined created a powerful therapeutic environment for me. Through the artists' own struggles and ambitions and the messages they provided, I connected and found comfort and meaning. Quinn and Goodman also became part of my therapy team.

Corey Hart's "Never Surrender" was released in 1984, a year before I would graduate from high school. I was stumbling through my life, dealing with a mother who was trying to control me by regularly grounding me for no reason and a father who had given up knocking me around but had significantly stepped up his emotional abuse and guilt game. I had some friends, was considered popular in school, and had a beautiful, kind girlfriend. Still, my head was a mess, and on most days, I could barely keep it together. This song was one of those that reminded me I was not alone in being alone and that failing was not an option. I figured that if this random Canadian singer was singing and writing about being alone, having perseverance, and never giving up the fight, then I should just realize and accept that I needed to not make excuses or feel sorry for myself and keep pushing onward. He wasn't offering me answers. Instead, he was offering me a subtle form of kinship, which was good motivation and another arrow in the quiver as I worked my way through the darkness toward what I knew would be a better place. As things were getting much worse, I began to accept that hoping for functionality at home was a waste of time. No amount of wishing was going to change my situation. Intuitively, it made sense to push ahead and not mull over my station in life. I am thankful to Mr. Hart for the message that self-pity and looking for sympathy was never going to get me out of this place. More gifts from a stranger, proving once again how much the Universe has helped me along the way.

I spent a considerable amount of time wondering about God as an adult, but less time as a child. My evolution in understanding faith and a higher power started with complete confusion and mayhem. This was the result of my parents arguing about attending mass every week, juxtaposed against the weekly mostly peaceful and loving messages from the priests at the Catholic church. Then I would rotate to anger as I equated pain and suffering with the absence of any God being concerned about me. If God was all the things the church said—with a finger touching everything everywhere—then it seemed to be purposely ignoring me. I felt abandoned. Messages of an actively compassionate and loving God didn't make much sense when I was living with daily evil and a deep desire for even simple things like a regular meal.

As a youngster, I attended mass at Our Lady of Victory on Wilkens Avenue. Usually, it was just me and my mother, as my older brother would stay home with my father. My mother wanted John to go to mass, but my father did everything he could to discourage my mother from taking him to church, while berating her regularly for having Catholicism as part of her life. I suspect that because John was older and could manage himself, that this was the reason that my father demanded he stay home. It allowed my father to get a win, but not have to do much work. His hatred for the church was real, but having to manage me full time, even for an hour, was still a worse option. None of us misunderstood my father's intentions: He would not be satisfied until my mother discarded her Bible and stopped attending mass. Both had grown up in the Catholic faith, but my father had an anger about the church I would never fully understand. His disdain for my mother's faith and for any notion that there was an "old man in the clouds" (his words) grew in intensity with each passing year. As with everything my mother had to endure in dealing with my father, she would keep her mouth shut, put on her lace head covering, throw me in the car unbuckled, and head the short distance to her one hour a week of "me time."

The lessons learned in church often went in one of my ears and out the other, as I suspect happens with most young children. My mother's efforts to increase our engagement in her faith were destined to fail as we didn't talk about religion and prayer in our home. This was primarily due to my father's strong resistance and that our family didn't have a tradition of conversation. When the topic did surface, my father would launch into an outburst on the church that was mostly directed at my mother. Her responses were distinctly different; she would either cry with no words or give him a look that said, *I hope you choke on your tuna helper*. Church was her one sanctuary, her one free hour of time a week, and he was slowly tearing it away from her.

I didn't mind attending because it was peaceful and a nice distraction from the volatile environment at home. It was also good to see that my mother seemed to find some peace while she was there, which was something I rarely saw in her at home or elsewhere. My father's regular insults and criticisms of her homemaking skills kept her in a stressful state from morning until night. It was easy to see that the short trip was a welcome break from my father.

As I grew older, my father began to be more vocal about his disapproval with my attendance at church and was unrelenting in his harassment of my mother every time we left and came home from mass. She did not give in immediately, but I imagine each trip must have been awful for her. If you're not religious, try to follow with this analogy: Imagine going to the gym to get your head and body right and your husband meeting you at the door to berate you as you crossed the threshold to leave, and then waiting for you to return to give you a heavy dose of ridicule. His attacks were ruthless but effective in slowly and methodically dismantling her faith. By all measures, he was a committed bully, and it seemed important to him to make her feel stupid for having faith in God and Catholicism. Any benefit she found in Sunday mass was stolen from her like piranhas stripping meat from a bone. Her once-a-week time away at church was actually much less than an hour, as it must have taken her twenty minutes to wash my father off of her while sitting in the pew, and another twenty minutes at the end of mass to get herself mentally prepared to go home to him. This left her with barely fifteen minutes for herself. It angers me to think that all his attacks were targeted to steal a measly fifteen minutes of peace from her. Clearly, he would not be satisfied until she was fully compliant.

As it was with John, the older I got, the more pressure he applied for me to remain with him. Eventually, that pressure led to my mom caving in and leaving me at home. I was OK with it because church was fast becoming less enjoyable for me. I hated the drama and verbal abuse from my father over my attendance and I was too young to get much value from the sermons. The wrath my mother and I received upon returning home made us extremely edgy and nervous in the car. My father's messaging was having an impact on me and the rosy, optimistic stories from the priests weren't giving me any real hope. It would take many years for me to decouple the strong association I made between attending mass and awful things happening in our home. The pain I was feeling in my life was not being cured by a Catholic God. Whatever interest I might have had in the uplifting sermons would never be enough to offset the trauma around our attendance.

My father also regularly interrogated me about my intentions with the church, which, of course, I was too young to understand or answer. I know now that his questions about church had the real intent of subversively criticizing me while selling me on his views about the evils of the church. He had no issue with making anyone in our family feel dumb and inadequate, so he didn't bother to dilute his feelings for a child. Despite my best efforts to give him the answers he wanted to hear, he began to use the same guilt and aggressiveness my mother was receiving.

My mother must have been so sad he destroyed yet another dream of hers, the dream that her children be raised in her faith, but she never said anything about it to us. She had lost again and soon after I stopped going, she also stopped attending, ending her connection to her church for the rest of her life. This must have pleased him immensely, but even with the win, he still never let up on berating the church and our earlier association at every opportunity.

I was forced to make a lot of grown-up decisions as a child. That happens when your parents are emotionally unavailable and make no effort to connect with each other or their children. In some ways, my forced independence is a positive as I have no issues making decisions and understanding and shouldering the work and risk that accompany those decisions. In my case, my parents' efforts, or lack thereof, were about as opposite of support as you could be. As a young adult, I made the conscious decision that the Catholic God was not for me. My belief at that time became that the world was godless, and the concept of God was what mortals used to have some hope beyond their miserable lives. After all, *weren't all families as miserable as we were?* Also occurring at the same time, a fuzzy picture of self-reliance and confidence about making my own fate began to form. It was only in the concept phase, but I was beginning to think I could find a way out of the darkness. The idea was scattered and broken like a large puzzle, but it offered the hope of form and opportunity. And I didn't need any God for that.

There are some benefits to growing up the way I did. One of the most important is that my mind remained open to most things, including the possibility of there being a God. More succinctly, I may not have thought God was part of my life, but that didn't mean I was convinced that it did not exist. Because I was not programmed with answers to anything and my primary focus was survival and accessing anything to achieve that, I was learning that anything was possible in just about any situation. I can't write this without clarifying that I was in no way an optimistic soul. Instead, I mean it more like a con artist with a keen ability to assess a situation, see the weaknesses throughout, and exploit those weaknesses for his own benefit. I wasn't a con artist, either, but I learned to study my surroundings and life operations in great detail. In those details, I learned the terrain, made mistakes, but always moved forward. It was clunky progress but I was beginning to see a path. I lived a lot of years lost somewhere between depression, anxiety, and loneliness, but my openness to any available data on any topic presented options and chances for a slightly opened door or window. I wouldn't realize how powerful this gift was until much later, after many years of mistakes and trials. This gift—call it an open mind—is what allowed me to eventually connect with God at a higher level than a priest or scripture had ever taught me.

Later in high school, I met my sweetheart. She was a beautiful girl who was very devoted to the Catholic faith. Being with her and her family brought great comfort to me. They informally adopted me, no doubt seeing what a mess I was, and I began to see what living as a Catholic could be in its best form. It was less about the Catholic religion and their version of worship than it was about this wonderful person I was spending time with and the good family that had raised her and was willing to accept me as I was. Family and religion were central themes in their pod, and that was something I had never witnessed firsthand. I had closely studied shows like *Leave It To Beaver*, *My Three Sons*, and *Father Knows Best*, and held moments of hope that if I could just be a better human, my family might turn into something like the Cleavers—happy, kind, and loving. I knew it was acting and therefore fantasy, but the fact that someone had written the scripts gave me hope that some of what I was seeing was based in truth. Like these shows, my girlfriend's family confirmed that loving and supporting families exist, and it had a powerful impact. Before I knew it, I was back in church again and going through the motions of becoming a real Catholic. As in my early years, I generally understood the value of their messages, but did not see an application for them in my life.

I continued to attend and got myself to a place where I was willing to take communion and get confirmed to create the possibility that my life might be enhanced in more practical ways. In taking these sacraments I knew I would win greater affection with my girlfriend because it pleased her to think of me as a fully inducted Catholic. It was not a requirement to date her, but it made her happy. Being a fully credentialed Catholic seemed like a small price to pay to please a person who made me feel better than I had ever felt in my entire life. I wanted more of that good, warm feeling in the center of my chest. It filled my heart with joy how her family celebrated this big step for me. I had never experienced the wonderful emotions that come along with being supported and loved.

Of course, no one in my family was there to see my confirmation or ever made a positive comment about it. By then, my mother was bitter about life in general, and my father's feedback was limited to his criticisms of me and my girlfriend for "recruiting" me into the faith. However, none of his sharp words could diminish my genuine love of her family and its powerful ability to lift me up. I didn't understand at the time that like the artists I respected, she and her family were another gift that arrived exactly when I needed it.

My relationship with the church ended about the same time as my relationship with my girlfriend. I never fully believed what I was hearing in the sermons and was achieving the sacraments only to please my girlfriend and her family. They had shown me the power of family and what unconditional and unselfish love meant, so doing this for them was a small gesture. Even today, I recognize her as one of a handful of beautiful souls who were instrumental in my life education and gave me important high test fuel for the next length of road I would travel.

While my father had many negative positions on most every religion, he truly enjoyed and respected the Unitarian church. He urged us to go many times, and there were times I conceded and enjoyed it. The Unitarian church was informal, had less rules, and didn't try to make anyone accept a rigid set of rules, values, or beliefs. It seemed to me that all opinions were respected, and that the intention was to bring people of all faiths and backgrounds together. Attendees were provided with a place to feel safe being themselves, while hoping collectively for a better world. At no point have I called myself a Unitarian, but I get the sense that Unitarians don't care what I classify myself as, which is testament to their open mindedness. My father enjoyed the membership as it was more intellectual and required no faith in the "old man in the clouds." The members seemed nice and a lot more relaxed than in the Catholic setting, and I enjoyed my time with the youth group. As introverted and socially awkward as I was, the youth group leaders were patient and accepting, with no demands of me to conform. There was no pressure to perform any rituals or get to a higher level of commitment. I could just be my normal, messed up self.

I'm not sure how the Unitarian church has evolved since the late '70s, but I never felt uncomfortable with the organization until a crazy retreat to Philadelphia my father talked me into. I had heard of religious retreats at the Catholic church but had never attended because my father and mother would never have allowed it, and there was no chance of them paying for it. In truth, even at the peak of my Catholic experience, I would never have wanted to attend.

Normally, I would run from any activity that involved hanging out with strangers. However, as a newly minted teenager, I could begin to comprehend the benefits of being in a far-away city with no adults. I could be parent free, and more than that, I could get a taste of real freedom. For these reasons, I warmed up to going with a group of strangers to a city I had never been to. It was highly unusual for my father to be interested in paying for something like this. So unlikely, I was almost shocked when he said yes and wrote the check.

My time in Philly was mostly positive and educational with one odd event that would be life changing. At the age of thirteen, I was entertained by heady conversations with topics like saving the world from our own destruction, being good citizens, and exploring the possibilities of a higher power while not being constrained to a set of rules or conditions.

It was intellectually stimulating, and I liked that I was not being forced or threatened by some terrible outcome like going to hell if I didn't believe in a God in a specific way. I liked that no one in the Unitarian Church ever tried to corner me or any of their flock to believe one idea about anything. I appreciated what was likely my first look at how tolerance and respect for all faiths can set the stage for acceptance of anyone.

Up until my trip to Philadelphia, I didn't know anything about sex. Most of my sexual knowledge was listening to the thumps and groans of my mother and father having sex in our townhouse and then later the same sounds with my mother and her boyfriend. They had separated, but my father must have believed that sex was his right as the primary financial provider for the family. He didn't yet understand that not wanting to be part of our family meant he didn't get the perks of sex with the person he left behind.

I also had an experience when I was about nine, when I stumbled across a couple having sex behind a thick canopy of bushes in our community park. I was playing hide and seek with some kids in the park and found myself wandering alone down a path I had never been on. I barely noticed the couple out of the corner of my left eye. They were about fifty yards from me to my left off the path, so I couldn't see much detail, but I could see a half-naked man mounting a woman from behind and pushing back and forth with lots of energy, moaning, and theatrics. This had the effect of thoroughly freaking me out and my instinct was to walk away quickly while stealing a couple confirming looks on my exit. I think they heard me because within a few seconds of me breaking a twig or stirring some leaves, they hastily got dressed, snatched their blanket, and dashed off in the opposite direction. It was startling while deeply intriguing, but nothing would prepare me for what I was about to see in Philly.

It was our last night at the retreat, and it featured a mixer complete with boy-girl dancing and activities. Afterwards, the adults left us under the watchful eye of the older kids who guided us to get cleaned up for bed and find a spot to crash in our sleeping bags on the gymnasium floor of the old school we were staying in. It was quite dark, but a couple of standard caged-in dome gym lights remained on, providing a steady buzzing sound and a hazy, low-light luminescence that enveloped the space with an early dawn feel. Many of the kids were joking until late and then one by one, we dropped off to sleep.

Never a good sleeper, I awoke a short while later with my foot shaking to the sight of a curious new landscape. Some of the older kids had begun to share sleeping bags, which was curious to me, and I didn't fully understand immediately why a boy and a girl would need to share

Never would have thought that I would have stumbled across a couple being intimate in the woods. It was funny to watch them scurry away.

something as small as a sleeping bag. I mean, I understood the why of it, but a church retreat seemed off limits. With sex on my mind, I fell in and out of sleep with the occasional squinting eyes to survey my surroundings. Either I went unnoticed or there was no concern for what I might see. As events progressed, I was faking sleep at this point. The buzzing lights helped mask other sounds, but upon hearing some familiar sounding groans, I opened my eyes almost fully to a scene of three coupled sleeping baggers within twenty feet of my spot. They were now on top of each other in their sleeping bags and moving and grinding in rhythm. While I had no personal hands-on experience, the sounds combined with my late-night Cinemax research gave me a fairly good idea of what was going on. I laid there confused, scared, and admittedly somewhat interested at the sounds of multiple couples performing sex acts around me. The couples later separated and clandestinely slipped off to their own bags, and we all eventually fell asleep.

To bear witness to something close to a live sex show at that age was something I could not easily come to terms with. My adult mind today says it was not a big deal and reminds me I never even saw any skin. However, the next morning after the event, I remained awkward and curious about the night's adventures. I'm sure a psychologist could explain my disposition, but my best guess is I just wasn't ready for it. This event combined with my childhood experience of listening to my parents regularly having sex, and making that connection, kind of doubledowned on my uneasiness. It's possible my discomfort was simply the result of a young kid in puberty caught somewhere between being turned on and disturbed. Whatever the cause, the event led to me not returning to the Unitarian church for many years despite my father's regular strong-arm persuading and doses of guilt. I never told my father about what had happened.

Going into my late teens, my experience with the two religions was obviously quite diverse. As a child, Catholicism was not something that gave me any spirituality or reason for hope. Rather, the most important benefit is I could be away from my father, a tremendous value. Later, the best part of Catholicism was the strong influence of my girlfriend and her family, of which a byproduct was their extension of love and support for me. With Unitarianism, it was the opposite: positive on the outset with my view turning negative after the event in Philly. It seems I was destined to find no spiritual home. I would attend a few services at the Unitarian church by myself later in life, but my ex-wife, Ann-Marie, was Catholic, and with no buy-in and a feeling I was disrupting the expected religious agenda, I stopped attending. Even in our divorce, the kids were to be raised Catholic. It was a "faith" that seemed only interesting to the kids because of the presents lavished upon them for achieving the sacraments.

But all was not lost. Between life experience and my sporadic attendance with the two religions and the bits and pieces I picked up along the way, I began to form a yet unfounded but resolute belief there must be some type of higher power helping me along the way. In a sea of dysfunction, abusers, addicts, alcoholics, and criminals, I was somehow being nudged to advance. Even as a beat down, much of the time resentful kid, there seemed to be too much that science and religion could not explain. This belief didn't mean anything spiritual to me; rather, it was just an observation that seemed to have some merit. I allowed myself to believe a God must exist in some manner. It seemed a logical and unavoidable conclusion, and one that I could not disprove. And so a God, unconstrained by any rulebook or "how to" guide, entered my life in the most general way.

I don't believe the God I have faith in has the expectation I follow what Catholics believe. It seems impossible that the same God responsible for creating the universes, all the species of our planet, elaborate complex ecosystems, and an enveloping interdependence of all things was also demanding I sit in a wooden box, confess my mistakes, and then go off to say an arrangement of words in repetition and ask for his forgiveness. I have come to believe that no religion has ownership of something as great as God. They each have their manmade scriptures and rules of worship, and these can have great value, but in my opinion, they do not offer any fast track or special access to God. The various religions seem to give us a portal to pay our respect and homage to something far beyond our comprehension. Religions are powerful and effective tools to help the masses develop a relationship with a God that can bring great benefit. However, I didn't need religion to guide, instruct, or even guilt me into framing my beliefs a certain way. Becoming confident in this revelation is calming and freeing to me.

I don't believe God grants the wishes we utter late at night and when we are under stress. Instead, I believe that at birth, God had already given me all the gifts I am to receive. And that when I use those gifts, I can climb any obstacle, weather any storm, and be resourceful enough to solve any problem in my life. I could launch into a largely uninformed discussion of the wonders that cannot be fully explained by science, but I would quickly be found out as knowing dangerously too little to carry the conversation. However, I am comfortable with being under informed because I don't need to get in the weeds on the details; I only need to know that the smartest people on our planet still have many unanswered questions.

I know the important parts—we are all wired to do incredible things if we want to and are willing to work for it. And that this wiring comes from a higher power always working in our favor. Part of the wiring is the work that is required to be done. Working for what we want and are meant to be is a critical piece —not self-pity for it, not blaming others for lack of it, and not throwing a silver dollar in the well and wishing for it, but to actually use my awesome brain and all the capabilities God has given me to solve whatever issue presents itself in my life. To me, that is much less difficult to understand and accept than to navigate the reams of material on how to follow a religion properly and the risks of not making it into heaven. As I have a long history of going over, around, or through obstacles, I have enough evidence compiled that confirms that nothing can stop me from doing what I truly want to do. All that it requires is for me to roll up my sleeves, commit to the work, and access some readily available average brain function. It is my responsibility alone to find out exactly what my gifts are, and they continue to be revealed each day. Understanding and accepting the sometimes grueling hard work needed to achieve exceptional results with no support, and in the face of extreme adversity, is something that I have learned I must face and overcome. I have been blessed from birth with all the tools I need...more gifts.

In April 2019, I was diagnosed with a rare soft tissue cancer that started deep in one of my glutes and metastasized to my lungs. The result of my scans is I can see many nodules hanging about like Christmas lights inside my air bags. It was found by accident and not the result of any direct symptoms. Because of the cancer metastasizing and not having any effective conventional treatment, they say my cancer is stage four. Fortunately, it is a slow growing cancer, and I have been gifted time to figure out how to heal myself. I do not accept the clinical prognosis and am comforted knowing I still have time to figure it out myself and set a course toward healing. Rather than feeling self-pity, an activity that only would drag me and my family down, I decided to use this time wisely to find my own path to achieve the end goal of NED (No Evidence of Disease).

And with that decision, in walked my God again, leaving me humbled and deeply grateful for the gifts bestowed upon me at birth. With the qualities of self-driven determination, grit, an unwillingness to fail, and reasonable intelligence, I know I am hardwired to address this issue exactly as I have done with other issues my entire life. I understand that doctors give prognoses based on historical data, research, and experience. For many patients, they will listen to the all-powerful white coats, and because of that, will do very little or nothing beyond what is prescribed to help in the effort. Research has shown that many of these patients, in simply following their doctors' guidance, often find themselves unsurprisingly falling into the stated life expectancy band. It's a bit of a self-fulfilling prophecy, driven both by Western medicine's push to radiate, cut, or poison cancer, and its lack of acceptance of viable, often complementary alternatives, that in some cases can rid patients of cancer. An ability to learn, persistence, and refusal to accept the status quo are all examples of more gifts—thank you, Universe. Meeting other doctors that consciously choose to be open-minded, blending Western and Eastern medicine with other integrative approaches in their method to curing cancer, giving their personal egos very little weight, are yet more gifts from God. Had God not blessed these physicians and PhDs with open minds and a willingness to help me hunt for a solution wherever it might lie, I might have felt lost and hopeless. Had God not shined on the techies that came up with the idea of the internet and the many others who made it what it is today, I couldn't get online and learn in one day of studying what would have taken me weeks to pull together just a couple decades ago. I am so grateful for the gifts that others have been given and how those gifts have enriched my life. The combining of gifts gives birth to a powerful compounding effect that rewards us all.

For me, it is not about pumping myself up with bubbly hope or prayers, my approach is pragmatic and just makes sense. There is lots of knowledge just waiting to be consumed. The nudge from my higher power tells me my job is to digest the most relevant information as quickly as possible. Also, my intuition tells me that fighting and healing myself even while my conventional doctor offers little hope is the right way to think. I've been overcoming large obstacles for most of my life, so I am comfortable with the mountain that lies in front of me. To sit idle was never an option for me, and certainly accepting the situation at face value would not be using my gifts. If the Universe could get insulted, which I don't think it can, I believe sitting helpless and following the herd while not using the brain power that was bestowed upon me would be the reason.

What are the gifts I am writing about? At the most basic level, I am referencing an ability to read, to ask questions, and to consider all options while trusting my intuition. I strongly sense that I have a responsibility to God to use my gifts to work toward a solution. I don't believe the Universe demands it or even "cares" in the way that we humans think of caring, but using these gifts, these things I was given even before I left the womb, seems like the proper way to show respect and gratitude.

As I solve for this problem, I must live my life fully and not wait on anything because the clock is ticking. The clock reference is not in reference to the cancer possibly shortening my stay here. The meaning is that each of us has a fixed amount of time to be on this planet and I feel my obligation is to use it wisely. I wish I would have been this insightful when I was younger, but all that matters is right now, not what is behind me. While trying to figure out how I can get to NED, I am doing my best to have as rich and connected a life as I can have. None of this is because I am in denial, as I fully accept that I have a disease that has the possibility of cutting my life short. But there are many things I can do to try to change the playing field, and I'm willing to try just about anything. When I give my mind the right messaging while following my intuition and trusting the gifts that God has given me, I am confident I am making the most of what time I have here. I also believe the Universe sees when I have light and hope. In seeing that, it will encourage me to maintain and build on my positive attitude while living a good life. If I am wrong and the Universe does not care, then I am satisfied knowing that being present and optimistic will never do anything but make my life better.

On another note, somewhat tangentially related to religion or at least a form of possible temporary enlightenment, I had a vision, which was encouraged by psilocybin, the psychoactive compound found in hallucinogenic mushrooms. The first stage of my six-hour journey was quite heavy and psychologically difficult. Some might call this a "bad trip," but since it only lasted about an hour and graduated to and became wrapped in something wonderful, I prefer to call the first leg of this experience an initiation. The hard part was as important and needed as anything positive that came after. Like everything in my life, I had to experience the bad so I could know what good means.

I had come into my "trip" somewhat down from recent news that my cancer was growing. Drawing on my very limited mushroom experiences in college, I knew it was probably not a good idea to swallow the magic mushrooms while depressed, but I ignored that fear, hoping for some radical relief from my sadness. I was mostly looking for a good time, a chance to detach from a darkish reality and find an escape from the monkey on my back. Anyone who has had cancer knows that the diagnosis is never far from the top of your mind. I had a lot of hard questions to answer and was working the problem as best I could, but I wanted a break from the constant processing, angst, and worry.

The front end of my trip sent me to a place that was as dark as any I had ever been before. The experience was like a black, lightless cloud pressing down on me, demanding that I yield to whatever it wanted from me. I found myself staring down a long hallway with many partially opened doors on both sides. With no way to exit behind me, I began to walk down this hallway. As I passed, the doors were opening toward me. I could not see what was inside the rooms until I walked to each door and investigated the opening. This forced me to uncomfortably commit to each door to inspect what was around the door's edge and within. As I passed each opening, the door would swing open and reveal an event from my past that played like a movie. It felt a bit like Mr. Scrooge in Dickens' *A Christmas Carol* as the events displayed were disturbing. Some went further and were horrifying depictions of events I had buried deeply. All of the scenes were difficult to witness, and it hurt to visit these moments I thought I had left behind some decades ago.

As the events stacked in my mind, the trauma uptake building inside me was palpable. Indeed, it was as if I was reliving it, and I was quickly becoming engulfed as if it were occurring in real time. I could physically feel my blood pressure rising and my body temperature seemed like I had a fever, so much so that I began sweating profusely. My sweat was not a hallucination as I was literally drenched to the point that my clothes were soaked through. While on mushrooms, a user is still able to check in with the practical parts of body operation generally controlled by the left brain. The right brain was clearly at the wheel, but I was being guided to give myself periodic check-ins at the same time, which allowed me to make certain I was physically safe. I was aware enough in the moment to know that severe sweating and an elevated heart rate are real threats, so I needed to make sure I was OK. I checked my pulse, went to the sink to put cold water on my face, took some breaths, and determined I was OK to continue. I am glad I arrived at that conclusion because discontinuing the experience was not an option. With no switch to turn it off, I went back to my chair where the horror in the hallway was still waiting for me.

As I visited each episode revealed in the rooms, I wondered in sadness and fear why this was all being brought up again. I had worked so hard to suppress these things. I knew that suppression was not a healthy answer but never opted to find therapy as an adult. Although I had entertained the idea many times, I knew that it would hinder my white-knuckle drive to achieve and couldn't risk opening a box that might unhinge me completely. I had boxed these events up and stored them away many years ago, but the detailed tours down memory lane certainly suggested they were present despite any effort I made to bury them. As I moved past the first ten doors or so, I was feeling close to a full breakdown. It was way more than I had ever handled in my life in one concentrated dose. I had experienced some pain in my life, but this was about as close to hell on Earth as I had come. While all this was happening, my left brain was also still actively processing stimuli and I had a real fear I might not be able to break out of this nightmare.

However, at the same time, a distant light at the end of the hallway grew just a bit closer and brighter. It sent me a message that no matter the pain, I needed to keep moving in that direction...moving forward, always a familiar theme in my life. It's interesting that even in the turmoil I was experiencing, I never once looked back to see if the door I had come through to arrive in the hallway had reappeared. In hindsight, I am curious what this means. Perhaps it meant that the Universe, through the gifts given to me, demanded I give these moments my full attention. That feels right.

Even though the light grew brighter and more inviting, there were still so many doors that lay ahead. With deep-rooted worry that the worst might be yet to come, I didn't know how much more I could endure. I was fearful I might not be able to handle much more but had no choice but to proceed.

Soon after, something came up from deep inside, telling me it was time to fight back and use the stuff I had used my whole life to take control of this trip or at least get the hell out of this imaginary hallway. It was a sense of hardened calm and decisiveness in the middle of a category five hurricane. I was scared at first as I internally debated how I would climb out of this hell. Then something extraordinary happened that I cannot explain: my father made an appearance.

My father died in 2012, only seven years prior to this event. Our relationship had somewhat improved by the time he passed, but we were far from resolving the pain and trauma he had caused me. To him, my offenses were equally bad when compared to his actions, so he easily and too comfortably summed it all up as a wash. He had two serious diseases that resulted in years of increasingly bad health, eventually causing his death. While I was not his caretaker, his deteriorating condition and an always present campaign of guilt made me believe I needed to visit frequently. Until the end, I did this out of a sense of trying to prove to be a good son, with my ulterior motives being that I might finally earn his respect and unconditional love before he moved on.

Locked in the hallway of my trip, his appearance was odd on one hand but fitting on the other. Since he was the lead perpetrator in many of these replayed scenes, it made sense he was involved in my journey down the corridor with the bank of doors. I didn't associate protectiveness or nurturing with my father during his life, but his appearance there in the hallway had the absolute effect of calming me and offering unfettered safety. What I saw was an image of him when he was in his late twenties. He had a beautiful smile and a lightness about him I had never seen while he was alive. In my state of panic, his presence made me feel secure, the opposite of any time I had spent with him in real life. There were no words, but the message he communicated was that I was OK to move away from all I was seeing in those replayed moments. My heart rate dropped, my sweating began to subside, and I began to gain control of my environment. I knew then that whatever was happening, I would be OK and make it through.

I believe, perhaps too optimistically, that his brief appearance was meant to show me that he wanted my happiness and to provide some relief from the pain he'd caused. There was no apology or other redeeming effort from him, but I felt real love. As he began to fade from the scene, I was happy to see my father at peace and I was grateful for his unconditional love and unselfish help. Inside of this trip, I had been shown the worst and again I'd made it through. As important, I had seen the version of a loving, supporting father I always wanted. This was powerful stuff, and no doubt more gifts were being revealed.

I began to slowly walk backwards as the doors closed before me, feeling happier, more content, and oddly fulfilled. I felt a warm brightness in my chest that was expanding and empowering me. The light at the end of the hallway was still out of reach, which I knew was OK, and I had no drive to pursue it. I was safe, warm, and protected and knew there would be no way I was going to slip into a psychotic break. Instead, I was pleasantly surprised that the opposite occurred as I moved into a seemingly enlightened state. That's not to say I had achieved enlightenment; rather, while on mushrooms, tripping my ass off, something very beautiful and powerful happened.

I looked behind me for the first time, and the single gray metal door that had been behind me and previously disappeared opened to accommodate my exit as I continued backing up and watching light and warmth washing over the phenomena of my past trauma and doors forever closing. The last thing I remembered before I entered the next phase of my trip was the light rushing at me in a flash and the entry door closing in front of me and disappearing as quickly as it had appeared in the first place. I then woke to the scene in the room filled with emotions of relief, confusion, and raw, commanding strength. It was as if I had changed the channel on the television.

My brain became flooded with chemicals that lifted me in a way I had never experienced. I'm certain some of it was drug related, but a truly miraculous thing had happened and the effects of it were cathartic. While still tripping, I began to study the total event with my left brain, deeply desiring meaning and understanding. The therapy, as it were, was potentially life changing and I wanted to make sure I didn't lose one piece of the experience. Even as the left brain was suggesting it was all fantasy resulting from the ingestion of the drug, I knew in my soul that what happened was too real to not be important. Later, I would become more confident in what I had experienced and choose to accept it as a gift from the Universe meant to provide guidance and new perspective.

Still tripping, another vision, this one much more positive and equally impactful, began to form. It might be hard to believe that anything could be more important than my father's visit and his desire to help clear matters up, albeit in the most abstract way possible, but the next leg of my tripping journey was even more meaningful and critical to my life than the first. I received a message from an honored soul from my past that communicated convincingly that I would heal completely.

The vision for my future came to me while in a fixed meditative *seiza* kneeling position for the better part of an hour. Where the previous adventure was all about my past, my brain had switched gears and was driving me to carefully consider all that lay ahead. I had learned the *seiza* position while training in karate as a kid, and I hadn't used that position since I was about sixteen. I have no idea why I chose that position as a fifty-plus-year-old with aching knees from early arthritis and a baseball-sized tumor in my ass cheek. That position just came to me as something I must do. I remained in that pose, barely moving a muscle, as I let the chemicals take me where they wanted me to go. I was no longer afraid and was ready to accept this path and not fight it. My meditative, trance-like state was not intentional, wished for, or forced in any way. It was what my mind wanted and needed, and my brain simply complied with the involuntary command.

My former karate teacher, Sensei Najib Amin, came to me with that vision, which was a shocking surprise as I hadn't talked to my highly respected instructor since I'd left his *dojo* over thirty years earlier. When tripping, parts of the brain open to all possibilities, and not just those you have some working knowledge of or are presently involved with. For me, tripping is like looking through someone else's glasses and seeing a new world in high definition. However, the other side of tripping is that I still always retain the ability to check in with everyday Daniel and make sure I'm OK. The everyday Daniel was like, "OK, this is weird, and by the way, Sensei Amin, what are you doing here? Why you? Why now?" It was great to see him, but if I had to write a thousand people on a list of folks I hoped to see on my trip, his name would have never appeared. I thought of him from time to time, but he was decades away from being top of mind.

In my vision, *Sensei* Amin appeared as I had known him in my youth, an early fifties, six-foot something, very dark-skinned black man. This was how he had looked thirty years earlier when I was his student. As he was then, he appeared chiseled with muscle from head to toe. Without a word, as in life, he commanded respect when he entered this bizarre domain. Training under the ninth *dan* black belt, one of only a handful of Americans to have trained under a Japanese master and climbed that high in rank, was one of my life's greatest gifts. Like my girlfriend in high school, he was one of those people who changed my life for the better. As a teenager, I remember feeling reverence toward him long before I learned what the word meant. At some point in the years close to when I met him, he had converted to Islam. I didn't know or need to know the significance of that event; I just knew that I loved and respected the man. He was strict, but when I earned his rarely given praise or just a simple nod, it meant everything to me.

When *Sensei* walked in the room, all conversation in the dojo would stop and we would take our formation in neat, well-formed rows. The class was all adults except for me and John. When *Sensei* stood at the front of the room in his heavily starched *gi* (the karate uniform), adorned with a black belt, it was time to train, and training was something *Sensei* took seriously. Most of the time he would train with us, and his moves were so swift and strong you could hear his *gi* snap, similar to a whip, each time he threw a kick or a punch.

John and I would grab a spot in the back of the room as we moved through various exercises and *katas* (Japanese word for a series of choreographed moves), and we would sometimes find ourselves just being normal, misbehaving kids. If one of us cracked a fart, the two of us were sure to be giggling clandestinely for a few minutes as we continued the sequence of moves and let the scent drift out onto the floor to be shared with our classmates. *Sensei* would never say a word, but as he walked the floor barking out counts and commands, all in Japanese, he would eventually work his way back to our area to observe our form and, at times, to encourage discipline.

I can remember *Sensei* asserting this discipline on one hot summer night when I was acting silly. It was a stark reminder that he never missed anything in his domain. It was a serious offense to disrupt training, and I was hoping he would forget my chuckling in the rear of the class. He walked the room patiently through the rows and columns of about forty grown men and the two of us kids, as we all moved in perfect unison to his Japanese commands and counts. Normally, he would watch me directly for four or five counts, then straighten me out in a deliberate way—countering my moves, straightening my stance, adjusting arms or footwork. Sometimes he would use his *bokken* (a Japanese wooden sword that I remember being called a "bow") he carried in his belt with him throughout the class as a tool to assist us. He would use the bow to tap the inside of a leg to indicate he wanted the leg farther out or lightly touch my back to show he wanted me to be more upright.

As he walked the floor barking commands, his voice got closer and louder, and I heard the pads of his feet working their way across the clammy concrete floor. There were no mats or protection gear in those days. As he walked, he counted—*"ichi, ni, san, shi"*—and seemed to move away and behind us to continue the drills. As always, I was nervous when he came around behind me, but I was especially nervous knowing John and I had moments earlier been snickering in the back of the group. Then, like lightning, I felt my lower legs collapsing and rocketing forward from a level quarter-powered swing to the bottom of my calves with his bow. As I fell backward, I felt his super strong hand grab the lapels of my *gi* to prevent me from falling full force to the ground. I went straight backwards down to the concrete with only his hand holding my clothing to stop me from crashing at full weight. I had landed firmly but safely on the floor, and the next thing I saw was the tip of his sword wagging just below my chin. I had never experienced anything like that from him, but of course, as a nine degree black belt, he was fully capable of taking any member of his *dojo* to the ground, least of all, a hundred-and-forty-pound kid. He didn't say a word, but I knew exactly what the message was. He made John and I do twenty-five push-ups and sit-ups each as he took turns putting a foot on our bellies and backs to make it more challenging. Still, with all of that, I only gained more respect for the man. He was a spectacular human being and one of my great teachers.

As I sat in my kneeling position, *Sensei* stayed with me as music played lightly in the background. Without a specific intention, my mind went deeply into thoughts about my cancer, wondering what would be next and how I could keep myself from being crushed from the weight of it. *Sensei* didn't say anything, but his purpose was important. When my head would fill too heavily with worry, his spirit seemed to turn my mind to where it needed to go, which was away from those things that did not serve me and more to the things I could control. In his presence, I felt solidly anchored and full of light, energy, and gratitude. It's a hard thing for me to write about, not because I am unable, but because it was such a beautiful happening that I am afraid words will not adequately capture the experience.

Of all the people in my young life, he was the one adult who did what he said and demanded the best from me while giving all of himself. I learned so much more from him than karate, including what it means to have a relationship based on mutual respect. I was the student, but he never took this as license to talk down to me or make me feel small. He was a true master. Master of karate. Master of life. A true rock solid hero to me.

Sensei Amin's companionship in that moment gently nudged me to help my own mind reveal what I needed to know—I will heal, the disease is a gift, and the greatest gifts are yet to come. I also learned it was time to access my gifts and to work more diligently on my self-healing. The early part of my trip (the walk through my trauma) bookended nicely with the message I was receiving on the back end of the trip from *Sensei* Amin. It felt like an example of a yin-yang application — one was clearly and integrally connected to the other, a circle with a dark and light side, but both components having immense value. Clearly, my mind was telling me I needed to deal with old issues before I got to the wonderful healing place, and that healing my mind is important to healing physically. I felt so uplifted and full. No matter what I did to try and dilute or second guess this powerful messaging, the positive energy along with the message remained and is still with me today.

The more I process this, the more I realize that *Sensei* Amin was the perfect person to deliver this news. If my higher power was in fact sending me a message, maybe it foresaw that I needed to be under the influence of psilocybin or in some type of non-normal state of mind. Otherwise, I may not have believed it or was ill-equipped to field such a powerful intervention. And by choosing my *Sensei*, my hero, a role model on a very short list, God knew I would find his message credible and would pay attention. I believe his involvement was intentional and more proof that the Universe works in remarkable ways. The Universe was actively talking to me and I was beginning to actively listen.

Up until the moment when I had one, I was not a "vision" type of guy. I am as practical as they come and could rationalize away anything that seemed other-worldly. I would read with great interest about someone else's vision and be intrigued, but I wouldn't have given it much thought as something that would happen to me. Visiting with my teacher while in a kneeling position for close to an hour is not something I can do under normal circumstances. When I was coming out of the trip, I was astonished that I had sat that way for so long and wasn't

John and I performing a kata during an exam. The discipline and focus that Sensei Amin instilled in me proved far more valuable than simply learning self-defense. Even today, his foundational lessons continue to guide me.

feeling any pain or discomfort, not even numbness. The entire experience was freaky, unsettling, and nothing like anything I had experienced before. At the same time, it was immensely inspiring and gave me great reason for hope. Undoubtedly, I was chemically impacted by the psilocybin, but there is no clear reason why the rest of my experience, including the resulting visions, played out the way they did. To this day, I remain convinced the vision was sent intentionally and recognize it as another great gift in my life.

The steps I have taken since this experience have ascended me to the best mental and physical condition of my life. Even if I am unsuccessful in finding my healing, the experience not only paved the way for me to find the conviction to fight this battle but also to live as a better version of me. It doesn't matter that I can't answer every question that comes to mind when processing the experience. What matters most is I had arrived at a place of clarity and peace, and faith became an anchor in the healing process. What a wonderful experience with a bounty of gifts. Mushrooms, clarity, acceptance of the power of the mind to overcome hurdles, stumbling into a new and different brain process, intuition, acceptance of messages from wherever they come, and a willingness to try something new—all are GIFTS. And all were offered up exactly when I needed them.

Around Christmas in 2019, another gift was granted to me—a Virgo entered my life. I met Jeff at a neighborhood holiday party. He was a former football player for the Air Force and a counterintelligence officer during the most recent wars. This was a man who lived a full, rich life and did so with honor and dignity, despite many threats to his own life along the way. Jeff had been blown up by a roadside bomb, was diagnosed with multiple sclerosis, had supported his wife through her own successful cancer battle, was a successful, high-performing entrepreneur, and had lived at Dana Farber in New York City for seven months while undergoing multiple surgeries and treatments for his own aggressive form of cancer. Later, he had the misfortune of being diagnosed with a different type of cancer. This was a guy who knew something about grit, survival, and winning. What drew me to him most was that in our brief discussion, I could tell he owned his life, not the sickness and the other challenges that had plagued him. His positive attitude was contagious and something I wanted and needed in my life. Even after the cancer came back, he never surrendered who he was at his core. I grew to respect this kind and generous man immensely in our brief but life-changing friendship.

Our first conversation led to a nice moment we both enjoyed. After that, our friendship became fast and deep in a short time. We did not see much of each other during the pandemic, but we stayed in touch, shared stories, and pumped each other up whenever we needed it. I felt like he had granted me special access to his boundless positive disposition and endurance. I respected and trusted his view, and it gave me hope. He helped me reunite with the qualities of problem solving, raw will, and persistence, attributes I had called upon my whole life but for some reason ignored after receiving my diagnosis. His influence was a key component to getting myself back on track and working the problem.

To my great sadness, Jeff passed away after another recurrence of cancer. It was a short friendship but extraordinarily meaningful and powerful to me. It was a reminder that as with most things, it's about quality, not quantity. The gift delivered to me wasn't just a friendship that fate allowed to come along at the right time. Describing it that way seems too simple. The gifts were stacked high in this case. There was the gift of a chance meeting with a man who had similar struggles and who over a lifetime had banked the stamina and willpower to challenge those struggles head-on with a high degree of success. Also, there was the gift of my intuition, to be dialed in enough to know I wasn't taking care of my emotional self and needed help. Then there was the gift of being born with a love of learning and being humble enough to know I knew too little and needed to get myself into student mode. There was also the gift of meeting this titan of a human who, despite being in the midst of fighting the last battle of his life, still took time to share his experience and be a friend. Then there was the gift of two guys talking and feeling safe enough to be vulnerable. In that shared experience, we discovered a wonderful gift of friendship. I sense that Jeff was a gift to many who knew him. I am honored to have met this man and am deeply grateful for the impact he had on me.

It's impossible for me to see all that has happened in my life, how highly complex and wonderful this world is, how everything delicately connects to the other, and not conclude there is some type of higher power at work. It starts with our complex wiring and with some self-awareness and work; we realize our gifts and use them to create a rich and fulfilling life. God's work is also in the people we meet, both good and bad.

It's my high school girlfriend and her family giving me affirmation that functional, loving families do exist in real life, not just on television. This gave me undeniable proof of concept and a model to achieve for my own life.

God's presence was involved in introducing me to a man suffering from late-stage cancer. Jeff was deep in the most important fight of his life, yet he found time to give perspective and wisdom to a stranger. This left a lasting impression that will help me stay energized in finding my own answers and I work to give back to others who I might positively impact.

It's knowing that great doctors and scientists are compelled to perform endless research and studies, willing to endure failure after failure and the certain frustration that comes with that process to find answers. They do this to save lives, and their important work leaves a trail of crumbs for me to follow as I search for my own answers.

It's the folks who invented the internet so we can all openly share information and rise from the perils of ignorance, allowing for most topics, to get a basic understanding of just about anything in only minutes.

It's a mushroom containing powerful chemicals that can offer a fresh and different perspective and the ancient peoples who somehow were compelled to eat these and other plants and discover and teach their value. It's the impulse to know that maybe psilocybin was something for me to reintroduce into my life.

It's the *Sensei* from decades earlier who never ceased to be my role model and life teacher.

It's my wife, JoAnn, showing me what true unconditional compassion, patience, love, and connection are all about.

The list is endless of the blessings that have been all around me for the entirety of my life. I was too bitter and resentful in my youth to understand that God was always on my side.

7

Painting and Vertigo

When I was ten or so in 1977, Fleetwood Mac released "Don't Stop." Written by Christine McVie, the song is reportedly about her breakup with her husband, John McVie, the bassist for the band. I didn't know at the time what the song was about, but I remember digesting the words and feeling optimistic about whatever future lay ahead for me. With everything so messed up at home, the idea of literally focusing on tomorrow, not all that had come before, and in doing so, believing my life might improve, was a poignant message I adopted and used to build inner fortitude. Christine's voice and inspirational message got me through a lot of hard times. Every time I hear her singing and playing the keyboard, I pay attention and realize there is always an opportunity for me to lift myself up and let the past go. This was another gift.

When I was eight, my father took up oil painting. In the eyes of a youngster, he was quite talented. His painting hobby started shortly after we moved into our new end unit townhome in Arbutus, Maryland. If purchasing a new house was the catalyst for my parents' reconciliation, it clearly did not achieve the desired result. Within a short time, my father was at part-time separated status again. Thankfully, he did not want to be in the house with us full time, and after only a week or two was back to his "come and go whenever I please" schedule. His part-time status was another one of those blessings from God I did not fully appreciate until years later. I was too young at the time to grasp that less of him or none of him was a gift.

In the early days, having his own apartment did not stop him from coming by frequently. It was not to play ball with us or interact in any way; it was more to assert control and authority, and that was joined with healthy doses of ridicule to the lot of us. Having gone through a divorce myself, I can tell you it would never cross my mind to even consider his level of autonomy in the home I left. It makes my stomach turn to think of how my mother must have processed this and how much control he had over her. On one hand, she wanted him back and loved him; on the other, she was obviously being used and manipulated. Perhaps it was a price she was willing to pay. If we by chance were having a relatively happy day, my father's presence, or even the thought that he was on the way, would bring a dark cloud over everything. I wonder if his doses of negative interaction were intentional because he couldn't stand the bliss of children or enjoy any time we might be having a happy moment. Maybe he unconsciously, or perhaps even consciously, thought that if he could not be happy, then no one could.

He would come to eat dinner, then paint, and then "meet" with Mom in her room for some time. These visits were complete with grunting, ceiling vibrations, and sheetrock nail pops. After that, he would go to his apartment or wherever he went on those evenings. I cannot explain why he couldn't have sat his large easel in the middle of his own living room of his own apartment and painted there, rather than set up his makeshift painting center in our home. Maybe he was showing off how worldly and educated he was, something he would do frequently. Unfortunately, despite his specific warnings about touching his completed oil painting, I could not resist the urge.

One evening after my father had left, I was alone in the living room with his artwork as it rested on the A-frame easel. After several art sessions, he'd completed his great masterpiece with triumphant exuberance. I could tell he was excited and proud of his creation. Even with his unusual bubbly disposition, his warnings to stay away from the painting echoed in my mind as I crowded the piece. The subject of the painting was a dark Central Park-like scene with sidewalks, fall-colored trees, people, and streetlights. To my eyes, the work was gallery worthy and quite large for a dad starting a new hobby. The canvas and frame were three feet tall and four feet long or at least seemed that way to a young boy. Overall, I was impressed, not just with the subject matter, but that my father could work from a pallet of cool, gooey oil paints and create such a pretty thing. Unfortunately, it was not enough for me to just look—I had to touch it.

Fighting the conscious reminders of his warnings and knowing the punishment that would certainly result if I did, I reached out slowly and

My father's masterpiece destroyed with the touch of my curious right index finger. The severe penalty for this crime is a difficult memory to forget.

carefully to touch a thick, multicolored oil swirl in the foliage of one of the trees. It was so beautiful and cool, I just had to see if it had hardened. After a couple of hours of drying, I assumed it would be dry to the touch. But my veins froze over with fear as the partially dried paint swirl became, instead, a large finger smudge complete with my fingerprint. As I whimpered to myself, becoming frantic and overwhelmed with panic, I did what any eight-year-old with no painting experience and no artistic abilities would do: I attempted to fix my mistake. My fumbling efforts made a less than one-inch smear into a multidirectional star-shaped obliteration that looked like a meteor landing had become an important part of the subject matter. My heart sank. I knew the painting was ruined. More importantly, I knew there would be a heavy price to pay for my mistake. In desperation, I went to my mother for "help." It was pointless to ask her for assistance, but it was my only option.

Being helpful and selfless was not done in our family, so seeking the protection of my mother from my father for this sin was a lost cause from the start. Aside from an unwillingness to defend and protect me, most times she seemed to enjoy telling on us to my father. I think it was the one way she thought she could stay connected to him. My request for protection, in this case, was no different and there was no benefit for the crow I ate in telling her my misdeed. Once again, I was reminded that being honest did not pay, and I was completely alone.

On a usual day, I dealt with heavy anxiety because of the unstable, violent situation at home. But on this day, knowing my father was going to be coming for me at some point made my anxiety almost uncontrollable. As I thought about my father returning that evening to dinner and ran through the likely course of events, I ran several times to the bathroom at school to cry and tried to keep myself from melting into a psychological break. I did not believe in God at the time, but I prayed to him a lot that day. I could barely eat as I was in terror watching the clock tick down to the hour my father would arrive for dinner and his rendezvous with Mom.

To my great joy, he did not make it home for dinner that night. It was not like it mattered much, because he would be there eventually, either that evening or the next; but it was some short-term relief. I went to bed and allowed myself to exhale a bit. I knew there would be no pass, but I was grateful for the possibility of having an extra twenty-four hours of good health. Still, I knew my father could come at any time. He might skip a meal from time to time, but he did not like to miss out on his alone time with Mom. Because he would park in the rear parking pad, which was accessed through the rear alley, I spent my evening looking out of my alley-facing window for the unique headlights of his Ford Falcon. I figured that if I saw his car coming, then at least I'd have advance notice, and could mentally and physically prepare for the worst.

As the sun went down and the possibility of his arrival diminished, I slipped into a nervous sleep. On its own, my body decided the best mechanism to keep me in a lighter sleep state and able to defend myself was to send an order to my brain that my right foot must continue to shake incessantly. I know it's weird, but it worked well. It was another way God worked through me to allow me to help myself. This defense mechanism, a side effect from stress and anxiety, would go on for decades after leaving my home.

Some time that evening I heard my father pulling into the parking pad. I woke immediately when I heard his loud rapping on the rear glass slider, giving my foot a well-earned rest. The sound of his gold college ring banging loudly on glass sent an "I'm here! Let me in now!" message through the entire house. I'm certain that, like me, the announcement of his arrival got the undivided attention of everyone in our home. It did not matter to him that we were all asleep with every light in the house turned off. He didn't care who he woke or disrupted, or that he could simply walk around to the front door and use his key.

As I sat in the dark silence, to my breathless surprise, he did not immediately come for me. When I heard him go into my mother's room and close the door, I allowed myself the luxury of cautiously exhaling once more. I figured that since the painting was right in front of him when he walked through the door, and he had decided not to come for me, it was at least possible he would postpone my punishment until the next day. I gave myself and my wagging foot permission to go back to my semi-sleep state. It was an awful feeling falling asleep knowing that a terrible thing could happen to me at any minute. Right foot shaking again, I dozed off and prayed for him to leave without a need to see me that evening.

Later in the night, I was suddenly awakened to excruciating pain in my chest matched with a complete failure to take in oxygen. As I pleaded with my lungs to fill with air, I could see the outline of his angry face, silhouetted from the hall light, directly above me. With my mother having obviously told him about my mistake, he had made the decision that a punishment was not only warranted, but that it needed to be carried out that very evening. Fresh with vigor from having satisfied himself with my mother, the punishment started as a punch directly to my gut while I lay sleeping and unprotected. With no immediate ability to breathe, I could not beg for forgiveness or plead for leniency. I was all tears and painful, oxygen-less grunts and gasps, with wide-open eyes full of panic and desperation. It's hard to imagine how a grown man could make the decision that punching a sleeping eight-year-old was deserved.

The inability to breathe was problematic, but, as I gasped for air, my focus was on trying to quickly graduate from my partial slumber into a place where I would have some degree of real-time cognizance about how events were unfolding. I also needed to develop a plan for how to defend myself from what would come next. With my foot shaking failing to pass the early alert test, I had obviously made a critical mistake falling asleep that night.

Unfortunately, the punch was just the beginning. As I was still sucking wind, my father grabbed me by my right ankle and dragged me from my bed. I tried to tell my hands to find the floor to cushion my thumping to the shag carpet, but I remained mostly disoriented as my head hit the floor, banging the bed frame on the way. I would have gladly walked to a designated area for my punishment if I had been given the option, but this was not offered. His highly effective intentions were to incite fear and powerlessness in his surprise attack.

Ankle in hand, we headed out of the room I shared with David, down the short hallway, and then down the steps. I was very thankful for the thick, red shag and low-grade padding as my body thumped down the steps one riser at a time. Fortunately, while grabbing door jambs or railings was forbidden, I was still allowed to use my hands to stabilize myself to some degree, so each step was greeted by mostly ass fat. From time to time, my head would knock on a step. It was painful, but I managed the trip as best I could as my breathing systems came back on-line. I learned within a few steps that the critical thing was keeping my neck bent forward so I didn't crack my head open.

At the bottom of the steps, my father hooked a sharp left in the direction of the painting and dragged me across our linoleum floor, which was a treat compared to the stairs. I thought it made sense I would be receiving the bulk of my punishment near his recently upgraded masterpiece. However, my father surprised me by making an immediate left, throwing open the door to our unfinished basement. He then dragged me down the uncovered pinewood basement steps, and then onto and across the dirty concrete floor. By now, I had regained control of my pulmonary system and was fully aware that I was awake, frightened for my life, and heading to some place very bad. Where words previously could not be heard as I was gasping for air, I now begged and pleaded as sincerely as an eight-year-old boy could do. It made no difference. I cried so hard my whole body convulsed. Begging was the only choice, but it was a catch-22 as my experience told me begging only made my father and mother angrier. True to form, he was incensed with my whining. While everyone, both inside the house and through the wall to our neighbors, must have heard my screams, no one, including my mother, came to my rescue. All just ignored my plight. He was enraged, and I was at his mercy.

After landing at the bottom of the steps, my father dragged me across the room to a wooden chair. He instructed me to take my pajama pants and underwear down to my ankles and lay across the seat face down and naked. This was not unusual for me as I had been here before. I immediately complied, while continuing to beg and sob. With my ass facing up, he used the next few minutes to wander the basement to find the perfect instrument to beat me with. He liked to smile and talk about what he was choosing as he went about the selection process—"Too easily broken, too flexible, ahhhh...just right!"—all with sadistic chuckles in between his statements. Sometimes, he would let us choose our own beating instrument. When this happened, we were smart enough to choose a weapon that was light and breakable, but not today. Today's weapon would be a sturdy piece of 2x4 lumber about four feet long. I could see from his sinister smile he was proud of the instrument he had chosen.

As he crossed the floor back to me with the lumber in hand, I could see a sick pleasure and satisfaction building inside of him as he prepared to disperse some real hurt. Something about this event was sickly entertaining to him. He uttered some words about the warnings he had given me and how what I was about to receive was well deserved as well as the usual rantings about how awful I was as a kid. As his fist gripped the wood tightly, his knuckles were white from lack of blood flow. He ordered me to stay still and shut up as I begged even louder. I had been beaten with a 2x4 before, so I knew it was not a weapon I should attempt to block blows from. Also, aside from the possibility that he could break my arm because when 2x4s meet bone, bad things happen, attempting to block the blows with my arms and hands would only extend the punishment. As a standing rule, if I touched the weapon, the strike did not count. This mattered because punishments often came with a specific number of stated blows. I was instructed to hold on to the bottom part of the legs of the chair. I followed the command while panicking and as he loaded up the first strike. I used all the strength I had to refrain from instinctively blocking the shots, which is hard to do given that the brain is wired to protect oneself from such things. It was one of those wired-in gifts at birth, but one I had to fight against in this situation so this brutality would take the least amount of time possible.

The first blow was crushing, making a loud slap on my ass—"Thraaaaapppp." I immediately dove to the cold, bare concrete floor, cupping my hands around my naked ass for some chance at comfort. It felt quite warm and was very painful, but beyond the standard whipping on flesh, there was an excruciating, sharp, specific pain that was not normal. When I looked at my hands, there was blood all over them, a new twist in my twisted world. My father saw the blood, too, but did not rush to look after the wound. Knowing he had hit me with the flat, broad part of the 2x4, and that this should not result in a cut, he inspected his weapon more carefully. He quickly determined the cause: the beating end of the lumber had an old, bent nail protruding from its flat surface. With the force of his swing, the steel nail had cut into my flesh, causing it to bleed. It was not a deep wound because the nail was bent over and almost flush to the surface of the board, yet the head of the nail was still raised enough to cause an open wound. It bled throughout the beating, which makes sense since blood was being urgently rushed to the area as my body tried to defend itself.

I was promised three distinct solid blows as punishment. My father articulated that it was a requirement that each strike had to be solid hits and up to his standards for pain and effectiveness. If my hands got in the way, or I got up off the chair, he would add another. My backside was already purple and bloodied from the first blow, but it seemed that the area was numbing somewhat by the cut and the raw power from blow number one. The body is designed to deal with pain, and mine was doing its best to protect me with its natural responses.

Blow number two came as hard as the first but was easier to take. My father smirked with pleasure as this blow hit. The sound of board meeting flesh was coupled with his comment, "That was a good one! Just one more. Don't move or I'll add one on." After the second blow, the pain caught up and I could not possibly lay across the chair any longer, so I rolled off the chair to cower in the corner for as long as I could in hopes of some amount of time for recovery. He was furious with me and dragged me half naked, pants and underwear still hanging around my ankles, violently out of the corner and across the floor to the chair. He was noticeably angry that his operation was not running as efficiently as planned, so he promised me an additional blow. Staying away from the chair too long also meant he might start slapping and punching me on top of the beating, so I had good incentive to comply.

On the third blow, I could not help but throw my arm around to block the shot; it was raw instinct at that point. The blow came down jointly on my under forearm and across my ass. Later, I would see how the 2x4 neatly left a welt halfway across my ass, and how I could match the high welt on my forearm like a puzzle to complete the image. He snickered again as he announced the fourth and final blow was on the way. This time, I lay there and took it without protest or pleading. With that kind of pain, you get numb, which is another gift we are all wired with. I shrieked in pain one last time as it landed firmly and loudly.

As I rolled off the chair, my father gave me a steady stream of helpful warnings apparently meant to protect me from him in the future. He was especially generous with these public service announcements after doling out these punishments. It was not that he felt guilty. Rather, he liked the control and having the power to do this whenever he wanted. Not only did he have the power to discipline us in any way he felt appropriate, but he knew he had our absolute attention in the vulnerable terrifying moments after. Part out of fear and part out of feigning respect, I was uniquely attentive to any words he had to say. After passing on his words of wisdom to me about how to be better and avoid situations like this, he threw the bloody 2x4 across the room and told me to get dressed and go to my room.

As I stumbled clumsily and painfully into my pajamas, he confidently pounded up the pine stairs to the living room. I struggled to stand as the pain began to take hold. I soon learned that walking and especially climbing stairs were going to be Olympic-sized efforts. There would be no rushing the ascent. My body was struggling but was working hard to respond to what my brain was asking—begging—it to do. However, when my father yelled down the steps that I had one minute to get up the steps or he would be down to give me more, you can bet I got as much gitty-up as was physically possible in my step.

Struggling to walk and in terrible pain, I came up the basement stairs, which opened to a scene where my dad was sitting on the couch watching TV with my mother. Neither said anything, but my dad gestured for me to continue my journey up the stairs to my room. There was no hint of regret from either of them. With both Mom and Dad out of my view, I crawled on all fours up the second set of shag-carpet-covered steps and across the floor to my bed.

It had been an awful night. There was the original offense, then the punch, then the loss of oxygen, then the friendly assist out of bed down the hall and down two flights of steps, then the drag across the floor, then the nail in the board, and then the bonus shot. Exhausted, frightened, emotionally tattered, and alone, I found my way under my blankets to my piss-filled mattress. I spent some time wondering if my father would come again and attack me while I slept. With my foot now shaking violently from anxiety, I gave in to my body's need to rest.

The morning following the beating, I woke up in a bed of fresh piss. As I was almost a nightly bedwetter, this was not something unfamiliar and it was not necessarily the result of the beating. I wet the bed so much that my bed had rotted through to the springs and the material and padding on my twin bed had deteriorated with the constant high-acid-liquid exposure and me feverishly scrubbing it on a daily basis. I stuffed towels and no longer used clothing in the mattress hole to soak up the urine and to put a layer between my skin and the steel springs, so that when I slept I would avoid getting bed sores. I searched regularly in the back alleys for a thrown away twin bed in hopes of replacing it but never had any luck.

The smell of stale urine in our room and throughout the second floor was a constant. The rare times a guest visited, I would be in a panic about them seeing my room. It was never that I wanted friends in my house. But I would push for a brief home visit at times because my friends and their parents would question why we always had to be at their houses and not mine. It was this pressure that made me concede.

Getting approval was hard enough, but the real task was getting them into the house and out again as quickly as possible without seeing the circumstances I was living in. It wasn't just my nocturnal enuresis (medical name for pissing the bed) that concerned me—it was the entire house and the situation we were living in. For example, there was rarely any food to make someone a sandwich, and what was there was heavily restricted; eating anything was by permission only.

Also, it was not uncommon for our two dogs to defecate in the house. A hot, steaming pile of German shepherd and cockapoo feces in the middle of our shag living room carpet was not what I wanted to show off to my friends. My mother refused to clean the dog mess up and my brothers were content in ignoring it. This left me as the only person in the home willing to take on the job. I can't give myself much praise for cleaning because getting shit out of two-inch shag is not an easy task for even the pros. Even my best attempts resulted in obvious shit stains throughout the house.

Our home, the dog shit, the people living in it, my piss bed; all of it, was humiliating and embarrassing. I couldn't have felt lower in those moments.

It wasn't that my parents didn't care about me wetting the bed. They did everything they could do to stop it, including more beatings and intentional embarrassment. The pain of the humiliation was fanned with more jokes from my brothers, as they got a sense that bullying me about this was a way to partner with my parents on something and gain their tacit approval. Nothing seemed to work, and my bed wetting continued. Of course, seeing a doctor of any type for the issue was out of the question. Having failed to control myself so many times, my parents agreed I would not be allowed to have any water or fluid of any type after five o'clock in the evening. After dinner, my brothers and I would go outside to play in the alley or ride bikes, and I was often quite thirsty, so such an early cut-off was problematic for me. I would sneak a drink from a neighbor's hose when I could get away with it, but generally, I went to bed very thirsty.

Like me, John went to bed dehydrated and begging for water, but his pleading yielded suspiciously too soon. I learned one night in one of my half-asleep states that he had a masterful plan to bypass the rule. After we were all asleep, I heard carefully placed footsteps coming from John's room. My door was open, so I peeked around the door opening and watched him make his way to the bathroom. The distance was only five feet or so. He had a sneaky look on his face, a face that wasn't normal for someone getting up to take a leak. Additionally, he was moving in a way to not draw my mother's attention, who was sleeping only feet away in the other direction behind her bedroom door.

After taking a short leak, he flushed the toilet and dropped to his knees. He waited a couple seconds for his business to go down the drain, and then when the fresh water poured in, and while the fill valve was still making noise, he cupped his hands and drank as much water as he could. As soon as the water reached the fill line and the rising float triggered the valve to close, he was done with the operation. This was gross even to a thirsty youngster, but admittedly, it was a great technique to hydrate. The brilliance was both identifying an accessible albeit controversial fresh water source and using the noise from the fill valve as cover for his crime. He turned his back, and we locked eyes. Without saying a word, we both went back to our rooms.

I processed the procedure for several days, and then decided to give it a try. It worked well, but it still grossed me out, and then there was the risk of my mother finding out and the consequences that would come with that. I decided on a different approach. I tested the flow of the sink faucets and determined my choice would be to urinate in the toilet, while at the same time running the water at a trickle and drinking from it simultaneously. The hope was that the sound of splashing pee and the eventual toilet flushing would mask the faucet running.

On the first night I tried this, my mother knew immediately the sink was running because the pipes knocked and whined, a sound unique to our bathroom faucet. She came bursting out of her bedroom door to berate me, foiling my effort to get hydrated beyond a couple sips.

Clearly, my technique was not going to work. Running water would be normal for most, but she knew we were not kids who regularly washed our hands, nor were we expected to, so the pipe sounds were about as good a tell of illegal drinking as could be.

Physically unharmed, I returned to my bed thirsty like most nights. From that night on, like my brother, I became a regular toilet water drinker. Obviously, the bedwetting continued until at some point, I grew out of it, but at least I wasn't going to bed thirsty anymore. My mother must have been dumbfounded that I was still wetting the bed while apparently having had no fluid in me for hours. I was always grateful to John for his ingenuity—another gift offered up to me.

The morning after my punishment for the destruction of the painting, I rolled over in my soaked pajamas. Immediately, the pain greeted me and was amplified due to the urine on my open wound. I struggled to sit on the side of the bed, which was excruciatingly painful. My assessment revealed I would not be doing much sitting that day and did not think it would be possible for me to attend school. We never missed school for any reason, but since I could not even walk, let alone dress, attending school was not tenable. Missing school was a much worse option than being at home, so it wasn't something I ever wished for. The wounds healed over the following week, allowing me to gingerly sit within a day or so. The cut was not deep but hurt when I applied any pressure, but this could be dealt with by shifting weight away from the wound when I sat.

An unexpected side effect that occurred was a severe case of dizziness that followed immediately and stayed with me for some time. I hated that I was missing school and being forced to be home with the wolves. I knew that being center stage and needy with my parents was something that made them incredibly angry and ultimately would only bring more pain. I could not wish the severe vertigo away as it continued for over two weeks. Now the reason to miss school was no longer because I could not sit, the reason now was because I couldn't stand for long without feeling like I might fall over. The issue persisted, and they were noticeably more agitated with me as they saw me stumbling about each morning.

Things must have been bad for me because my parents decided to take me to the hospital to get checked out. This was highly irregular because my parents rarely took us to doctors or dentists. They must have had great insurance between my father's federal benefits and those my mother received as a full-time state employee. For that reason, I don't think it was an issue of expense. Rather, I believe they both found it to be too large an inconvenience. This time, it must have been unavoidable, as even these two people saw my stumbling around the house for days as an unusual occurrence severe enough to require medical attention. In a rare showing of parental participation, my father drew the straw to take me to see a doctor at Baltimore General Hospital, the same hospital where I had been born.

As my father and I waited to be seen by the doctor, I pondered how he would describe the events leading to my condition. I was instructed to keep quiet and speak only when he told me. I worried he would tell the doctor how bad I had been for touching the painting. Just having that thought tells me how effectively he had twisted me into believing how the world would perceive my awful behavior. Most days, I already felt like the scum on the bottom of a pond, but I didn't need to have that message reinforced by a stranger. My father did not disappoint. He never specifically spoke about the smudged painting. Rather, he commented on what a bad kid I was, how long I had been a bad kid, the many crimes I had committed, and then slid comfortably into his rationale for why I deserved this obvious beating. *'You know these kids don't understand anything but a beating these days. I have been warning him for way too long, and I would do it again if I had to.'*

I doubt I was mature enough to understand how my doctor processed what he was seeing and hearing. The way my father spoke, his brand of discipline was the global standard, almost selling it to the doctor. I only know that judging by his up and down head nods, he seemed to be agreeing with my father's opinion or at least pacifying him. I'm not sure which it was but given that a man had just told him he had beaten me badly enough I had an open wound, swelling, and severe vertigo, the doctor should have realized I was in a dangerous place, and that he was obligated to do something about it. On that day, the medical profession failed me miserably as the doctor sent us on our way with no follow-up expected. At the time, it didn't bother me, because I had been programmed to believe with all my heart what a terrible kid I was, and that I had completely earned the beatings. I'm not sure what the physician did for me, if anything, but within a few days, the vertigo had gone, and I returned to my normal hell.

It is still a difficult thing to write about the terrifying moments I experienced under their upbringing. With most things in life, the more reps you put in, the less painful it becomes. We are designed to weather pretty much anything thrown at us and I think on most occasions, I can push through most anything. My parents were generous with dispersing terror to me and John, but even with all the occurrences, it never lost its razor-sharp edge. And because it didn't get delivered in the same manner, I could never know what was coming, how it would come, or how long the punishment would last.

My father described his brand of discipline as his own personal coping mechanism. Even with us begging him to stop ridiculing and beating us, he would never yield. The best he could offer to explain his actions was to wait when we were in a calm setting, and then attempt to diplomatically and sweetly—as sweetly as this broken man could—explain he had no choice but to do these things to us. With a gentle, "loving" look on his face, he reminded us his actions were the only way he could stay sane and keep himself from killing us. As was his view with most things he held to be important, this painting's health was much more important than mine.

8

Being an American Arbutan, and Some Guidance from the Universe

I was sixteen in 1983 when Elton John released his song, "I'm Still Standing" and just two years away from graduating from high school. In just a short twenty-four months, I could potentially do whatever I wanted, wherever I wanted, and could leave my family far behind. My father spent what little time we physically shared communicating how disappointed he was in our relationship and listing all the things I could do to make it better. He never grasped the monster he had been and still was, and how his actions might lead me to avoid him. It should have been common sense. However, even with me eventually telling him in specific detail how unhealthy I felt in his company, he couldn't see that his regular doses of undeserved guilt repulsed me. Knowing this, I still never gave up hope we might one day build a healthy father-son relationship. But just when I would think a door toward this objective had opened, the moment would be spoiled when I would discover all roads lead to one place, a place where I yielded to him, bowed down, and bent the knee. It would always be most important to him that I understood *and accepted* that I deserved all I had received from him.

Fortunately, his crimes were so egregious that even with my low self-worth, I never gave myself over to his school of thought. Our relationship was always "net negative," a concept I will talk about later. As a child, he programmed me to believe his propaganda, but as a more secure adult, I found his lobbying efforts overwhelmingly absurd and anger inducing. My failure to onboard his view only made him push harder. It would be an important win in his mind if he could get me to agree that our individual fouls against each other were all a wash. Repackaging this in simple terms, this was a man so narcissistic that he saw his years of severe abuse as a lesser offense than what "crimes" I had committed against him as a child. Realizing as an adult that he would never change his perspective, I look at my eventual rejection of this self-serving manipulation and the resulting wide moat I built to protect myself from him as more gifts in my life.

My mother was isolating herself much more frequently, using the only energy she had to go to work and to make visits to the liquor store. She was always a complex woman to understand, which makes sense since she never spoke of any issues in her life. She was also volatile and unpredictable, and we never knew what version of her we would get. But one thing was clear: The more the alcohol took control, the angrier and more dangerous she became.

"I'm Still Standing" was a song I associated with my future, and I was listening to it with the ears of an almost adult. After what I had been through, I did feel like a true survivor, so I could closely relate to the lyrics Sir John sang. Like him, I was anxious to move up and out to a better place. When I heard Elton John rock the world with this hit, I felt reassured and confident in my independence. Through my experiences, I had become resilient, driven, and more inspired than anyone I knew. It also reaffirmed a guiding tenet of mine: I had to keep getting up no matter what, and that doing so would eventually lead me to escape this place and these people. At sixteen, I was beginning to believe I could do something with my life and that a better future was possible even for me.

As a kid, I had no pride in being from Arbutus. Through no fault of its own, Arbutus represented the worst that life had to offer. It was a place to leave as quickly as possible and where roots should purposely run shallow. My father doled out regular incendiary commentary about the rednecks who lived in our town, calling them "Arbutans." He did this in a sarcastic, condescending way as if he came from much better or had forgotten that it was him alone who had intentionally chosen this town for us to live in.

Initially, moving from the city to our little brand-new townhouse was an immensely positive thing. The house and my elementary school were new and beautiful and made me feel like flowers were blooming in my life. Even though I was socially stunted and didn't make friends easily, that didn't matter much at the time. I was enjoying the feeling of being a bit like the Jeffersons, the family from the 1970s TV show.

Making the move from Wilkens Avenue to Selford Road, a home full of fresh smells, clean walls, and new everything, was like Christmas. The move, combined with the news of my parents getting back together, seemed to be a sign that life was improving, and, like the Jeffersons, we were "moving on up." I was filled with strange feelings of external event-fueled optimism that everything was about to be better and would only just keep getting better. Unfortunately, those feelings, like my parents' reunification, would not last long.

My father and mother seemed to separate almost as quickly as they reconciled. As before, he was hardly ever there, which leads me to think he kept an apartment in play as plan B. I'm sure their final separation crushed my mother, who I remember as also being noticeably happier with the changes in our lives; perhaps she also believed things were improving. After his departure, her drinking ramped up, and she would disappear into her room more frequently and for longer stretches of time. She was beginning to come home with bottles in brown bags and taking those right to her room. I would never see the bottles but was old enough to know what a wrapped-up jug of wine looked like without seeing a label. The strongest circumstantial evidence of their existence was the clinking of empty glass bottles when she took her trash directly to the curb. She got meaner and more unhappy as the years opened and closed. It wasn't long before the brand-new place on Selford was as unhappy and full of sad events as our rental on Wilkens. I was grateful for the short glimpse of what a positive event and the feelings that came with it looked like. If anything, it was a nice preview of how things could be, and having that short experience told me that under the right conditions, my life could be good. That stayed with me and gave me some hope for the future.

I followed my father's behavior of knocking Arbutus and let it become part of the reason for all that was wrong in my life. My grand idea was that if I could just get out of Arbutus, then everything would be exponentially better. In hindsight, I wasn't wrong about the importance of leaving home, but, obviously, it's how you live your life that is more salient than where you live. I knew that leading myself away from my parents was the most mentally healthy thing I could do for myself. However, I was wrong to think Arbutus itself had anything to do with the challenges in my life. I was just a kid projecting hard times onto a town that had initially promised so much and in truth was exactly as advertised: sleepy, simple, and consistently so.

While I didn't have much pride in my hometown until many years after I left, I've always had a sense of pride about living in America. I don't know when the genesis of this pride began to take root or exactly why. It certainly wasn't that my father or mother were patriots or even flew the flag on the fourth of July. It was more that my memories growing up were that citizens took being an American much more seriously and with a greater sense of pride back then. I saw that people believed in their hearts they were living in the best country in the world. I recognized early that America would provide if I did the work.

For me, chasing the American dream of making it on my own was my only hope, and seeing examples in the media of patriotism in full swing resonated with me. The actions of my parents cemented this belief by making it clear that if anything good were to happen in our lives, it would come with hard work and determination. That in mind, believing in the American dream aligned nicely with my personal situation.

My parents' planning involved saving for their own futures, not ours. As a teenager, I was jealous and resentful when I learned that other kids' parents had saved for their college education or were working to help in other ways. However, thinking of it now, it strikes me as nonsensical that I would have had this expectation of them as there was not a shred of evidence in our history that would suggest they would do such a thing. More to the point, the truth is there were many children in the same shoes as me, and this is normal. I was disappointed, but my parents had no obligation to pay for college, and I should have understood this. This aside, my parents' emphatic, sometimes spiteful, statements about their unwillingness to be a part of the equation was what stung the most. Even without tangible assistance, they could have spent energy inquiring about and encouraging my higher education dreams, but that positive support was not part of either of their makeup. I can understand this better now as I know what they came from—that they had their own dreams, and that they were only paying forward what lessons and experiences they had from their own lives.

I accepted that college was going to be my responsibility, but it was still hurtful to watch my father's unyielding commitment to his own needs while witnessing all of us struggling so much. My parents made enough money that we didn't have to live in poverty, but my father was so concerned about his own future that he made us all live impoverished so he could retire early and have the life he planned for himself. He lived frugally, but all the benefit of that frugality was for himself only. I have little issue with him looking out for himself and providing for his own future, but doing so with wanton disregard for the people he was supposed to care for still seems selfish. While I encourage our five children to achieve self-sufficiency and support their effort to carve out their best lives, I couldn't imagine standing by and watching them suffer while knowing I could help, even if it was just with words. This self-programming that I'm certain was encouraged by my higher power demanded that I be a different type of parent and human. This intentional divergence from these role models was another gift.

Through my eyes today, I know that an elderly person who saves for their own future is in actuality helping their children. It may sound spiteful or even retaliatory, but I had no plans to support my father in his old age. Of course, given his undying focus on himself, I never thought of him as someone who would depend on me to survive into old age, which was a relief to me. However, when I consider this point juxtaposed against knowing he had a responsibility to his children to deploy capital and energy to make sure we were at least fed, clothed, and cared for properly, I am still a bit irritated by his lack of vision and compassion.

It doesn't take much analysis to conclude he simply didn't want to do more, and his plan for himself was by far the greatest priority in his life. He didn't mind that he skied the Rockies once or twice a year and travelled to different places around the world while his kids were malnourished, poorly clothed and suffering at the hands of their alcoholic mother. He didn't care to counterbalance his horrible deeds with kindness or even minor acts of generosity as some abusive parents do to address the guilt brought on by their actions. This was not him at all. His mindset was he could ignore the pain he inflicted and turn a rigid, blind eye to our situation because his child support checks were delivered every month without fail. Even though we had no concept of money, he reminded us of these checks frequently. When we would complain to him that there was no food or that our clothing was way too small and falling apart, he was quick to fault my mother. He would follow that up by showing us the stack of cashed checks, a prop he kept rubber banded and easily accessible for many years. This was enough rationale for him to confidently sit by and do nothing. The diversion of blame worked because we would then focus our complaints on my mother, who was already sinking into a deep dark hole. I regret doing this knowing now that this must have hurt her badly.

My father must have been so confident he was doing so well by us that he exhibited not a whiff of discomfort in sharing all of his good times and good fortune. One example that stands out is that as an amateur photographer, he would commit all the pictures of his fabulous trips to slides. He would then demand my mother make time for him to come to her house so he could present a kodak multi-reel slide show to all of us, including my mother! He demanded we all sit at the kitchen table after his trips and allow him to give us the play by play of all his adventures and the joy he'd experienced. Narrating proudly about each slide, he would do this as we sat there with our empty stomachs growling. As a special bonus to my mother, many of the shots were of him and his girlfriend. My mother must have been sitting there watching and probably wishing she was in her room drinking. It is incredibly bizarre how detached he was from reality as he forced a presentation of all his good fun down our throats.

My mother must have been hurting badly watching as he displayed all his good luck in travel and relationships. This must have cut her especially deep knowing he used her like an Uber for drop-off and pick-up services from BWI airport at all hours of the night and morning. He chose cheap, weirdly timed flights to save money and didn't seem to care that this often meant her having to pull us all out of bed in the middle of the night or very early in the morning to pick him up. Of course, paying for parking was out of the question. Keep in mind, these were trips he was going on with other women! Trips he had never taken her on... even once. Like us, her trips had been limited to camping. This man had a giant set of *cajónes* and a serious case of narcissism.

Fortunately for me, my father and I had very different views on what it means to first have and then support a family. At all times, my children are part of my big plan. It is my greatest joy but also my obligation. My greatest happiness in life has been watching my children grow and thrive. Their zeal for life and seeing their progress is one of my greatest motivators. Being a great parent and building a great future for our clan are always primary directives. This self-imposed discipline came from something much greater than me, and I am blessed there was this significant difference between the two of us. Working in my favor yet again, God made sure I not only knew the importance of family and my responsibilities to them, but that I also enjoyed the great reward that comes with being an active and present father.

I was convinced that being away from Arbutus was the right path, which to anyone reading this must seem like the obvious best choice given the circumstances. However, with no support from family or community, breaking out of my living arrangement made this feat seem impossible, albeit an absolute necessity. What helped move the needle from impossible to possible was a faith that my country had laid the groundwork for me to do great things. I might have had no faith in small town values or God at the time, but whatever I was watching or whoever I was talking to in my youth, and everything I knew up until that point, began to converge and lay the groundwork of a belief I could be anything that I wanted to be in this country. With little else to believe in, it was enough. The mass marketing on the billboards and televisions about all things American and how great we were as a country, seemed like something I could safely put faith in. Maybe it was selective attention, but I honestly believed that when I figured out how to break out of this town, America would show me a path. My conviction that America provided an abundance of opportunity was an important foundation to build on and provided enough optimism to believe getting out and being something was possible. However, a general love of country alone was not enough to drive me; another important event helped set the course.

When I was around twelve years old, I was waiting for my mother to come home from work while sitting on the hill of grass that rose up from the public sidewalk in front of our home. It was a small patch of grass that was maybe four feet wide and to the right of an eight-step riser of concrete steps. It was a beautiful day, and I remember the grass being recently cut. It was as good a place as any to sit and wait for my mother to return home from work. My mother didn't trust us to be in the house during the summer, so she would lock us out and order us to be back by the time she got home from work. This wasn't all negative, because it meant full days of doing pretty much whatever we wanted outside of the home, and anywhere outside the home was my favorite place to be. Her expectation was we would attend a county-sponsored summer camp that was within walking distance from our house, but the camp only lasted about four hours, so there was plenty of time before and after to explore and be free. We didn't always show up at camp because we quickly figured out attendance was not taken and the counselors, if they even cared, had no way to communicate to my mother we hadn't shown up.

My brothers and I roamed separately during these long summer days. On this particular day, I was alone in the grass. As the most responsible of the three of us and always looking to impress my mother, it was common for me to show up early. The sky was blue with a scattering of clouds, and I found myself lying back in the fresh grass and enjoying the clouds floating gently by. Shortly after settling in, my mind dropped into deep thought about where I was in life and where I wanted to go. I know this subject matter seems mature for a youngster, but even at that age, thinking and dreaming about my future was not unusual for me.

As the grass cushioned my body and a gentle breeze blew, I fell into a state that felt like deep sleep, but it wasn't how I normally slept. I had closed my eyes, and in complete comfort and safety allowed myself to drift away, yet I was aware of my active thoughts. Except for the light wind that would swirl by me from time to time and the touch and smell of the grass, I had unintentionally shut out the rest of the world. My mind then drifted to simply being present. I was not stressed or anxious about the week's latest serving of drama or trauma. Out in the open, I somehow felt uninhibited and protected, which allowed me to feel at peace.

From my current experience with meditation, I know I had accidentally fallen into a deep meditative state. While floating in that state, not fully realizing of course what I was doing, I could still enjoy the smells and the sensations around me, but my mind had also landed in a place of freedom and opportunity. I had a clean slate virtually void of the problems in my life. It could have lasted a single minute or maybe it was twenty. While in this state, a sharp vision similar to what came to me when I saw my *Sensei*, was offered up and I listened intently. The message from the vision said I would be a great father, that I was deserving of better in my life, and that I would rise out of the situation I was currently in. I knew it would require hard work and commitment to get where I wanted to go, but my vision affirmed with great conviction that my ambitions were truly possible and not a far-off fantasy. Oddly, I did not doubt the message or question that something special had happened. It just came to me without any asking or expectation.

Using my mindset today, I know the Universe spoke to me and communicated that a path to happiness and stability was going to be a reality. Most importantly, it gave me great confidence I wasn't destined to repeat my parents' mistakes. As I opened my eyes and became more aware, the clarity the experience provided led me to promise myself and my future children that I would listen to this message and do my best for all of us. I would most definitely find a way out. That single day, in that handful of minutes, was another moment in my life that changed everything. I believe it was a purposeful, directional nudge by my higher power. I can't explain it any other way. There was no path offered in the vision, but it didn't matter. It was perfectly timed support.

I am deeply grateful for that pivotal moment and my Arbutus roots. There were a lot of positives I didn't recognize until much later that were formative for me. People from Arbutus generally aren't well off. They are the salt of the earth people who dig our holes, fix our toilets, and happily enlist in the Marines, never afraid to be the first ones in and the last ones out. They fly their flags high on July 4th and never take their freedoms for granted. They believe in big ideas like patriotism, earning everything they make, and always doing their part. They pull over to help when they see someone in need while not caring much if their Christmas lights are still up in March. As advances in technology seemingly help them, it is also quietly making them obsolete, as they are being replaced by cheap labor and microchips. They don't get paid much, can barely cover the bills in many cases, and aren't sitting on fat 401Ks when they are forced out of their positions. In fact, many will go back to work just a week or two after they "retire." They experience troubles a mile wide, but they always have time to say hello and lend a hand. I spent a lot of time trying to get away from Arbutus, never having a whole lot of good to say about the town, but looking back, it is part of who I am. I am proud to say I am from Arbutus, and that I am an American.

Me having a short rest on a beautiful summer day waiting for my mother to come home from work. The moment produced a life guiding vision that would stay with me for the entirety of my life. I am humbled knowing that a higher power had been with me all along.

9

Lock and Key and Oceans 1000

I'm certain that many listeners, hearing Tracy Chapman's "Fast Car" for the first time, felt a connection to it. It represents the down and out of American culture, and when I first heard it, I felt as if I fell in that bucket. She was singing about me and my people, those trying to do something better than what their environment expected from them. From her unique impassioned voice to the song's words that spoke of unrelenting hope, there was much in the lyrics for me to connect with. When Ms. Chapman made the decision to produce this song, she dropped down another gift for all of the world to enjoy. Her creativity and strength lifted me and helped me to, once again, move forward.

Growing up, my mother and father were extremely possessive and protective of their property. Much of my mother's property was under lock and key. It wasn't that we were born thieves, it was more that she valued what she had earned the right to buy, and she wasn't sharing. There were padlocks everywhere, including on her bedroom door. My mother and father did not even permit us to sit on our ancient threadbare couches because they were theirs. We watched TV on the floor our whole lives. It's funny to write this now and to think we just thought all kids lived that way. For items not literally locked up, my mother was vigilant in claiming ownership—a can of soup, twenty-five-cent frozen concentrate orange juice tubes, random pencils, a dusty unread novel on a shelf...everything belonged to my mother. Nothing could be consumed, touched, or moved in any way without her approval.

All of my early ambitions for stealing were centered around filling the empty space in my belly and warding off hunger pains. Food was my most prized target to burgle. As soon as my mother drove off to work, my brother confiscated my lunch money to buy cigarettes. This went on daily until I could eventually fight him off in high school. With very little food at home and no lunch at school, I was hungry all the time. Stealing was a dangerous mission with serious risks, but hunger combined with opportunity had a strong influence on these high-risk decisions. I was too young and immobile to steal regularly from a store, something I would get arrested for when I was fourteen, so I had to settle for stealing from home.

My mother's bedroom was off limits to my brothers and me. I had only been in my mother's bedroom maybe five times, and one of them was after she had died. My brother claimed to have entered undetected through a double padlock system several times, but I didn't believe him. I knew everything that had ever been confiscated from us was stored behind that door, but I was never motivated enough to try even once. Whatever was behind that door, even if it were food, would never be worth the penalty. Her room was a sacred place to her, and she spent most of her life locked inside it. In my mind, to violate that sanctified space would have resulted in the closest thing to death that she could muster.

With most of the food either heavily monitored or under lock and key, I began to wonder about the risk/reward relationship involved with targeting items that were locked away in our basement. In my youthful, creative but twisted brain, I began to believe targeting locked items was the way to go. I conjured up some good reasons for turning my attention that way. For one, it *must* be something good if it was under lock and key, and so while the risk would never justify the consequence, it made sense to focus on the most valued targets. Also, she seemed to visit these secured areas much less frequently, so detection, if it occurred at all, would be stretched out over longer periods of time, which meant punishments would also be less frequent.

After carefully studying the padlock installations, I noticed she had installed the padlocks incorrectly. This meant the hardware could be removed and items stolen without the padlocks ever needing to be opened. Fortunately, my mother didn't realize that the clasp must be installed with the screw plate on the inside of the hinged hardware, so that when locked the screws are inaccessible to a thief like me. My mother was not a handy person, and I was grateful she hadn't read the directions.

For a bit more aggressive but effective approach, John taught me that a brisk pop of the lock with the heel of a well-placed work boot would easily pop the lock open. After pilfering the desired items, he would close the padlock nicely back up and walk away undetected. This was a skill he had learned in school to gain entry into other kids' lockers. The technique also worked nicely on school supply closets. These two tactics seemed to provide the setting for a perfect, undetectable crime. I elected to target the areas where the hardware was incorrectly installed. It was cleaner and didn't have the risk of damaging or making obvious scars to the hardware assembly. Too much muscle could mean splitting a door jamb, stripping threads, or creating other easily detected clues of a forced entry.

My mother could have worked as a crime scene investigator. Her ability to detect change and find clues was uncanny, and she was rarely wrong. In the unlocked cabinets, she could spot that a bag of chocolate chips had moved a quarter-inch in the pantry just by looking at the dust pattern on the shelf and how the bag had been sealed up. Like Indiana Jones's attempt to steal the golden statue, despite our efforts to study the item thoroughly before we extracted the loot, we could never beat my mother at this game. We would attempt to return the item exactly as we had found it, label facing correctly, sitting and positioned in the same dust bed as before, and even puffing the bag with air before sealing to give it the same appearance of fullness, but our efforts were laughable to her.

We were all extremely anxious when my mother would go to the basement to unlock the storage vaults. If we were close by, we would attempt to watch carefully, studying her face. I attempted to act naturally and disinterested when she studied her loot. I wanted to give the impression that I had no idea of what was in those cabinets. From time to time, I could see the expression of puzzlement on her face when she suspected the inventory was light. Thankfully, the idea that one of us youngsters could have broken in and skillfully covered the crime was simply not an option to her...yet.

It was not because she thought we were good children. Rather, she was overly confident we could never outwit her security. However, between me and John dipping into the supplies, my mom must have become suspicious at some point, because I spotted various inconspicuous contraptions designed to foil our efforts. Trip wires and Scotch tape seals weren't meant to stop us but were designed to confirm her suspicions. I don't remember ever getting caught for these crimes, but I knew the traps were a good indication that she was on to us. She eventually started secretly documenting the specifics of her treasures, logging the debits and credits of food, school supplies, and other items. Her recordkeeping, combined with the various traps and bad timing, led to John being caught red-handed on at least one occasion.

What would happen after my mother stumbled onto one of our robberies was fairly typical. It would start with a howl of sorts, and then end with a string of curse words. She would say something like, "You motherfucking kids." And for clarification purposes, this would be followed by, "Youooooooooo thieeeeeeving motherfuuuuuuuuucking kids!!!!!!" It didn't start as a scream or yell, but rather a deep, guttural voice coming from way down in her diaphragm that elevated in volume with each syllable. Hearing the wind-up to her rant was terrifying and an indication that something awful was about to happen.

As we hid in our rooms, our heart rates increased as the volume of her voice went up. It wasn't just that she wanted us to hear the insult; she also wanted us to experience the crescendo of rage as it was building inside her. Our blood froze as we prayed she would just bark at us, and then get over it after a few glasses of win. Sometimes she threw plates or cups across the room to enunciate the discovery in case we missed the introduction. Hearing her voice and not knowing yet what the crime was would trigger me to make an immediate, anxiety-ridden mental reconciliation regarding the security of any item I had involved myself with in recent history. Because our small house made it easy to identify where her voice was coming from—living room, kitchen, or basement—I could easily determine her location. This allowed me to focus on a quick review of my own crimes that might be in the specific area. I would think, *I hope it's not the chocolate chips...did I eat too many? Did I go too far with the cereal or milk?* All crimes were serious in our house, but some crimes were treated less severely than others, so knowing what was stolen was often a direct indication of what the punishment would be.

Her raspy smoker's tirade would end with library-quiet. I could cut with a knife the apprehension that filled me in the seconds she pounded slowly up the steps to our bedrooms. My blood pressure would rise with each intentional loud stomp, each step meant to send us scurrying in fear. My next move would be to pad my backside with whatever was available, and to cover any bare skin so the painful and embarrassing welts on my arms and legs would be at a minimum. I would begin to ask myself, *Will she have a ruler in her hand or will it be one of the old 1x3s that have been lying around the basement? Will it be dry and break or supple with a whipping effect (this was the worst case)? Will it be bare-ass, and will I be able to shield her blows with my arms as I hide in the corners of the bedroom and accept the outcome? Or will the whole thing pass as it rarely but sometimes does (the best of all outcomes)?* In the cases where she decided to issue a pass, she would make a big production in her trip up the stairs, but then, with us fearing the worst, would hang a sharp right at the top of the steps and head to her room and lock the door.

Although retreating to her room would allow for a partial exhale, our anxiety levels remained high as John and I worried she might come out at any time and administer the punishment. In some ways, not getting the punishment right away was far worse because I would operate at high levels of anxiety throughout the day. It was already difficult that the status quo of my homelife was living in fight-or-flight mode, but knowing the lioness was angry and might be stalking us stepped up the worry by multiples. I can remember the anxiety would be so traumatizing I found myself knocking on her bedroom door inquiring if we should expect the beatings she promised; it was just too much to sit in a corner waiting. I would rather have the beating and get it over with than know that, at any point, she would come for me.

On most occasions, there would be an opportunity for a confession. Armed with knowing that an offense had, in fact, occurred, she would generously offer just one chance for one of us to confess. Given the severity of the punishments we received, and that the outcome was the same or worse for telling the truth, it didn't make a lot of sense to be honest, so confessions were almost non-existent. The whole practice encouraged the act of lying and finger pointing. Because we were kids and would be given the same punishment whether we lied or told the truth, I didn't feel a need to work on my integrity. However, pulling a brother in to share a beating, sometimes even lying to do so, was always better than going it alone. To our simple minds, having someone to share in the activities was a form of emotional support, and sharing the punishment seemed to split her energy and attention.

My mother's one-on-one beatings were long, terrifying, and brutal, and being alone with her in these situations was horrifying and devastatingly lonely. I didn't feel bad about outright blaming John for my crimes because he had been the one who taught me the value of false accusations and their reducing effect on the total individualized punishment output. I can remember my own shock accompanied by a deer-in-the-headlights look when, in full *Law & Order* dramatic fashion, John would falsely wag his finger in my direction. I received many heavy, undeserved beatings as the result of his finger pointing, but on some occasions, I was lucky enough to serve it back to him.

There were occasions where we could tell my mom was bluffing, because she had poker-like "tells," which communicated to us that she was not fully certain a crime had been committed. Still, sometimes, despite all parties knowing it was likely nothing had happened at all, she would still carry out the punishment. As the acting warden, she followed through because she didn't want her prisoners thinking she was soft or inept. Even if there was a low likelihood nothing had happened, she knew punishing us anyway would be an efficient deterrent to ward off future crimes and keep us inmates in line. If even the mere possibility of an offense resulted in serious consequences, her thinking was that we would be more likely to obey her rules. In most cases, this might be true, but since we were hungry, and stealing food was the most frequent offense, there were always crimes occurring.

One event that stands out to me involved orange juice. There was nothing special at all about this juice. It was just frozen concentrate, mixed from a cardboard tube, store brand, twenty-five-cent orange juice. Orange juice was a highly sought-after item in our house. My mom would pop open two of the frozen paper cylinders full of the delightful, sweet, pulpy slush, dump them into a plastic pitcher, and mix until ready to drink. My mother planned for the pitcher of juice, which was more like a glistening vase of nectar to us, to last an entire week. When we were very young, she almost always made breakfast. Each breakfast would be accompanied by a ridiculously small glass of orange juice, a societal standard at the time, which she would sit to the side of our egg or Cream of Wheat plate. We were never allowed soft drinks, so I couldn't imagine anything that tasted better than orange juice.

Before bed, I would have pleasant thoughts of that cup of juice at breakfast the next morning. I would also be plotting ways I could have some of that juice *before* the next morning. John was undoubtedly having the same dream. I couldn't help myself and began to hatch a plan for a late-night juice burglary. The idea seemed so simple to me, and I was determined to pull off the perfect crime. My plan was to sneak downstairs very late or wait for my mother to go upstairs for one of her extended wine and pill induced naps and for my brothers to be out of my sightline. The heist would take less than sixty seconds; despite the potential for severe punishment, the risk didn't matter to me. Knowing my mother would pencil-mark the balance of the liquid as she always did, I would simply enjoy a glass (or two), clean up any evidence that I was there, and then fill the container with water up to the predetermined level my mother had set. I thought of myself as absolutely brilliant while celebrating my cunning and prowess.

Everything went great and my plan was successfully executed to the letter. It went *so* well I even made a second trip to the fridge later in the evening. After all, since I had pulled off the feat once, there didn't seem to be any reason to believe I couldn't do it again. As expected, the heist again went off without a hitch. All likely would have gone well if John had not executed the same idea.

The next morning, we sat down to a plate of eggs and anxiously awaited our juice, or some much lesser variant of it. Half-asleep and in a darkish setting, my mother poured the juice into our three glasses. What I saw next made me lose my breath, and my blood froze in my veins. When she poured the juice, what filled the glass looked nothing like orange juice. It was quite obviously orange-tinted water, a distant cousin to the original content. After tasting it, I thought a better name would have been "Essence of Orange Juice." My brother and I immediately locked eyes, and I knew he and I had failed to account for another thief in the room. Our eyes then turned to David to see if he would make a comment that would bring the hammer. He drank the cloudy, virtually flavorless orange-tinted water with a big grin on his face at the start. However, as the taste caught up and he noticed the difference, he made a general comment about how bad it tasted. Fortunately, he did not belabor the point, and we sighed in relief as my mother hardly noticed his comments and went about her morning. The pitcher with the small remaining balance of evidence lay on the counter. We were almost clear of the crime.

Despite our pleading for another round so as to disappear the evidence, my mom reached for a fourth glass in the cabinet and poured out the remaining juice for herself. A small part of me was smirking inside thinking of her drinking the terrible mix of water with a splash of orange coloring, but mostly I was petrified and waited breathlessly for her reaction. Then came the worst possible outcome. Within seconds of the juice touching her taste buds, she let loose both the glass in her hand and a string of expletives. The vessel exploded in the stainless-steel sink with glass shards flying everywhere.

My mother owned a metal architect ruler. It was a long and flexible steel, eighteen-inch ruler that had various geometric shapes cut into it, along with the word *Pittsburgh* taped to it (she was a big fan of the Steelers). I'm not sure why she owned an architect ruler, but for us children, it was the best thing in the house for drawing a straight line. My mother also found it useful as an effective weapon, one that I feared more than any other she wielded.

After smashing the glass in the sink, her next move was to find the dreaded ruler, which she quickly located in our junk drawer. As usual, she gave John and me the chance to confess. Of course, we each pointed at the other, which in this particular case was 100 percent true. She became more furious, and her loud utterings caused spittle to shoot from her mouth like a mad woman. She ordered John and me to take our pants and underwear to our ankles and grab the legs of the chairs we were assigned to. We begged with every ounce of conviction we could muster for her to allow us to keep our clothes on. As angry as she was, we weren't begging to stop the beating, as we knew there was no chance of that happening. What we were begging for was for her not to whip our bare skin with this thin-gauged, virtually unbreakable stainless steel ruler. She ignored our desperate pleas, and we cried uncontrollably while apologizing and pleading for her to swing lightly and infrequently.

Those moments in my youth where I would find myself desperately begging were so sad and draining. Begging is an odd thing. If you have a fairly high emotional IQ and you have seen an actor performing this on a movie screen, you might have an idea of how sad *the idea* of having to beg is, but you would be missing most of the story. Unless you have experienced sincere begging firsthand, you will have missed the most important part. This is the part where you surrender being a human who is worthy of having his words listened to and where compromise is no longer an option. In those moments, I was so low on the food chain I had no voice or value.

At those points in my young life, I felt insignificant and worthless. Sometimes it felt like death would be a better option, but I never thought of killing myself. Many more times than this occurrence alone, I begged to be spared of the torture that would come, but it never worked, and in fact only made her more angry. Having my self-worth intentionally stripped away was a key part of her plan. Knowing that my own mother considered my powerlessness and desperation as wins made it much worse. Like my father, through her anger, I could see satisfaction in her face at her raw power and ability to take everything from me. Fending her off was unimpactful and only made her enraged and added to the punishment, so the only option was to comply. With nothing left, and crying so deeply I could not find oxygen, I would wait my turn, hoping for miracles that never came. These were the only times I actually prayed to God. I was not a believer then, but like the singer Jelly Roll, I only prayed when I desperately needed a favor. God seemed very absent in those times, but it was my only option.

The first round was on—she made John go first with three swings to his bare ass. In the midst of listening to John scream and writhe in pain, I shuddered with fear like a person overcome by freezing cold. Looking at the hard wooden chair, I obeyed her loud, crazed commands and bent my half-naked body over the seat, my belly at the edge and my privates below. As we screamed in pain, begging her to stop, she slapped us in the face and on the head for doing so. In a confusing gesture, she asked again if either of us would like to confess. As if on cue, we both fingered the other again. None of this was sane, but looking at it today, it was just two young boys trying to survive in the only way we knew how.

No ownership of the crime meant we were off to rounds two and three. In this specific case, since we both had committed the crime independently, pointing at each other was actually us telling the truth. By round four, we were bleeding from the edges of the ruler cutting into our inflamed skin. On our asses and legs, we had been decorated with small triangle, circle, and square welts, swelling caused by blood rushing to protect the impacted areas. My mom was careful not to leave the welts where the public might see them, but as we attempted to protect ourselves, she would sometimes unintentionally decorate our arms or lower legs with the shapes.

At around the fourth round, the script was flipped, and in desperation we both started confessing. In so much pain and distraught, our mixed-up thinking was that maybe this time a confession could lead to the light at the end of the tunnel. Eventually, the beating stopped because we couldn't physically follow her commands any longer. She left us with our clothes around our ankles in separate corners as she retreated to her room with orders to stay exactly as we were. Staring at each other half-naked, we didn't dare utter a word as we covered our privates with our hands. We sat there as commanded, almost afraid to breathe, whimpering, until she yelled down from the top of the stairs that we were allowed to get dressed and go to bed. It was late afternoon on a sunny Saturday, but we were thrilled to receive the order.

Half asleep and still reeling from the pain, I tried to find a comfortable way to situate my body on my piss-stained sheets. I remember my mother coming into my bedroom later that evening. As the acid from my own urine bit at my still-bleeding wounds, I pretended to be asleep, afraid of what might come next. Surprisingly, she sat on my bedside and gently touched my hair. I panicked inside, begging again, this time in silence, for her to leave. Instead, she combed through my hair with her fingers and softly explained why we deserved her attack. The touch and her words meant something to me, albeit confusing and unfamiliar. They were a morsel of humanity barely floating in a sea of despair. Looking back, she probably meant well, but my interpretation was that it was the explanation of a mad woman. At such a young age, and in serious pain, her touch and attempt at conversation felt good. and I allowed myself to partially exhale. Anything "good" at that stage in my life, even in this context, was a gift.

I fell asleep dreaming of a dry bed and leaving it to fly high above the treetops. I was a white bird that could visit anywhere I wanted, whenever I wanted. It felt like real freedom. This was an ongoing dream I experienced for many years, which always brought me some peace and calm. Cue "Freebird" by Lynyrd Skynyrd. God at work,

From our life experience to that point, and from watching our parents, my brothers and I became masters at personal property protection, defense, and concealment. Our home became a low-income attempt at Fort Knox-like security. We learned to lock everything we owned in whatever container we could find. Usually, the containers came from someone's trash in the back alley. A qualified container need only have the ability to accept the hardware of a padlock assembly. We spent the little money we had on locks and the necessary hardware to hide our most-valued items. Looking back, I can still remember when the rare friend would be allowed to visit and quickly noticed all the locks around the house. I never paid much attention to their queries as again, I thought this was a normal activity. Since we were rarely allowed in other people's homes, we didn't have any idea of how we were living.

Before long, my brother's skills and robberies were not limited to my mother and father's stocks. My bounty, as simple and worthless as it was, also became a desired target. It wasn't long before I also wore the same expressions of puzzlement my mother wore when goods would go missing without any proof of a break in. Later, John would be much more brazen in stealing from me. With no care about leaving evidence behind, he would simply smash a lock off with a hammer and take what he wanted whenever he wanted. It didn't matter that the crime scene clearly indicated I had been robbed and that everything I owned was gone. He gave up being concerned and would blame it on my mother, and my mother would blame it on John. Neither cared how badly it hurt me and that everything I owned was being stolen repeatedly. From how they unemotionally bantered with sarcasm and snickering, I was certain the few bucks and trinkets I had managed to squirrel away were never going to be returned. Mom's certain participation in the crimes and her nonchalance about the thefts were an indication things were getting worse at home. She was not protecting anything but what was hers. With no authority in place, my life was reaching a new level of mayhem.

10

Crime Lord

It's hard to listen to "Winning," originally released in 1976 by Russ Ballard and then later re-recorded by Santana in 1981, and still think of it as a Santana song; there is little Latin influence in the song and not enough of Carlos Santana's trademark guitar sound. This is more an observation than a true concern because I never listened to it for that purpose. Once again, I was drawn to the song because of the lyrics that Ballard committed to paper when I was about nine years old. I was fourteen when Santana released their version of the song, which is the one I remember. I could relate to Ballard's lyrics about being so far down that he couldn't get up and that there wasn't a friend in sight. The song's verses are mostly about bad things happening in his life, but the chorus is all about overcoming and winning. The lyrics felt real to me because there weren't a lot of wins happening in my life; my view was that my life was about struggle and loss. I had yet to learn there was a great world out there waiting for me and to focus on the reasons to be optimistic.

    Although I wasn't aware at the time, my higher power was working well, eventually allowing me to develop and then maintain a baseline faith that something better would come. I began to believe it wasn't just about doing the work; whatever was welling up inside of me was softly telling me I had to believe there was good to be had for me and there was good in the world. I didn't know what faith meant in my life and certainly wouldn't have considered my "cloudy with a chance of sun" perspective as "faith." But that is exactly what it was. I didn't know what a better future looked like, but knowing there would be one was the reason I gave myself permission to feel good some days. Gifts were happening to me in my life all the time, but I didn't know how to see them, and I had no real understanding and felt no need for gratitude. My God was at work when Ballard wrote this song, and then later when Santana's version came out on the radio. The message was telling me, "Yes, it's mostly shit for now, but it will get better. You must believe it. You will win." Get back up. Step forward. Take another punch. Get back up. Step forward. Repeat. And all the while, envision a future far away from where I was.

If I measured winning by my ability as a kid to commit various crimes and keep out of jail, then I could say I was successful. My friends and I committed many stupid petty crimes, but fortunately, I never landed in a jail cell. My first run-in with the law was for shoplifting. Most, if not all, of my shoplifting was for nutritional purposes—I had to eat. With no money and the fridge empty much of the time, theft became a requirement in especially lean times. I would often share my food with David, who, like me, was hungry most of the time.

The evening when I was caught shoplifting, I was in a 7-Eleven with some of my shady friends on Francis Avenue in Arbutus. My back-alley friends were my only friends at the time, but I was smart enough to know they were bad news and had no loyalty to me. The truth is we were all bad news. The plan we used had worked on several occasions, and I had little doubt we would be just as successful on this outing. The plan was simple—two or three of us would distract the cashier with questions and horsing around in one corner of the convenience store, while one person would walk the aisles, grabbing what they wanted from another corner of the store. Then, someone else would rotate into the distraction team, while another member went "shopping." I'm certain there were cameras at the time, but our focus was on keeping the cashier from looking at the convex security mirrors.

On this night, when it was my turn to load up, my friends indicated they were covering for me, but unbeknownst to me, they dashed out the front door with their bounty, leaving me exposed and alone. With no distraction element, the cashier could clearly see me as I confidently loaded up as if I was wearing a Harry Potter cloak of invisibility. On the way to the door, I realized I had caught the cashier's attention when I spotted his face checking me and my bulging pockets out in the mirror. With a jar of Green Giant button mushrooms, a pack of Oscar Mayer bologna, and a Baby Ruth candy bar deep in my pockets, I made quickly for the door. The cashier, anticipating my escape path and knowing there were no other exits, intercepted me before I could leave. He emptied my pockets onto the counter, and then sat me in a chair in a back room until the police arrived. As I sat sequestered in the back office of the store, I implored the cashier not to call the police, knowing this could be the last nail in my coffin for my parents. Having failed in my petition, when the police arrived, I sobbed loudly for my release.

My mother was called and immediately came to the store to pick me up. Despite being caught red-handed, she was defensive of me and had many choice words to say to the store manager and the police. It felt good to hear her stand up for me. She was particularly angry I had been locked in a dirty back room alone as I waited. However, any thoughts of coddling soon vanished as I listened to her angry words on the way home. As with most crimes, my mother threatened to tell my father of my sins. Fortunately for me, this communication could not happen immediately. Dear old Dad was vacationing in Aspen with his girlfriend, so I had a delay of a week.

Fear of punishment by my father fueled days of non-stop anxiety as I did all I could to convince my mom to keep our secret. However, despite us having to go to court and the circumstances dragging on for weeks, my mother never told my father about what I had done. We never discussed why she didn't tell him. I think sometimes she found a sick camaraderie in partnering on the administering of our punishment, so based on that, I would have bet she would tell him the minute she was able to. Perhaps knowing he was hanging with his girlfriend, confirming that she was fading out of his big picture, was the reason she let it go. There is also the possibility she thought this might be the time he would go too far with me, and her silence was meant to protect me.

I must have been around twelve the first and only time I ended up in handcuffs. My friends and I had made the poor decision to cut school and spend our time in the then vacant home of someone's grandparents. I had a new friend at the time, and he had introduced me to some boys I did not know well. These boys typically made me the butt of their jokes in passing, but on this day, they were convincingly sweet as they pushed their agenda. I wasn't just scared of cutting school and the possibility of getting in serious trouble with my parents—I was suspicious of this group of boys that I didn't know and who had always been bullies toward me. My introduction to them by my friend was possibly a good thing, but as an introvert who was afraid of everyone, I had a serious fear I would be stuck in a house with these guys and subjected to whatever they wanted to do to me. Poor judgment leading the way, I found myself walking into the basement of a small row home in Arbutus and a whiskey bottle being thrust into my hand as the door slammed and locked behind me.

Within a short while, we were all stupidly drunk, with some of us throwing up from drinking straight liquor. Vomiting is never fun, but I remember us all laughing together and being silly kids. For a short bit, I felt like I fit in somewhere. The phone on the wall rang multiple times while we were there. An elderly neighbor had heard all our racket through the shared wall of the rowhome and became concerned that someone had broken in. Rather than handle it like the grown-ups we weren't, we made fun of her and hung up on her multiple times in the middle of her rants. Within minutes, we heard a knock at the door and fear turned to panic when we saw multiple police cars in front of the house with their lights flashing. With that new data point, we did what any group of knuckleheaded kids would do: we hid all over the house. It was the best our middle school minds could come up with. When the knocks and demands of the police to open the door persisted, accompanied by threats of their imminent entry, several of us ran to the back door to see if we could escape through the rear alley. We were disappointed to find that the alley was occupied by several additional police cars.

With no possibility of escape, we returned to our hiding places. My hiding spot was an antique armoire full of old jackets. I closed the door and got behind the longest coats on the rack. It reminded me of a scene from *The Lion, The Witch and The Wardrobe* by C. S. Lewis, one of my favorite books as a child. I was scared, but I felt confident no one would come looking for me there. As I sat in near panic worrying about the consequences that would come from Mom and Dad and what would happen if the police found me, I tried not to breathe. In that tight space my breath seemed so loud I thought I might give my position away. My perceived safety, of course, meant nothing to the police K9s preparing to infiltrate the home and find me.

As we hid quietly in our spots, a lull in the outside commands would trigger the occasional far away loud whisper of a twelve year old asking, "Do you think they are still out there?" When we heard a loud, amplified voice demanding we exit the home along with a threat of sending in the dogs, we again did what all preteens would do: we froze and remained in our spots. However, when we heard the glass break and the sound of dogs barking through the rear basement transoms, I quickly realized our efforts were pointless and emerged from my hiding place. With panic on our faces, we headed up the stairs, away from the barking, and uniformly beelined for the front door.

We all had our own versions of excuses and finger pointing, as the police separated us and took us in different directions. I was distraught thinking of what would happen at school, and then later at home. The police officer put me in handcuffs and placed me carefully in the backseat of the car. When we arrived at the middle school, he took the cuffs off and walked me into the school and directly into the principal's office. Ms. Cheek was a nice woman whom I had *visited with* on several occasions. I found her to be fair and kind. She had a calm demeanor and was no different today as the prisoners were paraded before her. I'm certain there were some consequences through the school system, but I cannot remember what they were. Our parents were called to pick us up, and I remember my mother coming to get me.

My mother said little when we arrived home. I remember she slapped me around a bit and once again promised to engage my father for the real punishment. However, I don't remember him disciplining me for this. So I think that like my shoplifting escapade, she once again decided not to tell him. Skipping school, getting drunk, and then being picked up by the police and taken to school were all serious crimes that would have resulted in him raining some heavy pain down on me. Perhaps my mother, knowing that this could be the crime that might send my father over the top, made the decision to offer up another act of mercy. I think that her alcoholism coupled with a growing dislike of the man she had waited her whole life for, also played a part.

In another embarrassing act of greed and petty criminality, I was able to find a source of funding by exploiting the annual school cause related fundraisers. In the late '70s and '80s, kids collecting donations for organizations like UNICEF and the American Cancer Society were an important part of fundraising. Armies of kids poured into the streets knocking on doors, ostensibly to save lives, but the truth was we were all trying to earn vastly overpriced items like wrapping paper and toys from the companies promoting the fundraiser. Much of what I saw in the fundraising catalog interested me, but I knew almost instantly the greatest opportunity was not in the overvalued prizes, but in the cash collection itself.

I would walk the neighborhood for hours to fill paper milk cartons full of coins. I did this for whatever amount of time my mother would allow. My plan was that the non-profit would receive the bulk of the benefit, but I would skim from each carton as my own personal food and living allowance. Getting their cut of the take was exactly why the schools pushed so hard during these drives, so why shouldn't I also have a slice given that I was doing all the work? The fundraisers served important purposes, but they also were a much-needed stimulus to my personal economy. I didn't know it at the time, but this was another example of my gifts of resourcefulness and self-sustainability. I was not built to wait for others to help me or feel sorry for myself, so efficiently capitalizing on the few "opportunities" available to me was important to my survival. I know it was wrong, but I would like to think the Universe was OK with me using some of the funds to help with my survival.

When it came time to collect canned goods for the holidays, I also heard the call to help. Here again, my excitement had a selfish motivation, as keeping select canned goods was a much more efficient way to address my hunger than taking cash from a fundraising drive. With an abundance of food choices right in my hands, I didn't have to bicycle or walk miles to buy the food, and then try to explain where I got the money to buy what I had eaten when I returned. So my mother would not find out and to minimize thefts from my brother, I would hide canned goods in my favorite hiding spots around the house and in the woods. My brother would sometimes discover and seize some of the ill-gotten items from my room, there was little I could do about it. A complaint would only tell my mother that I was stealing, so instead, I had to be creative and outfox him. For this reason, the best items were kept far away from my room. Less appealing items were hidden in places John could find easily, thus keeping him from looking for my most prized items. It was nice to have a few days of food on hand and enjoy the feeling of a full belly as I ate from the cans in the woods. While I did enjoy the spoils, the bulk of my collections went to the school, and I was credited with collecting more food than most of my peers.

John was good at a lot of things: singing, writing, playing guitar, B and E (breaking and entering), fighting, and, not to be forgotten, bicycle theft and repair. My father would get us a bike from Goodwill from time to time, but with previous heavy use and our rough handling, the bikes did not last long or were stolen by other kids. Other times, the bikes needed parts my parents would not supply, so they would sit useless to us until we either fixed them ourselves or saved up for the parts. In response to this, John began stealing bikes around our neighborhood. Our unfinished basement became home to many locally owned bicycles whose parts were reassigned to other bike frames. It was an awkward conversation when parents were searching the neighborhood for a bicycle while I watched John go riding by with parts I knew he had lifted from the missing bicycle. By the time he finished swapping parts and painting the frames, the bicycles were unrecognizable to their previous owners. He had a large inventory of stolen bikes, so I'm sure the neighborhood was buzzing with the news of a serial bicycle thief.

Unfortunately, John was not a good sharer and like my parents, anything he offered came with a price tag that most times I could not afford. However, he gave me a gift he wasn't even aware he was giving—full transparency of his operation and the chance to learn how to do it myself. I learned from him how to break down and rebuild my own bikes. With this experience and what my father had taught me about basic bicycle repair, true to my independent spirit, I decided to start my first entrepreneurial venture.

My business model had some important differences compared to John's operation. I would not steal any bicycles that were near our home. Two of us stealing from the same hunting grounds would make the opportunities too thin while also increasing the chances of getting caught. Additionally, I made the decision to hide my bikes deep in some trusty woods because I didn't want John lifting from my inventory. Also, if he knew I was also stealing, I was worried this would lead him to leverage that knowledge against me.

To find acquisitions, I would take long reconnaissance walks and bike rides, travelling as far as I could get away with, surveying all the back alleys and yards. My search was for unlocked targets, preferably with no dogs standing guard. I was also looking for bikes that may have been sitting a while so their disappearance wouldn't be immediately noticed. Old spider webs and low tire pressure were good signs. After I identified a target, I would begin the planning and execution for how to acquire it.

Stealing a bicycle involved the highly risky but necessary tactic of sneaking down two flights of stairs to the basement window and slipping undetected into the black of night. On one such night, I had designated the target as a new looking metallic maroon ten speed Open Road brand bicycle. It had been sitting in the same spot for weeks, and I saw no evidence of recent movement. To complete another bike I had been working on, I needed new rims, a crankshaft, and tires, and this bike seemed to check all of those boxes. I proceeded through the network of alleys on a moonlit night and went to sit in the thick of a hedge bush I had predesignated as my surveillance point. I sat for a while to assess the situation. I needed to make sure there were no dogs and no human activity in the yard of the target or any adjoining rowhomes. Also preferable was that there be as little lighting as possible. Contrary to my discipline, this yard did have a dog, and he barked extensively at me as I sat in the dark bushes. He couldn't see me, but he knew I was there. I sat patiently only about twenty feet away while I watched and nibbled on wood sorrel, which grew naturally underneath the hedge.

Eventually, the dog's owners pulled him inside to end the incessant barking, bringing the moonlit night to an eerie quiet. I sat for a bit longer to ensure things remained quiet. When I was certain conditions were ideal, I hugged the shadows and made my way to the backyard of the target's neighbor. My reconnaissance suggested it was much smarter to hang over the fence from the adjacent yard and lift the bike over the fence, rather than walk brazenly into the yard and risk the owner releasing the dog on me. Once the bike was in hand, I could go to the next house, which was an end unit townhome, and make my escape to the street. From there, I would mount the bike and jet off to my safe spot for an assessment of parts and to find cover.

My heart beat out of my chest as I moved to execute on my plan. I carefully made my way up the sidewalk to the rear of the neighbor's rowhome. The lights of this house were out and darkness offered good cover all the way to the bike. Once within reach, I hung over the fence and pulled the bike quietly over to the other yard. I could hear the dog barking inside the house and the owner loudly reprimanding it, but no one came to investigate. With a few more steps in the opposite direction, I was over another fence to the end unit and had a clear path to the street. It looked like a clean getaway, but things were about to get bad in a hurry.

By the light of the moon, I mounted the bike and started to pedal away from the scene of the crime on almost flat tires. A short distance away, I saw a police car cruising very slowly down the street about one hundred yards in front of me, with its spotlight on and panning in multiple directions. Behind me, I picked up another spotlight from a different police car coming down the alley from a different direction, evidently triangulating my position. Someone had obviously seen me and called the police, and now I felt as if I was clandestinely crossing a prison yard trying to escape. I was in a tight, seemingly inescapable pickle as I felt my heart pounding in my throat. They were closing in on my position, and I needed to escape quickly. Assessing the situation, I could not go forward or backward, nor could I lie down in the wide-open lawn and hide in the dark; the lights would have found me instantly.

In front of me rose a thick and tall pine tree, which, in my two-second judgment, seemed like the only answer to my immediate problem. It was thick enough to provide cover if I could just get to the right height in its branches. At about five feet or higher, the branches looked to provide adequate cover if I could make it to that height, stay there, and motionlessly wait for the police to pass. However, if I got hung up in the lower branches, it could instead end up being a great way to present myself to the police. With no other choice, I dashed into the tree with my new bike in hand.

With needles in my face, climbing with my right hand, and the bicycle in my left, I fought my way to the center of the tree. Pine trees are easy to climb because they have many low branches, but sometimes the branches are so dense it can be difficult to maneuver and go higher. With the bike standing on its rear wheel and the front wheel pulled horizontally into the air and leaned against the trunk, I ascended to a branch where I could then reach down and pull the bike up. I climbed a bit more, slowly pulling the bike up behind me each time I cleared the next level of branches. Trying to keep the pedals, handlebars, and rims from getting hung up in the limbs was quite a challenge. When I got to a height and thickness I thought would provide enough cover, I pulled the bike up and used a broken branch through the front rim to hang the bike while I surveilled the police activity going on below me. Deep in the cover of the branches, my heart was beating almost as if it would explode. Minutes later, I watched from up high as both police cars slowly converged on the corner where the alley and street met, only about seventy five feet from where I hid. They continued to work their spotlights, but, thankfully, they spent no time illuminating the part of the tree where I was hidden.

I was shaking in fear, knowing what was at stake if I got caught. The ten minutes I spent concealed in those branches seemed like hours. If caught by the police, it would have certainly landed me in juvenile court, and worse would have come from my parents. Doing my best not to breathe or make any sound, I stayed in the tree until well after the police left. One positive about being in the tree was I could see in every direction. When my breathing returned to near normal and I was certain there were no police or others waiting for me, I started my descent. Once on the ground, I mounted the bike and shot across Elm Road to the graveyard, which could be accessed through a broken wrought iron fence. It was wide open turf from there, so I was potentially vulnerable to being spotted, but there were lots of options for escape if detected, so I knew I was safe at that point.

Inside the graveyard, I travelled the grounds and found my way to my stash spot in the woods. I hid the bicycle with tree limbs and forest debris as camouflage and made my way home, praying my mother was not up. I crawled back through the window and up to my bed. Despite all the excitement, incredulously, no one would ever find out about the events of that evening.

After several days, my confidence grew, and I went to inspect my bounty. I knew from the first look that I could not use the frame as it was unique in design and even if painted, that uniqueness would be easily recognized. But there were many other parts... The brakes, crankcase, front and rear derailleurs, rims, tires, inner tubes, seat, and handlebars were all common, non-distinct brands. I took what I needed for immediate use and buried the rest in a plastic bag in the woods. I put the unneeded frame in a dumpster at a local construction site. This most telling piece of evidence was soon taken off to the landfill, eliminating any opportunity for me to be fingered for the crime. It was quite an adventure, but that experience cured me of my midnight bicycle thefts.

There are gifts and reasons to be grateful for most everything. I am grateful I didn't get arrested that night or any other night for the many other things I stole or did wrong in my youth. Even though I committed crimes and felt bad for those who lost what was rightfully theirs, my thefts were always out of necessity and survival. I know this does not make my actions right, but perhaps I was a more honest crook for not making a profit on acquisitions. I am not sure exactly how to reconcile my respect and love of my higher power and morality with my criminal acts. I am also not naive enough to believe that stealing bicycles represented something necessary for my survival. However, for those who understand what it feels like to be alone and desperate for some showing of hope, then it may be possible to relate to how having a working bicycle might feel freeing. And further, how tasting that freedom might provide fuel to survive another day. It's not an attempt to rationalize what I did wrong, but my bicycle was allowing me to practice putting physical distance between me and my abusers. I wasn't leaving home, but in some ways, I was practicing for it. That is how it felt to me, and that contributed immensely to my willpower and ultimate survival. The opportunity that a bicycle afforded me to travel far and taste uninhibited adventure, while living simultaneously in the jaws of oppression and abuse, seems in hindsight like something the Universe wanted me to have. Knowing what was at stake, I can't think of any other reason I would take such risks. The gifts of hard-wired resourcefulness and initiative showed up and guided me in the way they had to. Maybe the Universe writes exceptions or doesn't care about right and wrong in absolute terms. Or maybe it was nudging me toward the greater good of things while accepting there are missteps and tradeoffs along the way. I know with certainty that all of these experiences and stories of survival gave me a keen set of tools and the right attitude to allow me to escape my home and build a life.

Me hiding in the branches of an accommodating pine tree with a newly acquired bicycle. A well-planned heist almost ends badly.

11
New Beginnings

When I hear the Indigo Girls singing "Closer to Fine," I am reminded of how profound an impact that song had on me as I compared the writer's experience with my own path of trying to learn what the world was all about. I wore an amiable face, but in my mind, I was broken and searching for direction and meaning in everything. I was driven to get out of where I had been and to make certain I would never return there. This drive, another gift from my higher power, was paramount, but I was seriously struggling to manage through the past trauma, deep insecurities, and a lack of any support system. There were days when freedom felt palpable, but most days I remained in survival mode. When I turned on the radio and the Indigo Girls were singing this song filled with lyrics I could understand, whether they knew it or not, they became my friends. Their gift became a gift I graciously accepted.

I don't know much about the singers but read recently they are gay. While their sexual status has no importance to me, I do wonder if when Ms. Saliers wrote this song if she was like me and dealing with her own struggle to find her place in the world. Being gay in 1989 was certainly more acceptable than in past decades, but the world was nowhere close to accepting homosexuality as normal. I can only imagine how difficult that was for her. In all of that difficulty, she was inspired to write a song that tells me it is OK not to know all the answers and fine to keep searching for my place in the world.

In thinking about big moves, I am reminded of when my family left city life behind. My father and mother separated at least twice, but ultimately divorced. As I wrote about previously, my mother and father had one of their reconciliations for a short period after we signed the contract for the brand new thirteen hundred square foot end unit townhome in Arbutus, Maryland. While the home was much smaller in size than our Wilkens Avenue rental, everything was brand new and the promise of no roaches, mice, or rats filled me with absolute delight. We would be moving to "the county," which was a huge thing for anyone to hear who grew up in Baltimore. In my time, the city was a place everyone wanted to leave. Neighbors and acquaintances thought we were rich or had come into some unexpected fortune. Things were really looking bright for the Wellingtons.

We drove by the new house at least once a week to survey the progress. John and I would spend as long as possible in our future bedrooms, fantasizing about how they would be set up and studying the view from our windows. The back alleys were like an ocean view compared to watching rats scurry across the parking lot of Gino's. The day the builders laid the deep, red shag carpet was a highlight in my memory. The smell of the nylon fibers mixing with fresh paint was a slice of heaven. We had never seen or touched anything so new. Our anticipation grew, and I could not wait to move into the home.

It was October 30, 1974, and with moving into the new house just days away, and the eve of Halloween upon us, I couldn't help but smile. It was my second-grade year, which would be my last full year at Violetville Elementary in Baltimore. Like every student at Violetville, I was excited about the annual Halloween party in the gymnasium. There was a costume parade through the halls and the grounds that ended with a visit to the haunted stage. The older kids had spent quite a bit of time putting together a haunted trail on the stage. Every student was allowed a tour of the gruesome Halloween scene, and many of us younger kids found ourselves crying at the end. There were coffins, creepy music, and plenty of black lights and flashing strobes. It was a perfect fall day, and the show was exactly as billed. I wore my Casper the Friendly Ghost costume my brother and I had taken turns using over the last several Halloweens. The Halloween show always ended with an opportunity to buy Halloween-themed cupcakes and other baked goods. My parents didn't provide funding for these things, so I watched enviously as my classmates bought the goodies and devoured them in front of me. I can still smell the thick, sweet buttercream icing as the kids taunted me by licking huge swirls of sugar just inches from me.

After exiting the show, we all stood in line to be led back to our class. A classmate of mine was straightening his costume and unwittingly put a handful of coins down on a close ledge to free up his hands to eat his cupcake. When he was done, he left the unused coins on the ledge and started carrying on with other kids in the line. The shimmering coins lying unattended had me fixed in a trance, and I was beginning to process the idea of a possible heist. My brain knew better, but it did not prevent me from convincing myself these sad coins were clearly all alone in the world. They needed the type of appreciation and respect only I could give, and if I didn't care for them, someone else would. We stood lined up for at least two or three minutes as the teacher gathered my classmates. My classmate's faltering memory and his willingness to leave behind the coins in favor of a position in the front of the line was all I needed to rationalize that the coins were in need of a new home. It was eight-year-old logic and completely made sense at the time.

As the line progressed and we slowly passed the ledge, I reached out and snatched the eighty cents in three quarters and a nickel and buried them deep in my Super Denim pocket. As far as I was concerned, my retrieval of the lost treasure had been successful, and while I was filled with worry at the thought of getting caught, I distracted myself by entertaining ideas of how I could spend the money. It was my first successful school grab, and I was too young to realize no thief is safe until he has cleared the scene and hidden the evidence. I believed I had very little risk, as the boy had purchased all that he desired, and this was just an unneeded and unimportant pile of "couldn't be bothered with" change. The single file line had almost passed completely out into the hall. If I could just make it back to our classroom, I would be in the clear. Things were progressing as expected, and I could feel my breath returning to my chest.

With just feet to go before I was home free, my heart came to a hard stop and my veins froze like ice in response to shrieks of panic from the true owner after he realized the coins were no longer where he had left them. The line came to an abrupt halt as our teacher came to his assistance and assessed the situation. He explained where he had placed the money in careful, accurate detail, and the teacher's helper went to more closely inspect the location. When the funds were confirmed to be missing, it was an easy deduction that one of the students standing behind the boy in the line, but ahead of the snatch point, was the thief. This left the teacher with about ten kids to choose from. She gave a small speech that ended with her giving the thief an opportunity to come forward. Whatever her words, they didn't matter; I was ashen with fear and well trained to stay quiet. In my world, telling the truth was not an option, as it only came with pain and suffering. This situation seemed no different.

As the search began, she promoted an air of fairness as she made her way through the ten sets of pockets of the students before me. When she turned to me and emptied my pockets, I looked away as if to act naturally, but she knew I was the culprit. I suppose she could have given me the benefit of the doubt and asked if it was my money, but she already knew I didn't have money for baked goods.

As she dragged me to the principal's office, the river of tears and wailing was as good an admission of guilt as she needed. She grabbed my eight-year-old arm, almost ripping it from its socket, and yanked me down the long, wide hall toward the principal's office. I was in shock and didn't yet have a true appreciation for where this series of events would lead. My focus in that minute was on maintaining my balance, and I don't mean existentially. I mean that physically, this enraged woman was only one tug away from dragging me on my knees down the hall. She twisted my skin so tightly it felt like the flesh would tear. I was mortified with embarrassment, but I was mostly concerned with my physical health. She performed the job effectively and with zeal.

As the teachers and students hurriedly cleared the way for us, she beamed with a hint of prideful vindication. The amount of energy and enunciation in our procession clearly told the spectators a great wrong had occurred. It was as if she, and only she, had netted the great Oliver Twist. This large, disheveled woman's level of stamina and determination meant that either I was a repeat offender, or she was a raving lunatic who derived personal satisfaction from physically abusing an eight-year-old boy over the theft of eighty cents. Having been in second grade for only a few months, I hadn't yet logged any other principal-worthy offenses, so it must have been the latter.

She dumped me on the standard government-issue heavy oak wood bench in front of the principal's office and proceeded through the frosted glass and wood door to give her accounting of the situation as the arresting officer. I stared at the floor in tears. Until that point, I had never noticed how shiny the twelve-by-twelve tile squares were. The bench seemed to be secured to the floor by the wax buildup around the chairs' legs that came from the nightly floor buffing. I doubted I would ever get the opportunity to explain how the shiny coins had called so softly out to me and how it tortured me to watch the other children shovel down the black forest cupcakes spread with orange icing and topped with candy corn and jimmies without having a single lick myself.

The arresting officer left the office, seemingly pleased with the principal's response to her debriefing. She flew by me on the way out of the office with no words and a spiteful smile on her face. Now I was alone and full-force wailing on the bench. Children walked by with various levels of interest. For the younger children, my bawling and obvious panic set the scene for how they would view the administrative offices for years to come. I was the perfect advertisement for what could happen to them if they made a wrong step. For the older children, I was an easy target for jeers and finger pointing.

Several times, the principal's secretary came out to me on the bench and warned me to stop crying. She had no words to ease my stress and made no effort to comfort me. This was 1974, well before ideas of compassion and understanding became the standard. Every time she came out of the door, my heart leapt with fear. I would attempt to calm myself by throttling back to a sorrowful whimpering, hoping that the moment of reckoning was upon me. The waiting is the worst in these types of situations.

The principal allowed me to sit on the bench in various stages of panic and anxiety for hours. Eventually, the secretary took me in to see the principal. He was an enormous black man I believed had been principal for as long as the school had existed. He was not an unkind man, nor was he accommodating in any way. He had only a few questions as he'd been told I had been caught red-handed. He asked for my confession, which I had no choice but to give. Part of me believed this would be like the confessions I had heard about in church. People skulked into the dark wooden booths, long faced and forlorn, and came out cleansed, confident, and with a clean slate—not like home.

After my visit with the principal, I was placed in the hallway again to sit out the remainder of the day. Dealing with my crime at school that day was traumatic, but my greatest fear had nothing to do with school. I was hoping the extent of my punishment would be to sit on that bench for the balance of the day and be forced to accept the public ridicule and darting curious eyes that looked my way. That I was still sitting on the bench at all was a positive sign. Maybe I was going to be able to ride this event out with public humiliation being the worst of it. As it turned out, this was wishful thinking.

My parents either could not or would not come to collect me earlier in the day. Perhaps it was because of work, or maybe they were teaching me a lesson. As the last bell rang and students ran for the exits, the secretary took me into the principal again. He wasted no time beating around the bush as he announced I had been suspended for two days and my parents had been notified. Again, my blood froze in my veins.

He also informed me my mother was on the way. I knew that interrupting her work was a capital offense, so with that news, my day went from terrible to terrifying.

When I climbed up into our Chevy Impala wagon, my mother looked at me with rage in her eyes. I slid as far as I could behind the driver's seat in case my mother felt the urge to smack me on the way down the road as sometimes happened. She turned abruptly on several occasions to check her mirrors, which I was sure was designed to check my reaction to her sudden movement. This teased me and kept my fear factor at a steady boil. In each case, I would dive behind the seat into the floor well with my arms wrapped around my head and my fingers locked together protecting my head. We had practiced bomb drills often in school, so I was confident this would be the safest position. To the cars sitting in traffic next to us, I must have looked like a deranged hyperactive kid, one moment sitting tight and close to the door, the next moment doing a tuck and roll to the floor.

My mother never hit me that day; however, she did something much worse. She said the dreaded words: "Wait 'til your father gets home." I begged my mother not to tell him, but she had no choice because of the parent-principal conference that both parents had to attend. The meeting would follow in the coming days, and taking their time in this way was yet another reason to incite my parents. I went to my room in a cold, panicked sweat and waited there quietly until I heard the knocking and sputtering sound of my father's Ford V8 as he cut off the engine.

He came into the house on Wilkens in his usual brazen, unconcerned, self-enlightened manner. He didn't notice I wasn't there to greet him and went about his usual routine: slippers, cigarette, drink, and then television, as he waited for dinner. I had to wait another hour before we convened for our meal, which usually consisted of some type of casserole made in a square bone-white Corningware bowl with China Blue-inspired designs on the sides. We covered the usual topics: my father's stress at work, an update on his least favorite coworkers, and an interrogation regarding Mom's productivity during the day. Her efforts were never good enough and certainly could not compare to the Atlassian load he carried each day. Eventually, he might get around to hearing how our days went. My mother was undoubtedly nervous herself, probably because his response to my theft would likely start with blaming and berating her for my actions. She decided to give herself a pass and instead forced me to tell my father what had happened. I had tears streaming down my face as I told him about the crime of the century—the pilfering of eighty cents.

He stared deeply into my eyes for a long time, and I could see his rage building somewhere deep inside. It was a look I knew, and it horrified me. News that his son was a thief was bad, missing hours from work to go to a school meeting was much worse, but being suspended and keeping one of them out of work to babysit me was cataclysmic. The rage grew to hatred as he got up and came across the table to me. I locked my fingers over my head to protect myself from what was coming.

My father had a long history of assorted violence with us. One of his favorite methods for on-the-spot punishments was taking a heavy handled butter knife and while holding the blade end, sharply cracking me on the head with the handle. The blow wasn't enough to split my skull, but it was enough to hurt badly for a few minutes and leave a well-defined goose egg on my head for days. Blocking the shot was not allowed and only meant he would demand our hands be at our sides so he could correctly administer the pain. Another block or failure to comply would lead to a worse punishment. So with his angry orders, I unclasped the fingers protecting my skull and took three knife knocks to my head. He giggled with each strike. As with other punishments, he seemed proud of his work—the placement and the dull thud. With his laugh and another dose of humiliation, I felt relief. The consequence was over, and, despite the goose eggs, I could let myself exhale a bit. Unfortunately, my assessment was wrong. When he was finished, he informed me there would be no trick-or-treating for me the next evening.

My father never reversed his announced punishments, but *this* was a giant punishment. At that age, missing Halloween was about as bad an outcome as a kid could have. The only thing worse might have been to miss Christmas. In hindsight, I might have taken several beatings in place of a lost night of trick-or-treating. Given the severity of the sentence, I hoped this might be the one exception. After a night to sleep on it, he would change his mind. After all, he enjoyed taking the finest selections from our take every year, so he would be negatively impacted as well.

On Halloween, we ate dinner at the old house and John rushed to put on his Halloween costume while my mother painted a clown face on David's baby face. The hours leading up to begging door to door for candy were some of the best moments of my young life. I would be smiling and dreaming all day of the night's take. Halloween was my first dose of gaining a kill-what-you-eat sales mentality, and that didn't bother me a bit. I was prepared to be out for as long as I was allowed, and give myself fully to the job at hand. In previous years, we had trick-or-treated starting as early as possible, and my dad kept us out well after the rest of the kids were gone. We would hit the garden apartment buildings on Wilkens and literally fill trash bags with our bounty. On this night, seeing John so excited and knowing I would be left alone with my father made me as sad as I could have been.

I sat there clutching my Casper costume, mortified I would be left behind and wishing for my sentence to be suspended. With no sign of a reprieve, we all got into the Chevy Wagon and drove the short distance to our new neighborhood on Selford Road in Arbutus. My father had decided to use the evening to do some work on the new house. We were happy about the plan to trick-or-treat in Arbutus because the townhouse community in Baltimore County was full of "rich" people and no doubt they would have better candy. Also, a sea of townhouses allowed us to cover a lot of ground quickly. Aside from that, Arbutus seemed friendlier than our neighborhood in the city.

Given my father's relatively calm demeanor, I was feeling some hope as we were finishing up dinner. The punishment just didn't fit the crime, and afterall, it was Halloween! We drove mostly in silence to our new home, with everyone obviously wondering the same thing. My mother and father talked quietly in the front seat, but there was no discussion about me.

The truth came brutally and quickly. When we arrived, my father parked the car at the curb and all of us helped carry in what needed to be carried in. Soon after that was completed, the streetlights came on, and my father gave the OK for my mother, David, and John to head out onto the street. His failure to include me was such a shock that it seemed like he'd made a mistake. When my whimpering met his eyes, I knew it had not been an error. I could not have cried any harder or any quieter as I watched my brothers and mother grow smaller in the waning light. When they turned the corner left onto Shelbourne, I knew Halloween was over for me.

There was little said between me and my father as we shared one-on-one space in the new house for the first time. He was hanging curtain rods, and I was sitting close by, slowly building up the courage to ask one more time to join my mother and brothers. He hated when we showed any resistance in any form, and any pleading for a sentence reduction was usually met with swift retribution. However, missing Halloween was devastating, so any risk was acceptable to me.

In a deeply anxious state, I tugged at my hair, trying to build up the courage to ask the most important question of my life. I rehearsed the tone and content of the question many times in my head, and, in as sweet a way as possible, let loose. I knew the chances of success were low, but I was still caught off guard when he verbally let me have every bit of his pent-up anger. Of course, he used the crime and my infractions to verbally highlight what he had always believed about me: I was a rotten, no-good kid, "a fucking thief and liar." It made him feel righteous and vindicated that he could connect these dots and punish me so harshly for the theft. It wasn't that I hadn't heard hurtful words before from him, it was the timing and intensity of his delivery that made the words cut so hard.

For a few minutes, I forgot about Halloween. I cried hard, hoping for some sympathy or maybe some affection. My effort had the opposite effect. Incensed, he picked me up and carried me into the living room, to a place that put me out of his sight while he was working. From his arms, he then threw me in a corner. He instructed me not to move as he turned off all the lights, leaving me in pitch black in the completely unfurnished newly painted and carpeted room. As he walked away, he threatened that if I continued to cry, he would "give [me] a real reason to cry." I didn't think he was joking, but I was so upset, it was hard to stop.

I was quiet for a short while, but then my weeping seemed to take on a life of its own. My crying combined with muffled moaning was met with only silence and the occasional far away verbal threat. When I realized I seemed to be getting away with it, I stepped up my moaning game and increased the volume. This got his attention! As I heard his cursing and footsteps moving quickly toward me, there was fear but also a dim light of hope flickered.

My father didn't bother to turn on the light when he came to address my behavior. He simply walked up to me, knelt down to my eye level, made sure I was looking at him directly, and punched me in the face. It was more like a sharp, surgically delivered jab than a full-throttle punch, but it was highly effective. My nose began to bleed profusely all over me. I was scared but was left with a dangerous decision. Should I risk stepping up my wailing from the pain of the punch and all the blood and attempt to capitalize on what might have been a mistake on his part, or should I instead attempt to gain control of my emotions and pain, avoid possible additional strikes, and sink back into the corner?

I didn't have to look too far or deep for the answer. A light from the hallway behind him dimly illuminated the side of my father's head. While I couldn't see his entire face, the fury that registered in what I *could* see of him gave me the definitive answer I was looking for. The evil I saw told me that the right decision was to cower submissively into the corner. I consciously worked hard to muffle my sobbing in the carpet, all while trying both to breathe and not to breathe. Controlling the nosebleed was not his concern at the time.

Fortunately, my father interpreted my effort as compliance and he walked casually back to his work, seemingly unimpacted by his actions. Moments later, I could hear him walking back toward me. My heart beat out of control as I braced for the next round. I was petrified with fear of a possible second strike or worse, and what might result from that. Mercifully, his return was for the purpose of callously throwing me a towel across the room and demanding I not get any blood on the freshly painted walls or new carpet.

I don't know how long I sat there suppressing my cries and listening intently. I had switched from sales mode to survival mode. My instincts demanded I pay attention and carefully track my father's every movement around the house. I had to be prepared to protect myself; surprise attacks were the worst. It was my mission to know exactly where he was and prepare myself in whatever way possible in case our paths crossed again. It was especially terrifying to be anywhere alone with him. The noises of his tinkering in the house were a relief to me; it meant he was thinking of something else, which was a good thing. The noises also allowed me to track him effectively. Exhausted, I allowed myself to fall asleep in the corner until my mother and brothers came home. Shortly thereafter, we all piled into the car and headed back to the city.

In the car, and now more awake, I watched as John gloated over his sack of candy and looked curiously at my swollen nose and bloody clothes. As none of us were sharers, I had no hope that John would share his loot, which made the bulging bag of candy much harder to see. No one bothered to ask about my condition. Life just went on as if nothing had occurred at all.

It is difficult for me to know my mother had that level of passivity when it came to my care. I want to believe she was so oppressed and so desperately clinging to the hope of a functional marriage that she painfully looked the other way. Sadly, it's also possible that, as a fellow abuser, she felt his actions were justified. Whatever the reason for her silence, what happened to me was never discussed again. You can bet I never got caught stealing after that, but this did not mean I didn't steal ever again…only that I didn't get caught.

That impactful Halloween jab was one of many conditioning moments for me. Because of this and many other attacks, I would flinch every time my father raised his hand for any reason. If he stroked his own hair or just simply moved his arm in my direction, I would immediately move out of his reach. I never stopped flinching when he moved like that, even well into my adulthood.

What I thought was going to be a wonderful new beginning had quickly started with a reminder that more of the same was in store for us, and now he was going to be living with us. What had seemed like good news now registered as a nightmare for me.

Fortunately, my parents separated only weeks later, and my father made his final exit from our new home. As is the case today, people were getting divorced back then fairly frequently, but despite the numbers, it was still thought of as odd in my circles to be part of a divorced family. When people asked me how I felt about the divorce, it seemed bizarre to even consider the question. Their final split was the best thing that happened to me at that time in my life and another example of how the Universe was working with me. It was even better than Christmas. After Halloween, I never had a single wish after that they would get back together; in fact, my thoughts were just the opposite. The idea of two physical, psychological and emotional abusers under one roof, collaborating together to affirm their belief of our awfulness, was about as dangerous a situation as I could imagine. In my case, their divorce and the hope that he would find a way out of our lives permanently, was a gift of hope.

12

Compassion and Understanding for Mom and Dad

My father loved Willie Nelson and that spilled over to me. Hearing my father play the *Honeysuckle Rose* soundtrack or the album "Red Headed Stranger" through a phonograph while he sang quietly along was a good memory for me. Whenever I hear "Angel Flying Too Close To The Ground," released in 1980, I remember how the song tamed my dad and had some secret importance to him. Hearing him sing and watching the song's physical impact on him was an opportunity to see my father as a human capable of emotions and not the dictator he most always was. I am thankful he shared Willie with me, and I still listen to his music today.

My mother loved Anne Murray and sang along to her tunes beautifully. On a couple occasions, she would play a song on her turntable and ask me to dance with her. Usually, she was a bit tipsy, with wine on her breath, but that didn't matter to me. My effort was more stumbling than dancing, but I immediately accepted when she asked. I loved hearing my mother's voice singing along with Murray, and, like my father, it gave me the opportunity to see the softer side of her; more gifts. The lyrics of "Could I Have This Dance" were written for lovers, but I wanted that song to be about her and I. It was one of those rare moments she would let me get close to her, physically and emotionally.

Despite the extensiveness of abuse and other mistreatment from my parents, it has been difficult for me to write so many disparaging things about them. It doesn't feel comfortable, and I struggle with putting these experiences to print. After all, these were human beings brought up in impossible childhood environments themselves; they, without question, gave a lot better to us than they received. Some might make a good argument that my comments about them should have stopped with me accepting my circumstances and being grateful. I still deal with guilt when thinking about it in this way. However, I ultimately arrive at a confident *knowing* that just giving better than what they got isn't reason enough to waive away their misdeeds and not find them willfully ignorant of the impact of their actions.

Another part of me wonders if the volumes of guilt laid upon me as a child makes me second guess myself regarding their conduct, as it did all those years ago. Back then, their cruel words were intended to make me believe without question that I was responsible for their actions, no matter how far they took things. I also think my nods of agreement about their assessment of my character combined with my lifelong willingness to do anything to earn their love and respect served as confirmation of their beliefs of who I was, allowing them to award themselves a guilt-free, unapologetic pass for their actions.

I know there are many books that could help me understand the impact their abusive practices had on me. However, I don't need the deep dive because I am healthy enough today to know I was not the person they said I was. Ironically, my programming by them has often made me feel a sort of twisted, contrived sympathy for them. I know the truth of my situation lies in the middle of two concepts: between the idea that they deserve some type of compassion and understanding for their personal traumas and the fact that these two college-educated people should have made different decisions. Whenever I find sympathy bubbling up, I offset that by recognizing the real truth: they both knew better and never cared enough to stop the physical and mental abuse.

I blamed my parents for my struggles and lived in anger toward them for more time than they deserved and for longer than these negative feelings ever served me, if they ever served me at all. All my struggles were the fuel that kept my disdain burning for them, but this anger and stress also served to push me harder to reach my goals, so perhaps there was a dysfunctional net-positive in play. I read that forgiveness was an important part of finding true happiness. However, being lost in bitterness, I found the idea to be foolish at the time and can still remember why: forgiveness seemed too much like a wonderful gift to offer them, a gift they didn't deserve. I was not yet Crutchless.

Fortunately, I learned how to forgive later in life. I had no idea how powerful forgiveness can be, but when I gave myself to it, a dense, heavy weight lifted off me. After being bitter and angry for so long and knowing these emotions were suffocating and limiting my life, I knew I had to do something different. Also, knowing my parents felt righteous in their actions against me, it became painfully clear it was only me being crushed by the experience.

I also felt that at times I was using that experience as an excuse for not moving farther and doing it faster, which never sat right with me. Sharing the negative experience might have been useful to garner some sympathy from a friend willing to give me time, which felt nice, but that sympathy wasn't helping me get over my history. Eventually the sympathy I could gain from even my best friends diminished with my repeated woe-is-me dark testimony. After all, there's only so much of a curmudgeon a person can take before they move on to happier people. This weight I describe grew less over time as ugly and debilitating emotions diminished, largely due to moving physically away from them and seeing them in only small doses. Negative emotions welled up on occasion but my forgiveness work paved the way to interpret the experiences and feelings as real but not a reason to dig up old bones.

I can't remember when forgiveness became important to me, but I knew the darkness inside me was a slow-killing poison. I read a couple books on the value of forgiveness and realized it would be a better use of my energy to let go of the anger I held toward them. After all, there was little value in being angry at people who had no desire to reconcile or seek out a healthy relationship with me. I truly gave myself to the effort and because of that, my emotional health improved. The books were right; by forgiving them, I was the biggest benefactor of the gesture. When I allowed for authentic (nothing in return) forgiveness, I could feel the benefit it created, and it made me want more. This created an opportunity to grow the space and fill the new cavity with good things. I also recognized that the Universe had shown me that something as seemingly flighty and intangible as forgiveness is in truth a practical, helpful tool.

The death of my parents was admittedly helpful in letting go of pain. It didn't make much sense to let ghosts steal my peace. With no more negative input from them or efforts to control the narrative, the benefits of forgiveness flowed unimpeded. With no ability beyond the grave to manipulate my genuine desire to forgive, I granted myself the freedom to finish a process I'd started when they were both still alive. I was happy that forgiveness did not mean I had to deny my history or morph my compassion into a version that served my parents' needs. They never knew I was working to forgive them, and it likely wouldn't have gone anyplace positive if I had told them. This effort was responsible for getting me to a place where the pain was a part of me but not controlling me, and this freed up more genuine love and compassion to be more available to everything else in my world.

Processing life events from a place of peace, even partial peace, is a completely different experience and one that has been transformative. I don't fall into the blame traps anymore and I stop questioning whether I deserved their treatment. Instead, I am confident I was a good kid and human, and know that they could have done volumes better for me and my brothers by doing very little. I will never know why they didn't course correct. Perhaps in their minds, they did make major adjustments. After all, when I would cry to my father after a beating or a mind-melting, ego-crushing verbal onslaught (the kind of verbal lashing that would have me wishing I could exchange it for a physical attack), and inquire why he went as far as he did, he would tell me it was all he could do to stop from killing me; to him, not killing me *was* the positive adjustment on his part. I took his words seriously when I considered the extent of the physical and emotional abuse he had administered and that he never walked back his comments. Abuse in lieu of death was another one of the great gifts in my life!

Many years later, after the physical abuse had ended, we would sometimes talk about the things he did. Interestingly, he would repeat the same sentiment in calm conversations as he had all those years earlier. While shocking, this reiteration of his position was the confession I needed for my adult mind. Processing this thought as an adult, specifically that I was so bad that I was worthy of being killed, and that my acts drove my father to murderous thoughts, is something I won't ever come to terms with. This man sat before me and discussed this like he was talking about what he had for breakfast. In complete comfort, he felt I should feel lucky to be alive with how bad I was. He did apologize for his abusive behavior later in life several times. Initially, the apologies would sound sincere, and I would feel hope building inside of me that he understood just how evil he had been to me, and that we could get to have a new start. But each apology was welded forever to his reminders that while it may have been difficult for me to weather those times, I deserved all that was given to me. This more than neutralized the apology and made me feel terrible and worthless all over again. It was clear his apologies were designed to help *him*, not me, feel better. His apologies were designed to get me to confess or at least acknowledge my great sins against him. He didn't care what he had done to me, he just wanted the opportunity for another swing at getting me once again to bend the knee. He was truly a sick man. Thank God I was working on forgiving him and that the world I was building was far from his reach.

Post death, without his voice on the other side trying to convince me of my crimes and seeking my apology inside of his supposed genuine apology, I allowed myself to develop and accept what I thought was a fair assessment of our history. Actually believing the truth about them, rather than the narrative they would sell to me, was a needed shift for me. This self-awareness brought more peace to my life and greater compassion for my father's suffering in life. It was also very freeing.

One thing that is certain is that we are all strapped forever to our life experiences and our own brands of nurturing, happiness, suffering, and adverse life events. If things are as dysfunctional as they were in my case, major change in just a single generation is a mountain of a task. However, this idea of *culture jumping*, what I define as making an accelerated generational improvement that far surpasses what likely would have happened in the normal course of events, was a mission I was passionate about and felt destined to execute on. I had great conviction I would do whatever work it would take to succeed at being a better human who was Crutchless and bringing a new empowered survivor persona to my future family. Much of this conviction was fueled by the strong message received on my front lawn as a youngster. I was not interested in small, multi-generation steps because I never wanted my children to experience *anything* close to what I went through. My efforts, win or lose, had to have the effect for my family of closing the valves of abuse and dysfunction forever.

I made a conscious promise to myself and to my future children to be a better human. Even with the many years of accepting my parents' message that I was not a good person, my greatest work in life will be breaking this cycle. I also knew that being Crutchless was a big part of turning a corner and not looking back. I define Crutchless as being blameless about my circumstances, while being independent and accepting of my flaws. To be Crutchless, I knew I would need to fail a lot while breaking through any obstacle in my path with or without help.

Through all of my efforts and best intentions, I know I am not a perfect parent or person. And I'm sure my own children have their own issues with my parenting and will seek to correct what they didn't like in my offering inside of their own families. This does not bother me. In fact, I applaud and encourage that not because I don't see myself as a good father, but because that is what I believe God requires from us: to give our best to ourselves, to those around us, and especially to the children we are responsible for bringing into this world. In return for the gifts, including the gift of living as a human on this planet, we are expected to learn through life experience and use the many gifts we have to improve our own lives and those around us. My belief is that every generation should want to do better than the last, and I believe this intuition comes from the Universe. No matter how many resources we are blessed with, or how well we are raised by our parents, nothing is perfect. It's all relative as they say, but I know that my children were spared the type of childhood I experienced. Having taken what I was given and done better, the bar is raised for my children to do even better with their own families. Working to be better humans, and as part of this—being better parents—is how we show gratitude for all of the gifts we have received.

The Universe has limited expectations, but I believe it expects us to do and be our best as much as we are able, while allowing for error, varied paces, and the many lessons we learn in life. What other way can we show appreciation for the life we are given than by being our best and giving back? At birth, we are given everything we need to do pretty much anything we set our minds to. This "everything" I reference comprises the complete package of gifts we are born with, that we can access at any time if we choose to. I must use life's challenges and be confident I am born to work through them and use the lessons so I can find my true path.

Humankind has shown us through the millennia that even in the worst of times, nothing can stop us from succeeding. With advancements in many areas occurring at breakneck speed, we are seeing things happen that my generation could only dream of and joke about. Not all of us can be astronauts, scientists, special forces, rockstars, and tech CEOs, but with every one of the advances, there is some person or group of persons who have reached inside and worked endless hours to pull up their God-given talents to literally change the world. It was the practical gifts of a strong work ethic, intellect, and a conviction to go further that got the job done. Yes, God is most definitely involved, but I don't believe our triumphs and success come from dropping to our knees and looking upward. It's great to reflect, but it's accessing all the tools in the toolbox that gets the results. I believe God is involved in both the good and bad in our lives. In the bad decisions, failed projects, and the falling down, we gain strength, experience, and will-power. In the good experiences, we gain affirmation, confidence, and trust. All are gifts moving us toward being a better human.

What I haven't written about enough in my journals or in this book is the value in growing up the wayI did. It's easy to write about my negative experiences and what came of them, but when I flip the script and ask myself what was valuable, even great, about that same set of experiences, I can see a lot of good. There are certainly many who have grown up much worse than I in the United States and millions more with far less opportunity in other parts of the world. For these folks, I know it would be a dream to have my childhood exactly as it was given to me.

Going further, I ask myself sometimes, as a person that has experienced a traumatic childhood, but through it all, has arrived at a place where I have accumulated enough financial resources to breathe easier, have a happy family, and a positive general disposition, then *could my life truthfully, in its entirety, really have been all that bad? And as a related follow-up question, how much credit do my parents deserve?* Again, I arrive at an unclear, confusing, and sometimes frustrating place, but ultimately land in a confident place. Years away from the most difficult parts of my journey has allowed the opportunity for some wounds to close and wisdom to grow. This creates a more positive outlook. When I marry this outlook with other life experience, including all the mistakes I have made along the way, I can be a bit more gracious about the experiences Mom and Dad provided. The circumstances that I lived under taught me to tap into my ability to be independent, resourceful, and resilient, which then paved the way to much success in my life. Also of great use, I learned to be prepared for whatever the worst-case event might be. This theme of preparedness and planning for the worst possible outcome has lasted my entire life and has provided many personal and professional benefits. All of this, including their 'involvement', eventually led me to a place of self-awareness and gratitude. All are gifts, and I am not sure how I would have obtained such a perspective without the life my parents provided. I don't believe all of this good was their intent, but yet, I don't think that matters. For that, some credit must be given to them. I wouldn't be here to write these words or kiss my kids or see a beautiful sunset without them having given me this life. Even though their behavior would have landed them lengthy jail sentences, these same behaviors had a role in getting me to where I am now, and that's a pretty good spot.

A strong work ethic was also something that was directly taught to us and was also something that was inescapable if I were to have any chance for a better life. My father and mother were hard workers, and there is no way they could have risen above their life in Pittsburgh without this quality. I can complain about my father's many trips, all places none of us ever enjoyed, while we were starving at home and waiting anxiously for his twice-a-year funded Goodwill shopping trip, but I can't deny he worked hard for everything he gave himself. So not only did I witness a strong work ethic, but their words and actions provided crystal clear messaging about the rewards and independence that comes from working hard. Their unambiguous messaging eliminated any reason to hope for assistance, which was a gift because I didn't waste any time dreaming of them coming to my rescue. It may seem sad or dysfunctional, but it made my situation easily understood.

While my two brothers focused their attention on how to bypass this edict and become adept at draining what little they could from my mother in the throes of her disease, I opted out of asking for anything except those things I couldn't earn for myself. The answer was frequently no for those things as well, but she was my only option. In the event of a rare yes from either parent, the expectation was I would pay heavily for whatever request had been granted. For example, if I needed a ride, it meant heavy chores and the possibility that if not done perfectly, the car ride would be rescinded last minute. If I had to have money for an event at school, my father might help, but only if I cleaned his apartment from top to bottom beforehand. It was clear his help was not a *quid quo pro* that ended at dollars for chores. Even when a transaction was completed—me getting something and paying the stated exorbitantly high price for it—it never stopped my father from coming back to the well for as much as he could squeeze out of me. For this reason, requests made to either of my parents were always a last desperate effort. When my parents gave me something, it didn't come with strings—it came with steel cables attached, the kind they use for bridges.

Later, when I was able to stop requesting the few things I did, my father recognized that his slave labor pool had dried up. His reaction to this was to leverage the small check he sent every month and gain our services by saying he was missing out on the cleaning services we provided to my mother and that he had equal rights to the same services at his apartment, and then later his house. I took the bait and found myself doing hours and hours of work on weekends for a bag of twenty-five cent McDonald's burgers. Still later, he would demand that his birthday and Christmas gifts come in the form of work order coupons. He would keep these coupons for years and stretch two hours of free work into a weekend of work, disregarding the term of the coupon. He was exceptionally comfortable with the narrative that he was owed more than we could ever pay.

Independence, resourcefulness, stick-to-itive-ness, and raw will were the required qualities to push through, and, fortunately, I had those attributes in abundance. More gifts. If I wanted to play football, I was responsible for getting to practice and games. This meant I would walk to practice and games by myself, a couple miles each way with gear in hand. The return trip meant walking home in the dark, through a stretch of dark woods and then through a graveyard. If I wanted to be in the school play or see a girlfriend, walking was the only answer, sometimes for hours, in all weather and times. Handling the logistics myself was the only way it would ever be allowed. I never complained because I felt lucky to be allowed to do these things and because I had many experiences where my self-supported activities, like attendance at a play rehearsal, were stripped from me randomly for no reason.

In a turn of good fate, when I was fourteen or so, I took on my brother's old paper route. John had moved on to either a plumbing apprenticeship or the local grocery store. His upward movement was an exciting event for both of us. It was especially beneficial for me, because it meant the start of my first-ever job, and I would finally have some money coming in. It turned out this was also positive news for my mother. Finding employment meant I was responsible for paying for food, clothes, and entertainment. One downside was that as the adult responsible for settling with the newspaper company each month, she managed the cash flow. She would parse out money to me upon request and "save" the rest. Receiving money after a request wasn't always a guarantee, which was immensely frustrating. I believe it was another power play to show who was really in charge. However, since I never saw most of my "savings," it was likely an income source for her, too. I embraced the work and took great pride in doing my job correctly. The successful management of this job showed me I could make things happen for myself.

Having a positive "can do" attitude as my primary driver worked for me. If I'd placed all my energy into hating my parents and keeping open wounds open, I would have never been able to move fully forward, and the pain of the past would have control over the outcome of my future. Along the way, I learned that being a victim and spending my life pointing a finger at my abusers never brought any real value to me. I realized self-pity is a valueless drug that only hinders my efforts to perform the work that needs to be done. It was helpful to understand early that driving my life by looking in the rear-view mirror was the quickest way to go nowhere. This helpful conclusion was another gift.

13

Learning to Fly, a True Hero Revealed

I can't remember how many times in my life I have played "Roll with the Changes" by REO Speedwagon, but with certainty, every time I hear this song, I experience a biochemical change that brings on motivation and inspiration. Even today, the song finds a way onto my playlists and demands my attention. This song was one of many that would offer me some perspective on my own personal journey. It was another song written about lovers but has often been the catalyst that would snap me out of a sad mood and transition me instead to positive, constructive emotions. Kevin Cronin puts his heart and soul into this song, as do all the members of the band on their instruments. The lyrics, cymbal crashes, power keyboard, and the lead guitar riffs are a high-adrenaline complete package.

When I first started listening to this song, it was on my brother's record player. Through the pops, hisses, and buzzing, what mattered most was the clear message being sent by the band. Between the lines, Mr. Cronin said to me, "Get up. Keep going. Get out. You will be OK. There is a better place waiting for you. Accept the changes in your life and don't get stuck in the past." Cronin will never know he has been my trusted therapist and friend when I had none. He shared his gift with me just as the Universe intended him to do from the beginning. His generous, unselfish offering shone a bright light in a long, dark tunnel.

Education was important to my father. He always made time to educate us on pretty much everything. It was irritating at the time it was happening, but I gained a jack-of-all-trades baseline education on many things and am appreciative of that. He had put himself through college at Pitt and continued to take classes at our local community college for many years. While I was resentful at times, wondering why he never took classes on early childhood trauma or parenting to help our situation, I admired his love of learning and inherited that quality from him. He took the opportunity to teach whenever possible, so much so that I always told him that he would have been a great professor. Some of his teachings were from a genuine desire to teach and enhance our intellect. However, many lessons were targeted so he could boost our productivity on the home front, allowing him to offload what he could of his adult workload as soon as possible. He completely dispelled the myth that we were too young for adult tasks like car repairs, fence building, mixing and pouring concrete, planting, heavy labor, professional level cleaning, and just about anything else that could be delegated.

At twelve, I could change the oil and filters in my parents' cars and could perform perfect tune-ups. This was back when people could still do this at home and cars weren't controlled by computers. I could use a timing gun, change and gap spark plugs, clean carburetors, change belts and hoses, and even replace head gaskets and torque down the covers properly on reassembly.

Because of this training, when I bought my first car in 1984, a 1972 Chevelle with a crushed driver's side door, fire engine red paint, and a white vinyl roof, I was more than prepared to maintain it. I bought the car from my neighbor for three hundred dollars I had saved from loading bags into cars at the local grocery store. Fortunately, she didn't mind me keeping the car on her car pad behind her house until I could get it on the road. It sat there for over a year while I saved up to cover the cost of passing a Maryland vehicle inspection and car insurance. Sometimes I would sneak out to the car and drive it through the alley network, pretending it was street legal. I wouldn't dare venture onto the street, but cruising around these alleys was a great motivator and gave me a whiff of what freedom felt like. I would push in a cassette, turn up the volume, and sit back and enjoy the cool vinyl seats while breathing in years of cigarette smoke still stuck to the interior and the scent of heated plastic. I wouldn't get the car on the road until I was nineteen, but every dollar saved brought me closer to independence. It didn't matter how hard I had to work; it only mattered that progress was happening.

Like most kids that age, this wasn't just a car, this was my ticket to a grown-up life and a ticket out of hell. My first real job was a "car loader," the person who would load the groceries in the car when a shopper pulled up to the curb. The money was much better than the paper route, and I received tips, too. I loved the idea that someone would hand me a dollar just for doing a job I was already being paid for. The idea that someone would appreciate my hard work enough to reward me was invigorating and affirming. It also gave me my first real view of the rewards great customer service can achieve. These early lessons taught me the importance of customer service, work ethic, and pride in work product. These values were the foundation that allowed me to put myself through college and be successful in business many years later.

Most of the time, I walked back and forth to my job, which again took me through the graveyard and past some unsafe places at all hours and all weather conditions. It was my normal, so I never complained or thought someone owed me transportation. From time to time, my mother would drive me if she was going that way (liquor store and bar across the street), but I would rarely ask. Getting a lift from her was a gift in her eyes, not a motherly responsibility or a form of support for my work ethic. She was always bitter about the effort she expended and sometimes would require gas money to complete the transaction like an early form of Uber.

Since I did not have a bank account, all my checks once again flowed through her. I became concerned the amounts would come in light as had happened with my paper route. Fortunately, I had gotten wiser since my paper route and would hold onto cash tips and kept an accounting of the check amounts deposited. Having an accounting allowed me to use real numbers when requesting a disbursement, but, like the newspaper money, there were never any guarantees. It was frustrating when the numbers would come up short or she would take a spontaneous deduction, but to argue with her meant getting nothing or punishment in the form of grounding. Grounding was a powerful control function she would deploy randomly or for any perceived minor infraction, even preventing me from going to work. Fortunately, her physical abuse had all but disappeared due to a heroic effort from John, one that I will never forget.

John and I were accused of committing some unthinkable crimes. There were so many "severe" offenses, like the diluted orange juice mentioned previously, that it is not easy to remember what crime went with which beating. Whatever the crime, on this day, all would change because of John taking an unthinkable risk and paying a tremendous price to protect me.

My mother was particularly unhinged on this important day. Her bloodshot eyes were filled with rage as she doled out our punishments with a flexible yardstick. With full force, she was taking turns beating us in separate corners of our dining room. Both of us were in bad shape, with some bleeding from cuts where the stick's metal edge connected and ripped flesh. She was also leaving many tall welts on our legs, arms, necks, and backs, not caring much on this day about what the public might see later. Our pleading and uncontrollable sobbing was not met with a hint of compassion. Rather, it only made her angrier and more committed to the effort. She screamed filthy obscenities at us as we took the pounding. Spittle flew from her mouth with each evil rant spelling out how awful we were as humans, wrapped in a promise to "fix us."

On my third or fourth turn as the designated target, I was wondering how much more I could take. I was cowering in a corner near the front door crying hard and begging her to stop, pleading despondently with her that I would do anything she wanted to end the pain. I did mean anything—nothing was off the table. At the worst moment, the moment when I was sure I couldn't last any longer, John surprised me and Mom and changed our worlds forever. Sitting bloodied and beaten as he watched me take my punishment, John got up from his corner, crossed the room, and boldly sat down directly in front of me. I didn't understand what was happening in the moment. John might have done some bad things to me and was responsible for many long days of hunger, but he was always my physical protector. However, until this moment, his protection had never extended to my parents. As he sat there with his body laying against me, Mom continued, more enraged than ever. No matter the intensity, he remained committed to my protection and absorbed blow after painful blow. His intervention infuriated my mother, taking her to a level I had not seen before. She swung harder and more tactically than before, searching for fresh flesh on both of us. But no matter how hard she tried, because of John's positioning to be my buffer, she could not reach me with her weapon. I was safe from her abuse while John's pain was doubling. Little did I know his unselfishness would create a pivotal point in our physical abuse history.

John's crossing of the room was the first open act of the rebellion against her by any of us. Sitting down and covering me was not his first act as my hero and protector, but in this act, his sacrifice was the greatest. After a few minutes, even John couldn't handle the frontal blows any longer, which forced him to turn around and offer up his back. Doing this meant his face met mine directly. Only inches apart, we faced each other for a few desperate moments. I could see the pain and desperation in his eyes as my mother stepped up her efforts. He must have seen terror in mine. Clasping his fingers behind his head and using his outstretched elbows to protect his head and neck, his folded, winged arms also acted as shields to protect my face and head. His body, already brutalized while in his position across the room, was now taking the full brunt of the attack for both of us. The pain was palpable as I looked at his eyes, wincing and crying with each blow. As the strikes reigned down, I could also see that his own brand of rage was building from somewhere deep inside. He was crying hard but not breaking. A tipping point had been reached, and I could see that fear was being converted to raw fury, similar to Dr. David Banner's transition to the Hulk. I had seen evidence of this behavior in street fights, but never with a parent. What I did know told me that there was no other possible outcome than for him to release this energy.

With John and I nose to nose, my mother wound her backswing to bring another blow to John's back. It was then that I could tell that he had too much; too much then and too much in life. He swung his body around and was face to face with her, rage facing rage. With lightning speed, like a car hitting an invisible concrete wall, his teenager arm caught her wrist in mid-air and brought it to full stop. After years of martial arts training, he was stronger than her and quite capable of subduing her completely. His rage- and despair-filled eyes were locked on Mom's as they both processed the moment. John must have known his actions were unprecedented and were taking us into unexplored territory. With my hero sacrificing everything to protect me, I worried selfishly at the type of punishment that would come later to me in response to him fighting back.

John's next step was to grab the yardstick from her hand and snap it into two then four pieces and throw it across the room. Like the exact moment the ill-treated circus elephant realizes his leather tether could never hold him, John took his freedom with determination. He was close to foaming at the mouth as he bit down hard on his index finger, a high-stress habit he had started years earlier.

With both of us considering our next steps, Mom and I reacted differently. She stood over us, panting from her workout, looking startled and confused. However, very quickly, her expression turned into raw rage. Seeing this in her eyes, I was close to wetting my pants with the fear I felt. Breaking my mother's weapon was an incredible act of bravery, but also an act my young mind feared we might both be killed over. It sounds extreme to think of being killed, but after having already endured a brutal beating and seeing the impact of John's actions on my mother's enraged face, I could not think of any other direction this new development would take us.

There was silence in the few seconds that followed, as even my mother didn't know quite what to do with this turn of events. It was new to all of us. John's next move was to push her out of his way while simultaneously throwing open the front door. In an instant, he darted through the opening with my hand in his. He could tell I was hesitant and afraid and allowed himself to pause his escape for a few seconds so I could steady myself, which was a difficult task while in the vortex of this situation. He stopped cold and looked me right in the eyes and said, "Come with me. We have to leave here." I didn't know what to do. I had seen some adult things too soon in my life, but at that age, I had never spent time thinking about living on the street. Questions came quickly in my head: *Where would we live? How would we eat? Would she find us and then kill us? Would my father hunt us and kill us when he found out?* I made it only as far as the front stoop just outside our front door. While processing the decision before me, my mother threw out many obscenities and threats. Her screaming at me, "Don't ever come back if you leave," was too great of a risk to take. Despite John's great sacrifice and display of love, I yielded to my mother almost immediately. I was forced to make a grown-up decision in a storm the likes of which I had never witnessed. With that decision, I allowed myself to step backwards across the threshold into our home and away from John.

Determined in his decision and no doubt sensing the circumstances that would be waiting for him if he returned, John held his ground, not moving forward or backward. As I stared at him, his eyes told an awful life story of pain, anguish, and desperation. I began to cry even more while entering the home, but this time without John's protection. John recognized I had made my decision and quickly let go of the idea that we might run away together. I felt the hurt and pain inside of letting him go. Barefoot, he turned and leapt down the two sets of steps to the sidewalk far outside of her reach. I suppose he knew he could never go back to that house, at least not while she was this hot.

When he arrived at the street, he looked up and begged me once more to come with him. He wanted a partner, I think, but I believe, more so, he feared what might be waiting for me when she closed that door behind her. I was momentarily caught between the two proposals again—go with him and be homeless and hungry or stay with my mother and have a roof over my head while taking the risk I alone might have to shoulder the fallout from his actions. Out of instinct and habit, I chose Mom again. Wailing as he ran, I watched as he turned the corner out of both of our sight lines.

I couldn't afford to stay in pity mode for too long, so my attention shifted to the business immediately at hand: protecting my physical well-being while attempting to anticipate what my mom's next move would be. I feared most that she would deliver the part of the beating John had taken but that had been meant for me.

I limped back behind closed doors and waited for the worst. My mother immediately locked and deadbolted the door behind me. The sound of the locks triggered more fear, but she didn't react the way I thought she would. She remained furious but distracted, her mind was obviously focused on John and what her next move with him would be. She was afraid, I think, as well. John's jailbreak was a brand new dynamic to our home. I'm certain she was afraid of what would happen if she did call the police, afraid of him being on the street, afraid of losing her son in total, and likely afraid of the impact this cataclysmic event would have on her future ability to control the inmates. I was grateful for the distraction and that more discipline seemed to at least be temporarily off the table.

With no more physical attacks, she sent me to my room, and then went to her own room and locked the door. She was there for hours, and I can't remember when I saw her next. My wounds hurt badly but I worried about where John was and if he would ever come home again. I also worried, selfishly, about what it would be like to handle this woman on my own.

She contacted the police, who searched everywhere for him for several days. It was about a week and a half later that John was spotted living in the trunk of an abandoned car in the driveway of a house across the alley only about eight doors down from us. His return to the house was awkward, and there was not much said between my mother and him for some time. I could tell she remained confused on how to handle things. John's demeanor was quiet, heavy, and distant. He walked taller and more adult-like after his capture and return, but he was lost, too, not knowing quite how to position himself after the *coup d'etat*. A permanent shift had occurred inside of him and because of that, the entire dynamic changed, benefiting me. His gift of bravery and decisiveness spilled over to me, paving the way for the physical abuse from my mother to come to an abrupt end.

There was never any discussion about the event amongst any of us. I was not surprised, because silence and siloing was the norm in our home. However, the stench of the festering wound combined with John's newfound defiance promoted an environment where he began to regularly test, and then soon outright ignore, her rules. Without any proclamation, there was one edict resulting from this awfulness that was clear to all: there was no way he was ever going to allow this woman or anyone else to physically abuse him again.

I can't imagine how scared he must have been. He left an extremely dangerous environment to live on the streets and sleep in the trunk of a car with nothing but the clothes on his back, not even shoes. I'm sure he wanted to be loved and held after being away from home for the first time, but affection was never part of our relationship dynamic even under the worst conditions. He came home to silence, isolation, and loneliness, which might have been worse than a beating to a young teenager.

Later, he became unmanageable and untamed. With there being no way for my mother to control him, he quickly moved to doing what he wanted with whom he wanted. My mother returned to threats of homelessness as the very last arrow in her quiver, but she never followed through with it. Putting him on the street was a low bar she wouldn't stoop to. That she would never allow any of us to be homeless was the threshold she would not go below; essentially this what love looked like in our home. Surprisingly, the police never questioned her actions.

John had done some bad things to me, including at times being my third abuser, but what made him different from my parents is that he had a knack for showing up in big ways at precisely well-timed moments. He didn't have to, but his instincts drove him to protect me. John has a kind streak in him not many will ever see. With their abuse, my father and mother stole from him the kind person I know he is capable of being. His experience with my mother and father wore him down to a point where there was little room for him to do anything but react and survive. Like a famished lone lion living in a deep drought on the Serengeti, John's only mission was to wander, look for something to feed his soul, healthy or unhealthy, and try to stay alive. John's drought started the day he was born and never seemed to stop.

Given everything he had been through, I can see no good reason why he would want to protect me other than raw instinct or an intervention from a higher power. I interpret this as proof of God's involvement yet again. Knowing he would pay a high price, he didn't run out the door alone to save himself. Instead, in a battered state, he made the conscious decision to drop down in front of me and take my pain and suffering, never yielding and never looking for credit. His shielding would have been more than enough to prove to me that he cared, but he didn't stop there. He grabbed my hand to take me with him, and by doing so, showed me he loved me.

I am amazed that someone would feel so much love for me that they would put their life at risk to save me. But I am saddened that any child would have to make this kind of choice. This was the type of after-school special you never see on TV, and certainly, there was no cliché happy ending. With blood, sweat, and tears, he sent a loud message that I could be loved and worthy of protection by another human and I have never forgotten his act or the profound lesson I learned from it.

Although my father's lack of involvement seemed to indicate he hardly cared that John was missing, I think his running away and resisting his oppressor, sent my father a direct message. As the more severe of the two abusers, John's escape and willingness to go as far as it took to shed his chains told my father that physical abuse was no longer on the table for his oldest son. John already held great disdain for my father by this point, so I'm certain that with some provocation, John's newfound independence and willpower would have led him to give a serious beat down to my father.

Although the physical abuse had ended, the environment remained volatile. As life went on, the results of John's rebellion forced my parents to rethink their management techniques and to develop different control mechanisms. Upping his psychological warfare game, my father grew to despise John openly and publicly with intensity. He wanted to keep John in the cage of worthlessness he had custom built for him back when he was still a cross-eyed toddler. Even with his newfound independence, John continued to fall victim to his own innate need to win my father's respect and love. I cannot judge because John and I were in the same position; no matter what the man did, we still wanted our father to be accepting of us.

My mother was already sinking more into the bottle, and after the event, she seemed to double down on that effort. She made half-hearted attempts to control John's movements, but he moved through the world largely on his own terms, wantonly ignoring her at will. They both lived under the same roof in isolation, and because my mother was never willing to throw us out, she surrendered her leverage to change John's behavior. All things considered, the halting of this type of abuse was definitely positive but ultimately resulted in absolute isolation for each of us, thus ending any thread of hope I had for a loving, functional family. With each of us in our imaginary concrete bunkers, I knew that whatever vision I had for a caring, nourishing family environment would have to be one I created myself.

John's transformation didn't just help us from physical harm on the home front, it also helped me in the neighborhood. I got into plenty of fights on my own, but John's reputation as a devastating brawler, and the bigger than life story of him taking up residence in an abandoned car, spread in our neighborhood like wildfire through dry timber. Knowing I had an older brother with this kind of pedigree effectively served as a protective umbrella over me. In some fights, as much as I stood ready and confident to defend myself, the aggressor would back down out of fear of the possibility of John retaliating. As John geographically roamed more, a function of his newly self-imposed unrestricted freedom, he found himself in even more physical altercations. Winning handily, the reinforced message continued like ripples on a pond: He was unbeatable and brutal. Throughout the neighborhoods of Arbutus, Catonsville, and Lansdowne, the kids knew he was untouchable and, because of that, by association, I received a similar status.

Most kids knew we were socially abnormal, even weird, but also knew we were well-equipped to handle ourselves in back-alley fights. John and I thought differently about fighting. I adhered to my training and only used my skills for self-defense. Because of that, when I fought, it was primarily to protect myself and stave off future aggression. John, on the other hand, fought to decimate and belittle and didn't mind being the first to strike. Winning, to him, was a foregone conclusion; he was only in it as an outlet for all the pain he carried inside himself. No one dared to challenge him unless they were ill informed, foolish, or new to the neighborhood of Huntsmoor.

Instinctively, John called up his karate training in each clash. His first target was always the face. If he could connect solidly with the victim's nose or an eye, he would leave his opponent vulnerable. If you have ever been in a fist fight then you know that a fighter's confidence is quickly impacted when an eye is sealed shut or a broken nose creates unstoppable tears and blood flow. In a whirlwind of energy coming from a leg that was like a hickory branch, John could land a kick or punch with high accuracy. It's intriguing to witness an opponent's wordy threats meet up with a foot or fist to the face. At first, it's a look of surprise, but then it's the expression one has when they've committed to something they cannot escape. I think of it like the terror I felt when I rode my first tall rollercoaster. Halfway up the first hill, I could think of nothing but how I might get off the ride. Knowing I could not escape made the fear compound. John's opponents were likely regretting their misjudgment of his abilities. Their inexperience and poor decision making didn't matter to him. He wouldn't stop until the other fighter ran away or yielded. He was a true badass and a dangerous young man.

Before John changed the landscape, my parents knew exactly how to control our every move and make us feel insignificant and powerless. They knew that, like all children, we desired their approval and affection, and they had no issue with using that wanting to their advantage. However, after John's uprising, it became virtually impossible for them to stop his movements, so they set their sights on me to ensure a different, more predictable outcome to satisfy their need for control. In our infrequent interactions, I still pointlessly sought out words of affirmation. I didn't think my actions would earn me love and nurturing, as that would be too high a bar. After all, I was trained to believe I deserved their hateful treatment; I was an awful, awful kid and what was happening to me was for that reason. I needed to look no further than that. With years of hearing that message, their programming was all very logical and made sense. When my father reminded me of this, and that this was the reason he hated having children so much, he never hesitated or took his words back. Even though this was one mountain I would never get over, I continued to try to be a good son and allow myself to hope for positive change or at least calm. This hope was my weakness, as it was the fuel they used to effectively control me. Comparatively, John had none of this hope, so they had no leverage and knew it. I was too young to know in real time to what extent their actions were psychologically impacting me. Unfortunately, keeping hope while simultaneously devaluing myself was exactly what my parents used to keep me in check.

Like my father, psychological abuse now became my mother's primary control mechanism. Since my brothers were both skilled at ignoring or reverse manipulating her, I was the primary target of her attention. The standards of isolation and negligence, and the absence of any affection or positive reinforcement remained. Threats to disclose our misdeeds to my father were always an attention getter but had become muted because by now my father was not wanted in our lives by any of us, including my mother. This meant that threats like "Dad's gonna get to you!"—previously one of her most effective tools—lost its impact. The older we got, the less we would want him around. When he came around, if we could not hide from him, his presence sucked away what little light I had inside of me, replacing it with fear and self-loathing. He would unapologetically openly belittle us on all topics. My mother was no exception to his criticism; Mr. Never-around would make certain to criticize her on everything from her career choice to her substandard parenting. Additionally, there was always the unspoken requirement that if his loins beckoned, then his urges must be satisfied. His narcissistic skill set served him well.

Mom's brand of mental abuse was nothing I had witnessed. Somedays, it was so debilitating and insane it made me wish for a good beating. She knew I desperately wanted to escape the trap I was living in.

Realizing this, she used this desire as a leverageable weakness. Perhaps, seeing my weak spot was easy because of her own dashed hopes in life and how hard she worked to escape her environment in Pittsburgh and then with my father. In that sense, she had firsthand knowledge of how highly effective limiting my freedoms could be. She also knew I had given up on asking her for anything, even the rare requests for transportation or food, so there were no material things she could leverage.

My attempt at independence gave me a sense of strength and an early look at organically created self-confidence, but it wouldn't last long. This was because, even with being mostly independent, she began to dial deeper into my pain points, which were all about achieving ultimate freedom from her prison. One time, she told me I had to call my boss and quit my job loading bags in cars for no apparent reason. It wasn't because she had to drive me or that my having a job inconvenienced her in any way or impacted my schoolwork. I can only deduce she did this because she could and because she knew this type of destructive intervention was a reminder to me that she was the one in charge.

After demanding I quit, she locked herself in her room and made me sit outside her door begging for hours to let me keep my job. The madness of it was that, without a reason for her actions, there was nothing I could do to cure the issue. It seemed her only intention was to hear through the one-and-a-quarter-inch hollow door the full surrendering of my dignity and self-respect. I can't imagine she enjoyed my whining and begging through the door, especially when she would intermittently scream at me to stop while threatening even more sanctions. After hours of pleading, through the door she gave in to me with an angry huff. Once she indicated I could keep my job, I showered her with praises and gratitude, hoping my glowing reaction to her generosity would be appreciated and remembered. Before she could change her mind, I gathered myself and took the opportunity to get out of the house and run as fast as I could to the grocery store where I worked. I arrived very late but fortunately was allowed to keep my job. Despite not being at fault, I was deeply embarrassed and disappointed in how this made me look to my employer.

Looking back at the event, this power play was quite ingenious. She picked the one thing that could hurt me the most and zealously concentrated her attack on this. My job provided resources and independence, but more importantly, it provided a path to freedom and an ability to get affirmation and feel valuable by my managers at the end of a good day's work, allowing me to build self-worth and confidence. At least subconsciously, she knew this and knew she had to hold her ground until I had surrendered enough dignity that I would be reduced to being a blubbering, whining child outside her door. Effectively, she was affirming that she remained in power.

This type of needless and hurtful interference gave her the control she wanted and became more regular as time went on and her drinking got worse. The worst part is I never knew when these attacks would come. This made living and trying to be a teenager that much more anxiety ridden and stressful. It was not rare for her to execute this tactic just minutes before I went to show rehearsals or sports practice. On every exit, my anxiety and heart rate would spike as I prepared to announce in the sweetest voice possible my intention to exit the prison. Often, I would set out to walk the four miles to visit my girlfriend, and she would order me to stay home. Like the work example, I would take my position on the steps and begin the begging process. Sometimes a positive response would happen within minutes, other times, hours, and still other times, permission would never come. I would not dare go anywhere without her permission. The fear of what would be waiting for me when I returned was just too great a risk. I believe in the cases where she could not respond that she was passed out from being too high or drunk.

While being sequestered in the house for no reason was something that happened through most of my childhood, the events that stood out were mostly when I was older. It was then that the penalty had the greatest impact because I was doing more grown-up things and desperately trying to find my wings. Often, my friends would be parked at the curb waiting for me as I desperately negotiated and pleaded with my mother through the door slab. Of course, they must have thought it was bizarre given I had gained prior permission to leave, and then suddenly I was running back and forth up and down three flights of steps while simultaneously managing two active negotiations—pleading with my mother to release me, while also imploring my friends to wait. Young, recently licensed teenagers are not generally built for being patient when there is a big night planned, so keeping them waiting wasn't an easy task. Eventually, my mother would either give in or stand her ground, but there was no way to estimate how long it would take for her to make a decision or if she would just pass out and never answer. Many times, I had the gut-wrenching experience of watching my friends drive away knowing I was stuck in the house and they were not coming back.

This was my normal, but for my friends and girlfriends, it must have been quite a spectacle to watch. Me, begging and failing, then running back out to the car to give an update and asking my friends for a few more minutes, all while in tears and trembling with anxiety, was as humiliating as it sounds. After some of my friends caught on to my predicament, they would ask to join my lobbying effort outside the door. This was always a last-ditch move and seldom used because putting her on the spot infuriated her. The worst part is that in the '80s, communications weren't like today. Back then, once the car pulled away from the curb, they were gone for good. Approved releases coming after my ride had already left, were the worst. There was no way to reach them and with no means to get to their physical location, I would sit in the house frustrated and alone.

One of my least favorite memories was when my mother told me last minute I could not go to my prom. I had done nothing wrong—she just said she had never given me permission to go, which was not true. Not only had I received her permission when she was sober, but I had saved up enough money to rent a tux, buy prom tickets for me and my date, buy a corsage, and still had just enough remaining to cover the cost of a basic dinner at the Rusty Scupper in Baltimore. I had even arranged my own transportation. She had to do nothing but just be quiet and wish me well.

Sitting on the deep, red pile carpet on our stairs, all dressed in my goofy rent-a-tux, I was ready to depart, but I was battling with polar-opposite emotions. On one hand, I was excited for the big night ahead. On the other hand, I was worried that since my mother was sequestered in her room, this likely meant that she was drinking and could also mean she might decide to randomly destroy my plans. Even at an older age, I never broke the rule that she be notified when I was coming or going. There were too many threats of homelessness to risk that.

When I saw my friends pull up to the curb, as calmly and sweetly as I could, and with inhaled breath so heavy I felt my lungs might explode, I told her my friends and date were waiting outside and I needed to leave. I waited a minute or so and with no response, I knocked ever so gently on her door. Hearing her grunt, I announced my plans to depart again, desperately wanting to hear any form of acknowledgment from her so I could fly out the door and down the street before she changed her mind. This time, her response was immediate. "You're not going anywhere." I could feel my heart sink in my chest as panic immediately set in.

The worst-case scenario had happened. I started a begging campaign that lasted close to an hour as I sat there in my tuxedo, crawling out of my skin with powerlessness and desperation. I eventually had no choice but to tell my friends and date to go to the dance without me. I was crying so hard and would have done anything to have normalcy for just that one night. She never even bothered to come out of her room. Realizing my efforts had failed, I gave up and went to my room to get out of the tux and go to sleep. Like many times before, sleep was a refuge.

To my surprise, a short while later, my mom cracked the door and yelled out crankily that I had permission to go. My heart jumped a beat with excitement and adrenaline. It didn't matter that I was going to be very late, and that the exercise was insanity inducing, I never bothered to waste energy getting angry with her. Doing so might give her reason to change her mind again. What was most important was that I connected with my date and enjoyed one of the most important nights of my young life. The new problem was that I didn't have a ride. This unfortunate fact set me up for begging session number two of the evening. Holding my excitement at bay, knowing she might be too drunk or unwilling to drive, I took my place on the shag carpet just outside her door and began pleading with the wizard behind the white hollow door for a ride. She might have given me permission to go to the prom, but without a ride, the pass was essentially worthless. Back in my tux, having reapplied my British Sterling cologne and ready to go, I spent all the remaining dignity I had begging. Either she was too drunk to immediately respond or was relishing the power she wielded, but eventually she gave in angrily.

The ride to the high school was quiet. Since we were heading in the right direction, it didn't matter to me that I could smell the strong scent of booze on her breath and that she was slurring her words. She made clear all the restrictions for the balance of my evening. I did everything I could to be invisible in the back seat (she never let us sit up front with her) and not trigger her to make a U-turn back toward home with me still in the car. Without any well wishes, she pulled up and dropped me on the steps of the school gymnasium.

I will never understand it fully, but with a few decades having passed since these events, I think she was trying to validate her role as a mother in the midst of alcoholism and drugs besieging her body and mind. She had little energy remaining for self-improvement, so to step up her parenting game was not realistic. But with not much effort, she could wield a sword of authority at critical moments to prove she still held the reins. It's not unusual to have erratic behavior arise out of sickness and dysfunction and just plain loneliness, especially when it comes to addiction. The combination of these things can make people do the unthinkable. I feel a deep sense of sympathy for everything she went through as a child, the pain of being married to my father, then the deep pain of him leaving her whilst still manipulating and controlling her. That's a big, painful hole to dig out of, and I won't pretend to understand just how deeply she was impacted. I have had some pain in my life, but having those experiences as a woman in a male-dominated culture is something I will never be qualified to comment on.

I wish I could praise more about her, but she seemed bent on taking what little I had, even if all I had was dignity and hope. She should have been impressed with my self-sufficiency and willingness to abide by all the make-believe rules in the asylum. Instead, it meant nothing, and she used my hope and drive as a fulcrum to control and debilitate me. I couldn't wait to get the hell out of that place. My next move would be to my father's house, but that was its own private kind of hell and ended up being as bad or worse for a different set of reasons. No matter how hard I tried to be a good son and person, these people I called parents had no intention of making one single day of my life easy. Fortunately, my therapist in the form of Kevin Cronin told me over and over again in our sessions that I must accept what is in front of me, pivot and move forward. Thankfully, that's exactly what I kept doing.

14

Dog Gone Nightmare

Steve Winwood's "While You See a Chance," released in 1981, was one of those songs where something inside told me to pay attention. The slow wind up on the keyboard reminded me I had to take advantage of every opportunity, while guiding me to do for myself because there was no one else. It seemed I was born ready to hear that song at the age of fourteen. I had seen enough in my life by that point to know the only opportunities that were going to come my way would be those I created for myself. It reinforced the idea that I needed to find my own way in a "get to work" kind of way. I needed to stand up on a clear morning and see what could be. It didn't happen immediately, but I eventually understood, through all the messages being sent my way, that I was being called to buck up and that my future was worth the effort. It was time for me to look for my chance and take it! What a wonderful, perfectly timed gift from Mr. Winwood, reminding me that anything was indeed possible.

My father had a love for German shepherds. Except for the need of company, I have no other reason why he purchased a large purebred version when he was living alone in Baltimore. He could have had us join him sooner but this dog and his personal freedom were priority. When my mother, John, and my father were finally reunited in Baltimore, Shep became part of our family and moved into our new home. When my father moved out, he conveniently left the dog with us.

Shep was largely untrained, often defecating anywhere when the urge occurred, including inside of our new home. My parents had both abused him with regular beatings but that abuse increased when he started relieving himself inside our new home. No doubt because of this treatment, he was prone to nip at people from time to time if irritated. He didn't bite anyone in our family, but he did draw the blood of visiting friends in our yard. We learned to be careful with him around everyone.

Witnessing my parents' behavior, I grew up having no love for pets. With the anxiety that he might bite someone and knowing that our new home was becoming his personal litter box, I couldn't comprehend why we even owned an animal. I wasn't angry with Shep but he lived to be very old and very sick. He became blind, could barely walk, and then one day, frustrated by his inability to follow her commands, my mother kicked him down the wooden steps of our basement. He stumbled a bit halfway down the first half of the steps, and then rolled the remainder of the way down, where he just lay still at the bottom landing. He was still breathing when I checked on him, but we were told to leave him as he was, which I assumed meant my mother was expecting a full recovery. Despite kicking him on a regular basis, I don't think she meant to kill him, but within an hour or so, I learned he had died. My mother sent me down the stairs to check on him after seeing him in the exact same position we had left him. I got down low to get a good look into his face. Given no body movement, a small puddle of blood from his mouth, a tongue hanging out onto the floor, and lifeless eyes still open, I was able to confirm with certainty that he had died. My mother did not show any emotion. She simply leafed through the yellow pages and called animal control. The next morning, a large man came with a heavy-duty plastic black sack. He stuffed Shep into it, threw him over his shoulder, and then tossed him into the back of his van. That was the last we ever saw of Shep. I don't remember feeling much pain or anything at all. If I had to guess, my emotions were that of relief—relief that he didn't have to suffer any longer, and relief that I would not have to continue to deal with the animal directly.

One would think that Shep's death and the problems that came with owning him would offer up a clear signal that our home was not a good place for pets, but this was not so. My mother almost immediately purchased another purebred Shepherd that she named Rex. Sadly, the story with Rex was almost identical to Shep's. Rather than train Rex correctly, she resorted to yelling profanities at him while resuming the physical abuse she had so generously doled out to Shep. I had more affection for Rex since I knew him as a puppy, but my mother's abuse made him more aggressive, and we were always scared he would start nipping people as Shep had. My father had commissioned John and I to help build a split rail fence for our end-unit townhome. It was a huge amount of physical labor for two young kids and our muscles reflected it, but the hope was that the finished product would contain the dog, and we would not have to worry about him attacking anyone. The fence was lined with cattle fencing to make certain nothing could get in or out through the rails.

At first, this seemed to work well, as only friends would get nipped once in a while when they played in our yard. Additionally, we kept Rex on a heavy chain runner in our yard to make sure he was limited in how far and fast he could travel. To place him on the runner meant walking him out the front door and holding him by the collar until we could clip the chain on him in the rear of the home.

A couple years after getting Rex, my mother's mother, my grandmother, passed away. We inherited her cockapoo. As he was a good-natured, quiet dog, Mom didn't have much reason to be abusive to Patches. However, because she was often too lazy to let him out and because Rex was openly displaying how he dealt with being locked in the house too long, the previously potty-trained dog soon learned to use the house to relieve himself. Soon, our home was littered with twice the piles of shit and urine pools to clean up. My irritation at the "shitty" circumstances gave my mother and brothers a regular laugh. As the only one in the house to take on the work of cleaning up these messes, it was just good fun for them to watch me scrubbing the floors and carpets.

Rex was becoming increasingly bothered by any non family member that he came in contact with. We knew we needed to be very careful with this physically strong, now animal, and we did our best to limit his direct interaction with others. When Rex put his front paws on the top of the fence, his shoulders were almost as high as the top rail. Even then, I knew he could likely scale the fence without too much effort if he wanted to. Then the worst happened, and I was blamed.

On a spring day, my twelve-year-old self walked Rex down our front set of steps with his collar firmly in my hand. He was a lot to hold onto, but I had done it many times. While holding him by his collar, my job was to open the front gate, hang a left at the corner of our end unit, and walk him to the rear of the yard. Once there, I would clip him to the steel cable line runner to ensure he wouldn't attack anyone. In a horrifying twist of fate, as soon as I opened the front gate and entered the yard, the "Gas Man" was walking up the rear alley yelling, "Gaaaaaaaaasssss Maaaaaaaan!" As was typical, he wasn't yelling to anger dogs; rather, he was being intentionally loud so everyone would know to put their animals away so he could enter the yard and read our gas meter for billing purposes. This usually worked perfectly, but not on this day.

As soon as Rex heard the gas man call out, he broke free of my grip effortlessly and ran around the corner of our house in a gray-black flash. There was zero I could do to hold on to him once he decided to go. Before I even realized what was happening, Rex was in a high-speed sprint toward the fence in the rear of our yard. By the time my eyes caught up to him, I could only see his tail as he easily scaled the fence and descended into the alley. The next thing I heard was a grown man screaming out in horror and pain.

I ran as quickly as I could to where Rex was attacking the Baltimore Gas & Electric man. I didn't know exactly what to do as I saw blood everywhere and the man pounding Rex in the head with a long, yellow commercial flashlight. There was flesh hanging off his arm in a sheet where Rex had inflicted one of his first wounds. Rex then moved to the man's leg and started dragging him down the alley with sharp, angry tugs. The flashlight blows only seemed to make Rex more committed. When Rex saw me close and heard my voice yelling, he let go of the man and jumped back over the fence like a little puppy that had gotten caught digging in the trash.

The moment was distressing. Time froze as just me and the seriously injured man saw each other. As blood gushed from the wounds and the man cursed at me loudly, all I could think about was the trouble that I was in. Terrified of what my mother would do to me, I ran to the house to get her. After that, it was all a blur. The man went away in an ambulance, and we went back to our lives. My mother, of course, guilted me for not holding him properly and completing my simple job and was not interested in my excuses and apologies.

Ignoring my genuine regret, it wasn't until we received notice of the lawsuit against us that my mother expressed directly how I was responsible for bringing this stress into her life. I apologized in every way I knew how, but it didn't seem to matter. As documents came in the mail, she would make sure I knew all the details of the case and how inconvenient and painful this was for her. The case went on for a long time, I think years, and she kept me updated with every letter or call that happened along the way. It was important to her that I share in her pain. I wanted nothing more than to gain my mother's approval, but this incident put me at an even greater deficit with her. I shifted to trying to earn her forgiveness, which, like trying to earn her love and respect, never came.

Oddly, after the attack, my mother never changed a thing about her animal management techniques. We never got rid of Rex, and she never changed her abusive behaviors. Additionally, I remained our dogs' primary caregiver. Aside from having to manage through the anxiety of dealing with my mother and father, I now lived on high alert with anything having to do with this animal. He ended up nipping a couple more people but fortunately, the wounds were not serious. I don't remember how Rex passed but leaving him behind was another great benefit of moving out of the home. Perhaps, the "gift" in this situation is that I had a deep respect and understanding of just how much damage a dog can do.

It would not be the last dog attack I was a part of. Twice, my children have been attacked by neighborhood dogs. Because of my experience witnessing the awesome strength of Rex, the gift is that I knew immediately to spring into action to defend my family. Fortunately, my aggressive counterattack on the dogs involved in these events gave them the appropriate notification we were not an easy target and they both retreated before any harm was done.

Given these situations and others, I never had any love for dogs. In my traumatic experience, dogs were just not worth the risk and maintenance, so for most of my older children's younger lives, despite many years of requests from my kids, we never had one. It wasn't until my daughter Kathryn was leaving for college that we purchased a chocolate Labrador. I'm not sure what exactly got into me. Perhaps it was a last effort to make a positive impression on her or maybe something else I can't fully explain. Whatever the reason, Bodhi was a fantastic dog, and I am happy he was part of our lives. I remained on high alert around dogs, including Bodhi, but he has taught me that treating an animal correctly can achieve very different results. As important, his loyalty, love and companionship to me and my family has been a beautiful gift.

That said, I never let my children get anywhere near his face with theirs and always kept a watchful eye on how he interacted with them or anyone else in our lives. I continue to have a healthy anxiety around dogs. I never forget it is always possible he could do harm to my family or someone else, but at least I can get to experience firsthand why so many people have such a deep, faithful love for their dogs.

15

Fight Club

Billy Squier rocked me in my youth with songs like "Stroke Me" and "My Kind of Lover." I loved his heavy emphasis on electric guitar and the way his lyrics spoke to me. "Lonely Is The Night," released in 1981, had lyrics that spoke of rebellion and fighting, and helped fuel a belief that no matter how dark my life was, if I fought hard enough, I would win. I knew I had endurance and drive and hearing this song was a solid affirmation I had at least some of the tools necessary to create real change for myself. The lyrics and the high energy guitar would create a feeling inside of me that nothing else mattered but freedom. Once again, a message of independence and not living as a victim resonated with me.

My father had taught me how to sew when I was eight. He wanted clothes to last until they literally fell off of us so this skill came in handy with achieving that objective. New clothes came only three times a year—birthday, Christmas, and a purchase in the fall with the start of each school year. There were also one or two supplemental Goodwill purchases my father would oversee and would proudly fund out of his pure generosity.

As an active and growing boy, new clothes wore out or were outgrown quickly, so it was a genuine gift to be taught how to make repairs and stretch the life of these clothes. Unlike today, gaping holes in pants were grounds for bullying, so in my young mind, even a poorly stitched-in patch was a better option than allowing my peers to see my knee coming out of a hole. This would get me the wrong type of attention and I had plenty of that already.

This new skill also afforded me the opportunity to bypass relying on my mother to do the repairs. Not depending on her felt exceptionally good, and learning to mend my own clothes was another building block for my independence. Seeing a threadbare knee popping out of my pants and having the skill set to get ahead of it before it split open also made me feel proud and responsible.

One of my most memorable sewing jobs was on a matching set of new winter coats David and I received. The jacket was dark green on the outside with a bright yellow liner. It was from the Montgomery Ward's latest fall line, and I was thrilled to have something so new. Unfortunately, the puffy, faux, down-filled jacket was made of a very thin polyester shell and pulled threads quickly led to multiple holes. For this project and then to be used for all projects, my father bought several spools of black super-strength thread he said was used to sew parachutes. The thread was strong enough that it could not be broken in my hands using full force. His thinking was that it made no sense to sew with low gauge thread, as any repair would deteriorate quickly with our level of play, and he wasn't wrong. I was tasked with repairing David and my jackets. I was proud of my work, but the finished product made our jackets look like a Dr. Frankenstein project. The thick, black, triple-looped thread stitching was very effective in closing holes, but the heavy thread was so prominent, it made the repairs very obvious.

Other than when the kids made fun of the stitch tracks, the only time I ever felt bad about my sewing was when my father also laughed at the "Frankenstein" stitching, a name he coined as he poked fun at me about my work regularly. It wasn't enough for him that we were being abused and belittled regularly in other forms by him—he enjoyed being one of my bullies as well. He did this with enough frequency that it seemed like he needed this to feel good about himself, while making me feel small. As a father myself, I can't imagine how he got to a place where making fun of his own children was so rewarding for him.

While repairing a hole or sewing in a patch became one of my skills, I had received no training on how to cure clothes that no longer fit. This was especially troubling during growth spurt years where hand-me-downs were not available, but where my body clearly could not fit into the clothes I had. However, equipped with my new sewing skills and feeling industrious, I confidently came up with a solution for pants that were too short. The seventies were known for bell bottom style pants that would often cover the shoe, so having pants that came four inches above my ankles was solid fodder for jokes and more reason for bad attention. With no new or used clothes coming, I decided that the best remedy would be to find an old pair of jeans that could no longer be worn, cut the bottoms off, and then sew them onto the bottom of the short pants as an extension. I did my best to match the denim color of the extension to that of the target pants, but there was limited inventory to choose from. My new creation seemed to be a much better option; however, while the kids at school didn't exactly know what to call my creation, they ridiculed me on every wearing. Unfortunately, I had to wear them several times a week while counting the days that more clothes might arrive. I would have been grateful for a father-son Goodwill trip, but I was scared to see him, and the price of a simple five dollar Goodwill purchase meant an entire day of cleaning.

Today, I am still mending our family's clothes and am grateful for the skill, and that learning this afforded another opportunity to *not* ask for something. Sewing, changing car oil, heavy labor, and many other jobs were all tasks that gave me my first taste of what being Crutchless could look like. I didn't put it all together at the time, but God forcing me to recognize I could do this and so many other things on my own was a powerful gift.

Kids in the late seventies could be relentless bullies. Bullies were accepted as part of life, and, even though irritating and troubling to the victims, there was never a drive then to stop these practices. It was the age of fight back or shut up and take it.

Wearing Frankenstein-style stitched clothes and sporting my mother's special haircuts made me a favorite target in school. I would do my best to walk away and ignore the bullies as I had been trained, but that only made me seem weak, and the attacks intensified. This makes sense now because the softer targets are always going to get the most attention. Soon, I seemed to be in tussles weekly and full-blown physical fights once a month. I hated going to school, but I hated being home more. Due to my karate training and my experiences at home with direct physical contact and pain management, I had little fear of being physically hurt. Training and instinct took over, and I rarely lost a fight. There was nothing a kid could do to me that would ever come close to what I was already experiencing in the dojo or at home. In fact, seeing my opponents throwing a wild emotional punch was almost a joke.

While it didn't show on the outside, fighting was where I was most qualified. Winning should have been an ideal result, where the victory meant I would earn respect and privacy. But the truth is that winning fights didn't earn me any of this. Popular kids get ego-pumping credit when they win, but if they lose to a weird and unpopular kid, it is thought of as an anomaly, and the outsider kid gets vilified even more. Being bested by me, a quiet, introverted, odd-looking kid, had a way of making me out to be a monster. Generally, even with some street sense and some experience under their belts, my opponents were no match. It sucked to be great at something and not have it lead to something positive in my life, but it was a gift that I could keep myself safe from an attack outside of the home. I did lose a few fights and one of them was to a group of six girls. However, that loss led to a surprisingly happy "the world can be good" affirmation—another gift granted to me by the Universe.

I was an oddity by any measure in middle school. I was seldom clean, frequently disheveled, and had no social skills. I was at best an average student, and most of my headspace was dedicated to surviving what was happening at home and trying to navigate school to just get through the day. My "best friends" were often part of the ridicule, and I found myself lost as to who was an enemy and who was a friend. This was partly because I had such low self-esteem but also because my friends were not always kind. This may have been what happens with all kids at this age, and it also could legitimately be that I was such a freak, they could only take me in small doses.

I was deeply insecure and with no guidance or role models, I remember waking each day to fear and trying to figure everything out right as my eyes opened. I would be afraid there would be no breakfast, afraid there would be no lunch because of John's daily pilfering of my lunch money, afraid there would be no clean clothes, afraid of who would come after me in school, and then later, afraid of who would come after me at home. In the midst of my fear, I was constantly trying to work the problems thrown at me and keep my head above water.

Inside all of the trouble, I did find a silver lining from time to time. One of those was when I wrongly perceived a girl's affection for me and allowed my heart to go all in. It was a very short courtship in middle school, my first, and it ended very badly for me.

Patty was a raven-haired Arbutus beauty with smooth ivory white skin. She was a beautiful eleven- or twelve-year-old, taller than me, with beautiful '80s-styled feathered black hair. We had made eye contact a couple times in the halls, and for some reason, she didn't look away like most girls did. I interpreted this as a very positive sign and took to keeping an eye out for her everywhere I went. I would make eyes at her, and she would kindly look back. Eventually, I got up the courage to talk to her, which took everything I had. Unfortunately, telling her I "liked" her was forward enough that she felt the need to clarify our relationship. She let me know loudly and publicly that I was not her type and that she had no feelings whatsoever for me as friend, boyfriend, or any other possible connected status. Apparently, my instincts couldn't have been more wrong.

The entire interaction happened in front of a pack of her girlfriends. It was clear that she wanted anyone within earshot to know she was rejecting me. I was crushed, and her effort to humiliate me while eliminating any thought that she had any connection to me was highly effective. In those brief seconds, the anthill of self-esteem that had grown inside me was obliterated. The one reason I had to look forward to school was gone in an instant. With her stinging words, I had not only lost my first shot at love in junior high school, but also ended up giving the bullies another arrow in their quivers. I received and abided by the message loudly and clearly. I slinked away as she and her posse left the scene. Thoroughly embarrassed, I realized that whatever I thought we had in those few stolen glances was over.

Unfortunately, with the increased taunting and jeers at school, her heartless, mean rejection was starting to grow some anger inside of me. After my brief interaction with Patty, her friends would join in the fun, calling me names and laughing whenever they saw me in the halls. I had done everything to blend in and not be noticed in school, but news of my interest in Patty, a popular girl, and her subsequent rejection of me, spread throughout Arbutus Middle School, and I had another reason to be the butt of kids' jokes everywhere. While I avoided Patty from that moment on, when I did see her and by chance made eye contact, she literally scowled back at me. On one such occasion, I was so angered by her aggressiveness and the added difficulties from the fallout, that I gave her the middle finger. Witnessing my gesture, her scowl led to a heartless glare as she turned a corner. I had the feeling I had made a mistake in how I responded, and soon I would find out just how terrible my judgment had been.

Traversing the school hallways to avoid threats was challenging, but, of course, not all confrontations were grounds for an immediate physical conflict. I had been trained by my *Sensei* to never initiate a fight and was terrified of what might happen to me at home if I got in trouble. Oddly, my father was proud when I would win a fight, but only if I didn't start it. Also, the other kids had their own risk to consider about how their parents might react to their son starting a fight with the weird kid at school. With my training mandate and the many witnesses looking on, the parents of my opponents were certain to find out that their child was the initiator, so blaming me was a lie that could not be sold.

However, the opportunity for bullies to engage without consequences was much increased on my commute home. It was not unusual for fights to break out in the areas surrounding the school yard that were not part of school property. Many times, the fights would be announced, and the school would be bubbling with excitement for the after-school-fight event. I never called anyone out but was called out myself several times. Not showing up to one of these events would result in ridicule for weeks and didn't make much sense because if someone was after me, the fight would eventually happen at some point. It made better tactical sense for me to know where and when I would be fighting rather than be surprised somewhere. I felt fear building all day knowing I would likely be fighting after school, but I always showed up because fighting and winning off school grounds was the best way to put it behind me.

It was not difficult for a boy on the hunt to find me because I had to walk the same path every day—out the back of the school, across Sulphur Spring Road, through a county recreational park, navigate a path through a quarter mile of woods and then emerge from the wood line to walk another half mile or so through the graveyard adjacent to my neighborhood. Because of where I lived, there were no options to travel any other route. This meant that anyone looking to connect with me knew exactly where to find me. A rift with a would-be opponent filled my days with anxiety and stress knowing that my predictable path home made me highly vulnerable to an ambush. It was a similar feeling to how I lived at home; it was hard to live in fight or flight mode twenty-four hours a day. Getting the fight over with was a much better option than taking weeks of a kid and his friends stalking me in the hall while promising me the worst. We were rednecks, and sometimes rednecks need hard lessons. Winning fights didn't make me popular, but as each kid took a loss, more learned to steer clear of me.

Scheduled fights in the park, or wherever the agreed upon meeting place was, always began with a boy mostly talking trash and pushing me. This allowed me to check the box that the fight was started by the other guy, and I knew that if it continued, I could soon give myself permission to defend myself. These fights almost always ended with a boy on his knees or laying on the ground with his face bleeding, pleading with me to stop. I knew how to break arms and legs and dole out all sorts of serious injuries if I wanted to, but I never resorted to that. *Sensei* Amin had taught me not just discipline in life, but also discipline during a fight, and so I had limits to how far I would go.

My opponents could recognize I was both organized and outwardly calm. Despite my adrenaline pumping wildly, I had been trained to stay in control. Fighting was as much about the mind as it was the body. I would be patient, allow for some pushes and shoves because they caused no harm, but I would not succumb to anything that would put me on the ground, which is the place any fighter is most vulnerable. When the time was right, I would send a small volley of sharp, direct punches direct to the gut or nose. If the boy was bigger, I might crack him with medium force in the ribs with a roundhouse kick. The effort was to not only defend myself, but also to send a message to my opponent, and their friends cheering them on, that this was going to be a different type of fight.

On some occasions, my opponent would realize he might be outmatched. When that happened, he would just talk more rhetoric and use it to back out of the fight. If he didn't walk away, the next move was usually a desperate attempt to tackle me. I could not allow this and used my training to keep my distance. My plan was to defend myself on my terms while staying upright. I have been struck many times in these fights, but these attacks were weak in comparison to those I experienced from my parents and dojo sparring partners. Being more afraid of the embarrassment of yielding than any physical harm they might receive from me foolishly kept them in the fight. On almost every occasion, I would win either by forfeit or clearly besting my opponent. This meant that kids would generally accept their defeat and go on about their lives. The fight involving Patty and her clan was a strange exception where I chose not to strike back during a surprise attack, and where all were attacking at once. It was also a reminder that gifts come in all sorts of packaging.

I remember it being a warm day and, as usual, I was walking home alone. Always keenly aware of my surroundings, I kept a close eye open for any threats around me in all directions. I felt that I was in the clear as I crossed the school grounds and made my way to the public park. Some distance behind me, I noticed Patty and her girlfriends were heading in the same direction. This was their path home as well, so this was not unusual. I knew that if I kept my current pace, they would not catch up to me. Despite girls fighting each other regularly in my school, I never thought of Patty and her friends as a threat. After all, she had achieved the goal of publicly humiliating me and all she'd received in return was one flash of a middle finger.

With my eyes focused ahead, I watched for traffic so I could cross over Sulphur Spring Road to the park. To my complete surprise, Patty and her gang of five had closed the gap quickly behind me, and we were all standing on the patch of grass to the right of the school exit, but still on the school side of the road. With traffic moving by, I had nowhere to go and was feeling anxious and awkward to be surrounded by my daily female tormentors. One of the girls started verbally assaulting me about my flipping the middle finger at Patty. Patty stepped back and away as the older girls managed the engagement. I was quickly surrounded as the girls began to get physical by taking turns pushing me around while throwing out insults. I did nothing but take what they were giving, hoping for a gap in traffic so I could dart across the street. A few quick, well-placed punches would have sufficed for a clean exit, but hitting girls was not an option in my mind.

One of the girls knocked my books out of my hands and I went to the ground to pick them up. While on my knees, one of the girls punched me in the face and another kicked me in the ribs smartly. It wasn't the hardest I had been hit, but with six girls surrounding me, and with no intention to strike back, I resorted to curling up on the ground while protecting my head and face. With no resistance, the posse then went about the business of punching and kicking me right out in the open for all of the traffic and school administrators to watch. Cars were exiting the parking lot and passing on the main road with apparently no concern. No one made any effort to stop the attack. Yet.

Setting aside what my parents did to me at home, it was the worst private beating I had at that time in my life. My only option was to pull my knees to my chest, protect my head and face, and wish they would stop soon. The kicks and punches kept coming with no end in sight. The circle of girls closed around me as they did their work. After what seemed like a couple minutes, I noticed a hole appear in their encirclement. The space allowed in some light, and my peripheral vision picked up what looked like one of the girls getting thrown backwards and away from me. I could see her lying on her back on the ground, our eyes briefly meeting each other. Another girl was shoved hard in the chest and landed on her ass, joining her friend. As the other girls tumbled and fell away, I realized someone had come to my rescue: a complete stranger. The oldest attacker exchanged sharp words with my new-found hero and promptly received a punch in the mouth. This was enough encouragement for the group to disengage, gather themselves, and cross the street to the park.

When I stood up, there in front of me was Claudette. As the girls walked away while mouthing off to her, vowing to finish this with me later, she promised them all an ass beating if they re-engaged me. I knew who she was by reputation, but she was the last person in the world I thought would rescue me. She was taller than me and wore a wide-brimmed, floppy leather hat with tassels hanging from the back, and a Jack Daniels logo on the front. This was the style at the time for the "heads" (partiers). After collecting my stuff, I looked at her for a couple seconds while leveling my breath and dusting off. My hope is that I thanked her, but I can't remember for sure. I don't remember her saying anything to me, but I do remember her lighting a cigarette and walking away with no desire for praise or gratitude. An angel had shown itself to me in this heartwarming, self-sacrificing act of unselfishness and I think I was speechless.

Writing about Claudette and the gift of her involvement and protection makes me wish I could see her again to thank her. She took on six girls by herself and won, all while rescuing me from what could have certainly gotten much worse. Something inside her must have told her this complete stranger needed to be saved and kept from harm. I remain both grateful and fascinated. Maybe it was her own nudge from God. Whatever the reason, it seemed obvious I had received yet another gift from the Universe just when I needed it. It wasn't just a gift in the moment to save me, it was a gift that sent a message that in the sea of darkness that was my then existence, here was proof of kindness, unselfishness, and light from someone who wanted nothing in return. Thinking about Claudette walking away with the floppy leather hat with tassels and feathers as the last intimate interaction I would ever have with her, I am reminded of how the Universe acts in strange ways and how gifts can be found anywhere in any situation. It also reminds me that we must stand up for those who cannot defend themselves.

My brothers and I were all fighters. David was the type who would take a lot of aggression and ridicule until he eventually snapped into attack mode. Whenever that happened, whoever thought that their continued ribbing was going to go unchecked found out just how wrong they were. While David never had any formal training, he had two older brothers to tangle with and a lot of his own pent-up emotions, so inflicting some pain on a bully wasn't something he had an issue with.

John, on the other hand, took nothing from anyone. If someone even looked at him wrong, he would stand them up. Most ill-informed kids who would test John's conviction would get the message right away that engaging him meant swift and aggressive physical contact. They would often pass on him in favor of softer targets to satisfy their small egos. The ones who didn't accept the rumors about John would quickly discover they had made a grave error. I don't think John went looking for fights, but he never shied away from one, either. Walking away was considered weak, and John was anything but weak.

Me cleaning up my books and papers after being assaulted by a group of girls. Claudette, a person I did not know, was yet another guardian angel sent to help me. She saved the day, showing compassion and a willingness to help with no expectations and no need for praise. We never had another conversation after that day. I remain deeply grateful for her help and will always remember her as a model for what unselfishness and standing up for those who cannot defend themselves looks like.

There was a deeper meaning for why John was so aggressive and thorough. Each of his fights was an opportunity to release some of the pain and hurt he was feeling at home. It was hard to hold so much sadness and trauma inside, so a street brawl offered him a release and a chance to project all of his anger to the wrong target. Also, given his experience of being ridiculed and bullied at home, there was no way he was going to have any tolerance for that type of behavior outside of our walls.

Lastly, winning fight after fight awarded him a reputation as being tough, strong, and even powerful. With no words of affection or affirmation at home, being known as an accomplished brawler was something positive and an ego builder of sorts. He was not a large kid, but he was well known as a merciless and gifted fighter. His experiences with my parents combined with his karate training turned him into a weapon.

We dressed weird, had few friends, and were as introverted as we could be, which was directly related to our home experience and specific instruction to keep everything secret. As such, we were great targets for bullying, so there were many opportunities to prove our grit. I witnessed John fight several times when we were children in the back alleys of our neighborhood. His results were decisive, quick, and emphatic. Later, when he was more free roaming and became more distant, I would only hear through the grapevine about how psycho he had gone on another willing victim. While his timing and patience in the fights may have been due to his karate training, the energy and commitment to each altercation appeared to be almost out of his control. With his reputation broadcasting far, the kids in the back alleys of our rowhomes knew John was not someone to pick a fight with. Even the older kids stayed away from him out of fear, and possibly respect.

More importantly, whether he intended it or not, he became well known as my and David's protector, to the point that I am sure my mouth at times was writing checks I was hoping my brother would cash. John and I did not have a close relationship in the sense that we confided in each other, but he did not tolerate anyone bullying or putting hands on his little brothers, and that was all the closeness I needed at the time. This brought me some security, and, in a world with none, I was thankful to have some protection from threats on the streets.

There were times when John would be in proximity to me and could see from a distance that an older kid was picking a fight with me. I would handle my own business, but if the developing situation looked unbalanced—my opponent was an older, heavier, stronger kid—John would be paying careful attention in his own way. He would sit about fifty yards or so away, smoking (always smoking) and acting innocuous and disinterested. From time to time, he would lift his head and glance in my direction, while never saying a word. To the outsider, it would seem like he was impartial or unengaged, but I thankfully knew better. I knew he had his eye on me, and I was certainly a lot more confident because he did. If a kid became more verbally aggressive or started pushing me, and John had a sense I was outmatched, he would pick himself up and move into the threat zone. From there, he cast a long, wordless stare in the aggressor's direction. This would usually send the right message, and the boy would back down in short order. If that didn't work, John would take an unyielding position directly in front of the boy, almost nose to nose. He would stare him in the eye, often blowing smoke right in the boy's face. There would be no words, but his bloodshot, rage-filled eyes told his opponent what was coming. If he were really incensed, he would bite down on the knuckle of his right index finger, a sign he was beginning to boil inside. Like hairs standing up on the back of a dog's neck, all of these tells meant John was gearing up for fight mode. More accurately, he was in win mode. To most, the unusual quiet but confident confrontation was all that was needed for the boy to gather his good sense and go elsewhere. Those who were ill informed or new to the neighborhood would have to learn the hard way.

On one such occasion, a new older kid moved into the neighborhood and a rift over a pick-up wiffle-ball game broke out in the back alley immediately behind our home. The new kid was trying to redefine the rules of a game we had been playing for years, and that did not sit well with me. I was being unusually mouthy with a much larger opponent, not my normal keep-to-myself self. It seemed I had grown too confident under John's protection. I stood my ground, but it did not take long for things to begin to heat up. Billy was a tall, confident boy three years my senior, five inches taller and thirty pounds heavier. With a solid shove to my chest, he put me on the ground with ease. This aggressive offensive move caught me off guard as I met the pavement. Somewhat disoriented, I got up from the concrete and attempted a strike or two but did not make solid contact. When Billy saw a break in my ineffective counter, he used his weight advantage to send me to the ground again.

Hopping up to defend myself yet again, I received my second blood-drawing punch to my face (the first was from my father on Halloween night years earlier). My nose bled immediately with Billy's well-placed strike, and I recoiled with the impact. I rose slowly while carefully considering my options. It was apparent this was a fight I was not going to win. I was normally able to avoid a pushing match by being tactical with my punches and kicks, but this kid was physically more than I could handle.

Contrary to my training and in an act of desperation, I tried to tackle the kid. It felt like hitting a wall, and his response was to throw me into a pile of trash like a bag of rags. As I climbed out of the garbage bags, it occurred to me I wasn't necessarily scared of the physical pain I was feeling. After all, I had experienced plenty of that before. My fear at the time was based more on my inability to back down fueled by the belief that I had a responsibility to defend myself to maintain my reputation. After all, being beat down in front of a group of kids by a relative stranger was not going to be helpful to my credibility as a fighter. Things were looking bleak, but I was determined to figure out this obstacle.

As the crowd gathered round to watch the beating and my situation getting more hopeless by the minute, I coincidentally looked up at John's bedroom window. I did not see John himself, but I saw the telltale puff of smoke coming from just above the sill. John and my mother blew their cigarette smoke out of the windows thinking no one on the inside would detect their habit. Of course, some of the smoke got pulled into the house and recirculated through the HVAC system, so we always knew when either was smoking.

The smoke I witnessed from John's cigarette produced a small wave of hope for me. If the kids kept loudly heckling Billy the way they were, the noise would rise to his open window and John would have to take notice. As I got pushed to the ground again, gathered myself, and looked up, I saw something that brought relief. This time, John's head was poking out the screenless second story window with great interest and focus. With his hands resting on the sill and his head hanging outside the screenless window studying the situation, I prayed for some assistance. His cigarette was still hanging from his mouth as he watched and assessed the situation. My vision was good in those days, and what happened next was music to my eyes. The feeling of a knight saving my day didn't happen often, but I knew John was not going to be happy with seeing his brother being beat down in the back alley.

After putting the pieces together of what he was witnessing, John established that I was in the process of receiving a serious beating. His next move was to flip his cigarette into the yard and disappear into the house in a flurry. The still-lit butt threw sparks as it hit the patio below. Tracking John's movements, I could see through the window that he was unmistakably making the motions of someone wriggling into a pair of pants. It took less than a minute for him to transport himself from the window cavity to my location. He was down the stairs, out the back glass slider, and over the split-rail fence that backed up to our alley in less than thirty seconds. He had no shoes or shirt, and his face showed only rage as the crowd parted with his arrival. With his mouth biting down hard on his bent index finger and his face flush with blood rushing to the surface, I knew Billy had a different problem now. Having seen this face before, I felt sorry for what would happen to Billy and the role that I played in the punishment he would receive. True to form, John didn't stop to check my injuries or ask for my account of the situation. He wasn't built that way; his approach was action not compassion. He sized up his opponent and likely noticed that Billy was taller and heavier than himself. As with all of his opponents, size had no bearing on the decision he had already made, so he set about the business of engaging the target.

With Billy's decision to not walk away, John started into his work with zeal. His fists were white with rage as he used a quick combination to punch the boy twice in the face. He sent a left jab followed by a typical karate front punch. Next came a straight right kick to the chest and Billy was introduced to the concrete for the first time. It was the perfect mix of ancient martial arts and street brawling. Obviously outgunned, Billy was not smart enough to swallow his pride and walk away as he noisily rose for a second helping. Still stunned, Billy threw two punches that were just short and wide of his intended target. Next came a kick, which made some contact with John's leg but had little noticeable effect. John waited patiently for Billy's flailing to stop, while easily avoiding contact. We had been trained that these types of moves are energy burners and if not a threat, just let them play out and wait for the opening. I had seen the look in John's eyes before when he sparred, and I knew this kid was in the process of learning an extremely valuable lesson. Several punches later and a hard roundhouse kick to the boy's ribs, and he went down hard again. John was on one knee and about to finish him off like the symbolic closing of a Japanese karate *kata*. (*In a karate tournament, it is common for a match to end with a very close no-contact punch to the face or other critical area. In loose terms, this move is what tells the judges who won the match.*) This was very different because John was not taking an exam, and this was a real live opponent. Emotions were high as Billy lay just under John's hammer of a fist.

Before a final strike could be made, the brawl ended when Billy's mother screamed hysterically at John from a second-floor porch across the alley. John rose from his opponent's chest, and, with only a glance toward me, walked away. I remember him purposely being only inches from Billy's face and spittle spraying the boy as he told him that if he ever touched me again, he would kill him. Of course, I don't think he meant he would actually kill him, but after witnessing John's rage and witnessing the pain he had inflicted, I am sure Billy would at least give his words some serious consideration.

John left me there with my bloody nose as he returned to his room. There was no effort to console me or pep me up, then or after, but this was not needed or expected; his actions did all the talking. This was John's style. He was not flowery, and he wasn't about hugs or trying to be my therapist, but he protected me again that day in the only way he knew how. Despite all of the pain he was experiencing in the house and the inaccessibility to role models or any lessons about love or family, similar perhaps to Claudette, his intuition (the Universe) still spoke up and told him to protect me. John's gift of physical raw ability, quiet compassion, and, indeed, his propensity toward violence, were all called up to protect me. I didn't ask him to protect me, and if he had not come out on his own, I wouldn't have called out for him. This was because we were not comfortable asking for help ever. We were taught as a rule by our parents that they would not help, and that we must rely on ourselves in any situation. This in mind, whatever mess I got myself into, I was expected to clean it up.

Today, I interpret his unselfish acts and my family's unwritten rule of unrelenting independence as among the many gifts that I took for granted in my youth, but that I know now were so formative for me. John's unique presentation of compassion arising organically from someone who was in no way wired by experience to protect me was also another gift as it showed me, albeit much later in life, how God works in all people in all ways. I have also come to understand there were many real benefits to being so self-sufficient at a young age. Lastly, his engagement showed me the stark difference between actions and words.

With everything working itself out, I took my battered self into the house with no feeling of embarrassment whatsoever. John had corrected an imbalance in the Universe and without saying it, or acting in any conventional way, he was telling me he loved me and that I had worth.

While I had lost the fight with Billy, I had won many fights in my times roaming the back alleys of Huntsmoore, Arbutus. A fight with a boy named Chris a couple years after the Billy episode was proof I was my own brand of weapon. I was less violent than John, but I could put most, even bigger kids (usually), down with not much effort. Most kids had no idea how to fight, so they were easy to deal with. Chris was a year older and taller and started mouthing off. Like my altercation with Billy, Chris's first meaningful push caught me by surprise and sent me to the concrete. I knew I could not allow for another Billy-style beating, so I got up off the ground and readjusted. I waited for the right moment, dipped down, and swept his legs. Losing balance, he fell backwards to the ground. I did not move in to attack him while he was in this vulnerable state but was hoping he would receive the message that this engagement was not going to be easy and walk away. Letting him up may have been a mistake as I watched him stand up confidently, physically unimpacted from the fall. He was ready for more, and I was ready to oblige.

Getting punched in the dojo and beat down at home gave me a high threshold for pain. I had literally been trained to endure beatings and, by rule, to get back up when knocked down. When I was outside of the dojo, there were very few opponents who could match that experience. Most kids melted with the shock of a first strike. There is an adrenaline rush and the flood of blood and chemicals as our sympathetic nervous systems trigger us into fight-or-flight mode. Having had plenty of experience managing through this primitive instinct is a huge advantage over an opponent. To the rookie opponent, the surprise bio-chemical tidal wave is what induces fear. Someone without experience is managing all this new information going on in their head in real time, while trying to make decisions under duress about what is next. This processing is an issue and a distraction from the task at hand. In this state, flight becomes a real consideration. False bravado and poor decision making are also common outcomes of this confusion, which adds to a novice's vulnerability. Everyone is brave and articulate until they feel their face being impacted by knuckles. It is a terrifically eye opening (or eye closing) experience you can't possibly understand unless you have been there. The more emotion, the poorer the decisions. The human brain is not good at making good decisions while being angry. All that the experienced fighter must do is recognize their own adrenaline surge, harness its power, be patient, and wait for mistakes; the opportunities will present themselves to the trained fighter. Much of what you see in movies is false, of course, but there is some truth to watching the decisive outcomes of a trained martial arts student against an untrained bully.

I assumed a standard defensive position and waited for him to send something my way. When his swing missed wide, I countered with a punch direct to the eye (eyes and noses are the best targets to end fights quickly). My fist accurately found its target when the knuckles on my right hand landed squarely on his left eye. It was a solid, straight punch, angled up to meet his height advantage, and its impact was known immediately. Chris's hands instantly went to his eye, and he started wailing loudly. He didn't fight back after that, and I could see that his eye was quickly closing shut, with the surrounding skin already turning black and blue. Still whimpering, he ran across the alley to his home to seek medical attention and rat me out to his mother and father. He promised his parents would make sure I was punished. I was anxious and realized my actions might have consequences and was hoping it would all be forgotten. The idea of another parent engaging my parents was more dangerous to my health than any harm Chris could do to me.

Less than an hour later, there was a knock at the door. When my father opened it, Chris's parents stood there with the now black-eyed boy. There were a lot of emotions on the landing of our front steps as my father exchanged words with the other dad. He called me from my room to join him on our front stoop. In front of the other father and Chris, he asked me for details about the fight, and I told him the truth. Chris told essentially the same story but tried to reason like a child would—that his attack on me was deserved because I supposedly broke the game rules. In his blunt, direct style, my father looked at the other dad and said something like, "Your son started a fight. My son defended himself and your son lost. If your son is hurt, it is his fault." The two men exchanged some insults and threats, but they led nowhere. My father was not easily intimidated and closed the door on them while Chris's father was still in a rant. We were now in the house together alone, which was never a good thing. There was some history of my father siding with me after fights where I had defended myself, but bringing mayhem to his doorstep was a much different experience. I thought this new element might be the trigger for him to discipline me, more than for the fight itself. Instead, my father looked at me and said that there was nothing else I could do in that case and said some words that made it seem like he was proud of me. I don't remember what the exact words were, but relief poured over me knowing I would be OK. I felt supported by his words and enjoyed the rare moment when my father stood with me. Feeling joy and pride in his children was not something that bubbled up much with my father, so this was a gift to hold on to.

16

An Unexpected Flashback

The Greatest Showman is a 2017 movie that I doubt my brother John has ever seen. One of the songs, "This Is Me," off of the soundtrack, makes me think of him. With the treatment from my parents, especially my father, John had a very difficult time finding a place in this world. He struggled at every turn, and the people who were supposed to protect him made it nearly impossible for him to survive, yet he did just that. The lyrics and the movie send a powerfully convincing message that there is a place for all of us, no matter the obstacles. I don't know if anyone in John's life was able to teach him that, but I know he deserved to find his people and a safe place to be himself.

I was sitting recently at a table working on a puzzle when a past event inexplicably popped into my mind. It was not subject matter I was thinking on intentionally and there wasn't any topic that would have segued naturally into my consciousness from some other thought. It was a memory I had filed away for many years that somehow worked its way up to the surface like a painful splinter working its way out of a wound. After I visited with the shocking memory, I found that the ripples kept rolling for the hours and days that followed. This dark scene, and others like it, sometimes find a way to bubble up, even when I think I have said goodbye to them forever. In doing so, they remind me of where I come from, even with decades having passed. When it hit me, I could feel hairs standing up on my neck as if I were there, and the emotions came rushing back like I was a young teenager again. The scene that popped back up was one of a Wellington family get together—good times.

In my youth, I would spend considerable time trying to understand my role in the pain I was experiencing. If I could find reasons that would clarify why I was legitimately deserving of the abuse my parents so generously provided, then my world might be easier to digest. I just wanted to make sense of it, and, in the spirit of wanting to earn their love and affection while staying alive, maybe I could cure it. Working toward fixing myself seemed much more useful than trying to understand how two people could bring children into this world and treat them as they had. The efforts to fix myself and be a better son were, of course, unsuccessful because I am not to blame for their actions. However, I still sometimes fall into bad habits and go back to a place where I am not fully convinced I did not play a part in the abuse. Of course, in my adult, reasonably educated mind, I know that these people should have done better. However, sometimes their programming still finds a way to be heard. In these moments, I hear their comments: *"You never had it anywhere near as bad as us," "You have no idea how good you have it," "We gave you the rules, you broke them, so you pay the price," "Good kids don't break the rules," "You are such a bad son and person that the only thing that can keep me [Dad] from killing you is to call you filthy, degrading names and physically discipline you this way."* The list of quotes like this could go on extensively but hearing these things with no offsetting positive comments or walk backs made these thoughts more believable. On days where I would let thoughts go too far, I believed their comments and gave them permission to fester like an infected wound. Eventually, common sense and consciously choosing to switch the channel led me back to the truth, as I doggie paddle back to a safe mental space. Durability, neuroplasticity, and a willingness to be kind to myself (after a lot of practice) are more gifts from a kind Universe.

I can find value in most everything I have experienced in my life. Even this kind of flashback presents an opportunity to gain perspective. The value I find is that a review of these flashbacks offers up proof about the environment that we were living in without outside influence, and the chance to process these thoughts with a much healthier mental disposition—a clearer, more accurate lens. It affords me the ability to conclude in absolute terms that I lived in a dangerous and dysfunctional environment. With no voices remaining to attempt to convince me otherwise, unfettered access to the truth is needed and healthy for me—another gift.

As I concentrated on connecting the puzzle pieces that lay out in front of me, this came to me.

I heard the chairs bouncing off walls and other articles being thrown around the kitchen area. Things were breaking, the result of two men arguing and pushing each other around in a small space. There was loud screaming, and I began to feel my face and head warm from the blood rushing to it, brought on by general anxiety and a fear that I might be pulled into this event. I didn't need to be told to put myself on high alert; it was virtually how I lived my daily life. Whenever these types of sounds were in the air, I was frightened and afraid for my safety. I knew I was not involved in whatever was happening but had known my parents to pull me in before, if for no other reason than to enunciate their power position. Knowing that it was better that I know what's going on, rather than being pulled into it and then being surprised, I made the decision to get a closer look. At least I could know the evil that was at hand, rather than wait for it to come to me.

I moved from the corner of the living room of our small townhouse toward the kitchen and gave quiet instructions for David to stay where he was. I crept down the kitchen hallway and began to watch the father-son battle in live action. I was about fourteen, but it was not the first time that I had seen this happen. They were pushing each other around and my brother was threatening to fight my father. John had the skills and the determination to finish him, but unlike the alley fights, his always persistent desire to see their relationship reconcile kept him from going the full distance. My never-wrong father, who at no point had any desire to reconcile, used John's insatiable desire for affirmation against him (his greatest weapon), as he grabbed John's throat and restrained one of his arms. He leaned his body into John, effectively cutting off any chance for him to strike back meaningfully. My mother must have been genuinely frightened because she began begging my father to let him go and even physically, in a rare act of intervention, tried to pull my father off of John. Her efforts were weak, no doubt because she herself was afraid of getting struck. I sat cowering in a corner of the kitchen, watching the whole escapade play out while I sobbed in fear hysterically. David had managed to make his way into the room also, and he sat in another corner. As always, David didn't really know how to express emotion, so he sat with his eyes locked unemotionally on the mess unfolding in front of us. Neither of us were stupid enough to say or do anything to stop this.

John's face was blood red from the restricted oxygen and rising blood flow. Despite barely being able to breath, he would not yield. Sadly...very sadly...it was clear that my brother would rather die than concede to him. When my father slightly loosened his grip on John's throat, my brother used the break to tell my father how much he hated him while daring him to finish the job. Spittle was flying from his lips into my father's face as each of their eyes screamed hatred for each other. Me, my mother and now even David, were all crying *intensely, scared of what might happen next. John also took a few moments when my father softened his grip to criticize my mother for letting it get this far, adding that she should have never let the man in HER house. Oddly, I saw no fear in John's eyes. My father likely knew his son wanted more than anything to have a father who loved him, and with that knowledge surmised that John would never go further than some pushes and lots of words.*

My father eventually let my brother go and in doing so, John fell like a sack to the floor. Dear Old Dad let loose a string of obscenities and searing insults as John lay there. They were designed to create pain at the deepest depths of John's psyche. My father had spent John's whole life making him feel worthless. Seeing him lying there, he chose that moment as the perfect opportunity to look to the future and announce that John would always be a loser and amount to nothing. Collapsing into himself, John ran up the stairs and locked himself in his room, crying loudly and painfully. My father left shortly after, but not before he carefully explained to everyone how right he was and how it was him who was really the victim. John stayed in his room for hours. When I saw him next, he was withdrawn and speechless.

Living this memory again brings back many emotions, but mostly it makes my heart feel so deeply sad for John. So much was taken from him, in such a sweeping, complete way by our parents, that it's hard to envision how he could have climbed out of the hole they dug for him. His experience was like the wiping out of rainforests that can never return to their previous state. I am a big believer in independence, making my own fate, and being Crutchless, but for someone with his experience, the task of finding happiness and a rich life can be forever elusive or even impossible. My heart is also sad for my whole family. We all deserved better.

As with everything in my life, in hindsight there are other gifts to be found in re-experiencing this sad moment. For one, while John was my protector in many ways, he was also another frequent abuser in my life. For much of my life, I had a lot of animosity and anger about how he treated me. But by reviewing an event like this and having the opportunity to first-hand experience again how horrific things were for him, I know that how he treated me was all that he knew. Reaching this conclusion, and believing it, has afforded me the chance to be softer and kinder with how I look at our relationship and opened up the pathway to forgiveness. And further, all this time later, I feel true gratitude for him in my heart, rather than the years of resentment and bitterness I had held on to. I am now interested instead in finding ways to provide unconditional love and friendship to John, something I was not emotionally available to do before.

The other gift is that a flashback of this nature provides me with clear proof that what I lived through was not my fault. This event was part of a long history of many bad acts that were just a part of a systemically dangerous and volatile living environment. Having been conditioned to believe the worst about myself, the positive affirmation and reframing are the gifts that offset that negative thinking.

As John got older, he and my father became fierce opponents. I believe that John secretly wanted to find his way into Dad's heart, but, despite all the abuse, my father always found good reasons to justify his actions and the awful things he'd say about his oldest son. This lasted far into adulthood. It was despicable how he never came to terms with the evil he brought down on John. I wish that I could give him that gift and somehow convince him that none of this was his fault.

The unfolding.

17

The Middle of Things

Whatever Gary Newby of The Railway Children was going through in the early '90s, I connected intimately with the lyrics of his song, "Every Beat of the Heart." I related strongly with the message and optimism found in the lyrics of this relatively obscure song about leaving angry clouds behind in search of clearer skies ahead. Once again, an artist I will never meet used his gifts to play a role in saving my life. Hearing this song then and now, I am reminded of the gifts resulting from the wiring that God gave Mr. Newby and myself. I knew I could persevere, find independence, and, above all, never QUIT. The lyrics of the song also are a good lead into this section about leaving my childhood behind and moving into my adult life.

I call this section the "middle of things" because it roughly correlates to a time when I began to see that the end of my prison sentence was approaching. With this news, a loose understanding was taking hold, suggesting to me that hard work, focus, and commitment really could lead me to somewhere better. I didn't yet have any direct evidence to support the theory that I could create a functional and happy life for myself, but survival instinct and an unwillingness to give up had kept me alive and generally on a positive trajectory to this point. With that, I began to suspect that these qualities would be useful outside of the nest.

Telling more traumatic stories has not been fun for me. I'm happy to move through this section to get to the end—the life lessons, which I consider much more fun and fulfilling. There is much left in the middle that will not be talked about—building a career, my journey as an entrepreneur, my father's psychological warfare well into my adulthood, two marriages, friends made and lost, and a continued struggle while dealing with insecurity and low self-esteem. But in recent years, the bad feels more distant and I have a strong desire to write about all of the good that has resulted directly from my life experiences.

My freshman year of high school at Lansdowne Senior was like my last year at Arbutus Middle School. As before, I did my best to survive and be invisible at home and in the hallways. The more I could go unnoticed in both places, the better off I was.

High school offered something else I had not experienced previously—school activities. Middle school had clubs and a chance to become involved, but I never saw myself doing more than just trying to get through a day without a physical altercation at school or at home. School activities to most were a great way to meet friends and build a resume ahead of college applications, but my motivation was very different. I knew my grades were not going to be good enough to get me into a university and even if they did, I couldn't afford it. Instead, to my pleasant surprise, I quickly realized that the more I became 'involved', the less time I was forced to spend at home. It didn't matter that I frequently walked home from high school or had to deal with my mother's constant threat of disallowing my involvement; the more I could be away, the better. She did ground me sometimes just to spite me, but even for her, this was difficult, as the clubs and sports I was involved in were legit and positive impactful organizations. In my mother's world of alcoholism and loneliness, her children were all she had. And when she saw me slipping away and doing all that I could to be as far away from home as possible for as long as I could, she was resentful and, at times, infuriated. Pleading for most things, even doing so to participate in a game or a play, gave her the last vestiges of power and attention that she had over me, which in turn gave her a sense of worth. It was undoubtedly a twisted, dysfunctional way for her to find self-worth in her self-made cave of darkness.

I can't take credit for spontaneously signing up for these events. In fact, I may have never done so if it wasn't for my first girlfriend, the one who took me to church. Being active in school came naturally to her, no doubt because of the positive encouragement from her parents. She talked me into trying out for lacrosse and track, of which I was a solid six out of ten in both sports. I made the teams and found that being part of a group that wanted to collectively win had a lot of positives. Bullies existed but coaches even then frowned on players picking on teammates.

And being on a team provided community and belonging, something I had little experience with up to that point.

I was also heavily involved in musicals and other theatrical productions that were also the result of her influence. In addition, I was actively involved in student government and graduated as the vice president of my class. The implication would be that I was super popular. Indeed, I think if you were to ask some of my former classmates, they might describe me in that way. Certainly, getting enough votes to win would seem to indicate some degree of popularity. However, in my head, I continued to believe myself unworthy and unaccepted. Looking back, my girlfriend did everything she could to counter these thoughts, by making me believe I was worthy of love and friendship. I wanted to believe her and, at times, allowed myself to. However, my parents, still the most impactful influences in my life, were still around to let me know I was lacking as a son and human.

Beyond providing sanctuary, these activities did become the place where I would build some friendships and find common interests among peers. The clubs and sports collectively showed me my first real-world application that human interaction could be positive, inspiring, and healthy.

My father enjoyed the shows I was a part of, but never once attended a lacrosse game, and only once attended a track event when it was held at the community college close to his house. I fell and was hurt running a hurdles event, which ultimately led to a hospital visit. I remember feeling that I had failed right before his eyes, giving him more confirmation of just how poor of an athlete and human I was. He blamed his lack of attendance at my sporting events on me leaving karate, but the more likely truth was that it was not convenient or interesting to him. This rationale was much more in alignment with how he had fathered my entire life. His model of no support or encouragement was at least consistent, and I don't remember ever being disappointed he wasn't there.

As the four years progressed, my mother's control waned. My confidence had grown, but I was still addicted to trying to earn her affection and acceptance. I was gaining more friends and acquaintances, and my relationship with my girlfriend was on solid ground, but my mother's jealousy and resentment was becoming more aggressive. She could no longer physically abuse me, as I suspect that she feared my newfound independence and confidence might lead me to retaliate or report her. But, as mentioned before, she could still spontaneously ground me without cause. This caused me to miss rehearsals and games, and I was not permitted to explain why to my coach or play director. Even if I could, how could I begin to explain such a complex situation that I didn't fully understand myself. Teachers and friends called the house phone asking me why I wasn't at rehearsal, and my only response was that my mother wouldn't allow it. Of course, they would ask why I had been grounded, and I never had an answer because embarrassingly there never was one to be found. Through the phone on the wall, they received the equivalent of a shoulder shrug.

It was a new brand of insanity that brought with it a completely different type of sadness and powerlessness. I might have been plotting a course out of her home, but these acts were crushing and disruptive to the life I was trying so desperately to build. In time, she realized her abuse was now becoming more public, as random absences from events brought many questions and outside efforts to communicate with her directly. She regularly listened in on my phone calls, and she must have heard me being just as confused as the other person on the line as to why I was sitting there doing nothing, when I should have been rehearsing or practicing.

My father, on the other hand, was getting everything he'd always wanted. He had kids who were soon turning eighteen, so his financial commitment was ending. And there was nothing he had to do to be involved in our lives. With greater financial freedom and no interest from us in having him in our lives, he continued with the business of perfecting his self-care. He did pop in from time to time or call us periodically. His calls were ostensibly to check in, but the real purpose was to check off a list of my shortcomings, and to remind me that I still owed him something, either in chores or in relational capital. The list was inexhaustible and I was saddled with guilt from any interactions with him. Fortunately, my school activities provided enough qualified excuses that I was fortunate to almost avoid him entirely. Qualified reasons to not see my father were just another of the many gifts in my life.

As I moved closer to graduating from high school, I was gaining some control over my life and starting to assemble the building blocks needed to construct a positive self-esteem. The dark influences of my mother and father were becoming less gripping. I still lived in fear of spontaneous meddling, but I was beginning to feel something unusual: a normal breathing rhythm. It seems so basic but having moments where things felt in balance and normal was yet another beautiful gift. It was a nice break from the anxiety-filled moments associated with spending so much of my time in fight-or-flight mode. In these moments, I could see more clearly that my life was approaching a place where I would be beyond their control and that felt great.

Even with the feeling of hope growing inside of me, I wasn't much prepared for the life I hoped to create for myself. With such low self-esteem, no money and almost no tools to navigate life outside of my prison walls, I walked through the daily motions of life as a nervous and uncertain person. I saw opportunity ahead, but my fear perspective was beginning to shift from a fear of the unknown within my four walls to the fear of the unknown of the entire world and all that waited for me. At times, this was engrossing and even paralyzing, but there was no way to go but forward and through. Fortunately, I had been gifted with the instinct to know that despite anything I had experienced in life, there was something better waiting for me. I didn't know what "better" meant, but it was a voice that said it was time to leave and find out what that meant for me. I am grateful that rather than silence this voice or take on an alternative voice trying to convince me to stay with these crazy people, that I was curious, even excited. The Universe purposely wanted me to have better, and it was letting the positive influences and feelings unfold in my life, providing some self-support.

I moved from my mother's house to my father's house right around the time I graduated from high school. He had built a single-family home in Catonsville, which was thought of as a more upscale town and neighborhood. Times with my mother had gone from bad to insane as her alcoholism took over. Spontaneous, rapid-fire, reason-free groundings and verbal attacks became the new normal from behind the door of her bedroom. I was a kid paying for most everything on his own and asking for nothing, and yet she still sought to keep me on a tight leash. My father knew my mother's condition was worsening and offered me the *opportunity* to live with him. I hadn't seen "new" in a long time, as we had really done a job on the townhouse, which was now badly in need of repair. Given that my father had his own brand of manipulation and abuse, I didn't immediately jump at the chance to move in with him. However, after careful thought and knowing that Mom's house was intolerable and a cesspool of dysfunction, I felt I had little choice. Living with my father would be a completely different set of fears and challenges, but, with a choice of two bad options, I chose what I hoped was the best of the two.

By this point, John and David had rejected my mother's manipulation and attempts to control them. They had flipped the script and were instead turning the guilt on her and massaging my mother for any resources she had left. Both were highly effective at this tactic. It was an ugly scene, as John and David were simultaneously struggling with their own substance abuse issues. David took things a step further by having his friends move into her basement full time without asking permission. He was young, but she was silent on the matter as he turned her home into party central. People came and went freely, and no one seemed to care how bad things were getting.

My mother was almost completely isolated and lost in her alcoholism at this point, spending almost no time outside her bedroom. However, when she saw me stuffing my last load of possessions into my '71 Volkswagen Beetle, she ventured downstairs. As I said goodbye and hugged her, I can still remember her sitting on a chair at the kitchen table, tearing up in a way I had never seen before. I told her I loved her, embraced her, and she gently but awkwardly hugged me back. Hugs were rare, and she felt fragile in my arms. We never said I love you in our family, but in that moment, it felt right.

Today, it's peculiar to write about the use of these endearing words because my family uses them frequently and sincerely. The few times I gave them a try with my mother back then, it was obviously uncomfortable for her. She would just stare at me and not respond, as if I was speaking in another language and the sounds were confusing her. However, on this occasion, she shocked me by repeating the words back. The surprise of me hearing the words coming out of her mouth at all, let alone directed toward me, must have been apparent. I can't remember if hearing those words made me feel better or worse as I turned the key and headed the couple miles to my father's place. But one thing I knew for sure: I would be homeless before I ever moved back into that asylum.

I had some optimism about the move, but the reigning emotion was anxiousness. My apprehension about the move was justified, as I realized almost immediately after moving in with him I had made a whopping mistake. I had traded the asylum to live in the lion's den.

The surroundings were more functional, clean, and new, but my father was still my father, and there was nothing that was going to change that. I quickly discovered that living with him came with a more sophisticated yet subtle level of abuse. What I had failed to calculate was that my moving into his house, like everything else he did for me in life, was considered by him to be a *huge, huge, huge* give on his part. In as positive a way as he could deliver the message, he let me know he had disturbed his whole life by allowing me to live there. It was important to him that I believe his motivations and great sacrifice were purely for my benefit alone. And with my acceptance of this premise, he believed he had license to do and say as he saw fit. As such, I received regular guilt trips about not being around enough and not servicing the home near to his expectations. When these issues weren't top of mind for him, he used his guarantee of an audience (because I now lived there and was trapped) as an opportunity to air a wide range of old grievances. As an adult, I was now being forced to find ways to make reparations for old infractions I didn't agree were real. Still stuck in old habits, I went along with this, believing his words that he held demigod status for allowing me to live in his walls.

Most comments from him during my short stay in his castle were intentionally designed to make sure I believed in his great sacrifice. I fully accepted that being under his roof was grounds for a life of servitude and a baked-in understanding that I would have to continue to not only accept his evolving methods of abuse and ridicule, but also must give myself to the idea that I was deserving of it all. Most interactions would be inclusive of some type of criticism and a highlight reel depicting just how little I had been doing for him historically and in real time. Every week, there was a list of chores that he himself had never done prior to my arrival. He was highly skeptical of my ability to be a functioning adult and son, but clearly the man believed my potential as a laborer. He was expecting payment in multiples for his overwhelming kindness, and there was no limit to how far he would take this expectation.

On a weekly basis, a typical chore list was to clean and wax his car, vacuum the home throughout, clean the bathrooms, scrub all floors, mow the lawn, and then complete whatever other side jobs he had. I know that a "good son" might have felt obliged to do these things, and maybe I should have had less issue with it. However, I was working full-time while also going to school full-time, so I had little time for being a houseboy. I made genuine best efforts but could not keep up with the work.

When not completing the tasks, or not completing them to his satisfaction, he continued with showers of guilt over my inadequacy, his primary tools for driving the performance of a lackluster son. This was a man who felt himself to be in a much higher class than me and considered me to be the lowest parasite feeding on his amassed riches. For these reasons, he thought I not only owed him, but *owed big*. The debt was so big it could never be paid off and just grew and grew like credit card debt. When his sharp condescending words rained down on me, it didn't matter to him if got upset or hurt. All that mattered was that he had done so much for me and that I had a debt to pay.

The barrages were consistent and potent, fueling my false belief that I was deserving of his behaviors.

Even knowing it was an impossible task, I worked hard and desperately wanted to satisfy him and gain his approval. In my twisted but hopeful young mind, I began to think that living with him presented a great opportunity. Being one on one with him in the home, with no outside interference or data points from my brothers and mother, I thought

I could prove to him that I was a much better person than he thought I was. Through my labors, I might just be able to pay off this massive relationship debt, and earn the "family" and unconditional parental love I longed for. As the fantasy continued, I had even grander thoughts that he might even find a way to like me. I knew I was a good friend and person to others, and that if he witnessed this first-hand, he might see the good in me. Being alone allowed me the chance to prove my merit and that I was so much more than he gave me credit for.

It didn't take long to realize that given all the pain and anguish I had caused him over so many years, there would never be a way to make right my wrongs. I could never come into full compliance with his desires as a house servant and punching bag and determined that my last shot at winning his favor was always destined to fail miserably. This seems sad, but, fortunately, the Universe would provide again, and I received another gift I didn't know was a gift at the time.

One night, when my father was declaring a list of inadequacies he had written down, particularly those around my failure to repair our relationship, I became distraught with sadness. Knowing I could never please this man, I broke down in tears. I had physically shown up as much as I possibly could, did my chores earnestly, and tried to show love and appreciation for him at every opportunity. It was a cool fall night, and I was crying hard as I asked what more I could do to prove how sorry I was for everything I had done to him. Knowing that I was a twenty-year-old adult at the time and how much I remained emotionally impacted and controlled, provides some context into just how bad I was in the head. Through my tears, but with sincerity, I let loose *the words* he never said with a small hope that I might finally convince him I really did care for him. For all the pain he caused, I still wanted his approval more than anything. They'd had a confusing but positive impact on my mother, so maybe if said with sincerity, they would work for my new warden.

This entire conversation took place with my father's face stuffed in the Baltimore Sun newspaper, while sitting on his rear porch in the early evening air. As we talked about our relationship, he nonchalantly continued to point out my imperfections and failings even while he read the front page. Without emotion, he dispersed his matter-of-fact sharp critiques of me and seemed surprised when I became upset. In a practical way, he explained that I needed to accept his words as absolute truth, and only from there could we begin to build. It was the same way that he used to tell me that if he couldn't beat me and call me filthy names, then he would kill me—a simple, unbendable truth to him.

The only time he shifted his attention from the newspaper during this berating and crushing conversation was when he heard *those words*—"I love you"—come out of my mouth. I may have written those words on a card when I was very young, but I had never said those words to him in person until that moment. When he heard the phrase, he intentionally folded down his newspaper and allowed his glasses to slide down his nose so we had unmistakable direct eye contact. This indicated to me that my words must have landed as I hoped, somewhere deep in his heart. I sat there in front of him snotting and crying all over myself, waiting in anticipation for an affirming response. I didn't expect the words to be returned, but I was hoping for some compassion.

I must have been a pathetic sight for him, as his satirical face displayed multiple reactions—curiosity, to sarcastic curiosity, to irritation, and then to cold, laughable disgust—all without saying a word. After a thorough head-to-toe condescending look, his reply came with a sarcastic chuckle, "You don't love me; you just want something. You should know the difference." He went on to say, "Maybe it's the fact I'm letting you live in this house, and you feel you have to say it…but probably it's because you want something else. You are just using me to get what you need." Then, with a smirk, he put his face back into the paper, wholesale dismissing me, the mess that stood before him.

I suppose his response shouldn't have surprised me given our history, but I was still shocked that he would be so heartless. Taking that risk and having it fielded in the worst possible way was soul crushing. There was no sweet talking my father, and, even though I was saying the words with complete sincerity, using a cliché phrase that meant nothing to him was no exception to ridicule. He took pride in saying exactly what he thought of everything, and it didn't matter if my feelings were crushed in the process. It was always more important to him to be right rather than to be compassionate and loving.

I cried even harder and more sadly as I loitered, hoping that after processing for a few more seconds, that he might offer up a more affectionate response. True to his normal, he looked up with the same sarcastic smirk, almost pleased with his dismantling of me, and then went back to reading the paper. As I walked away distraught and emotionally shattered, he didn't apologize at any point or ask to talk further. He just said, "Come on, Danny, you know it's true…stop living in a fantasy."

I went to bed early that night feeling very lonely, crying myself to sleep. The lion had been fed a full meal of the weakness it desired, and slept soundly that night. I knew then that no amount of effort was going to change his mind. The opportunity I had wished for would never happen, and I felt further away from him than when I had been living with my mother. I drank a large bottle of cheap red wine in my bedroom to numb my pain. As the alcohol took hold, all that I felt as I closed my eyes was empty, isolated, and trapped.

The gift from the experience would come in the morning as the sun rose. I woke exhausted from all of the crying and energy spent the night before. My eyes swollen, I processed the new information garnered in the interaction from the night before. My father and I were never close, so the feeling wasn't as if I had lost him—I had never had him to start. The greatest loss was that I took a shot at being vulnerable and it had failed spectacularly. Putting everything on the line, I took a chance and allowed myself to buy into the concepts of "love conquers all" and the power of "forgiveness," themes I had learned in movies. My failure had been absolute, but, as I further digested the previous evening's events, I felt a strong pivot was in order. Although I didn't think of it as a "gift" at the time, my father's blatantly direct response to my words had offered up needed clarity on two points. The first was that there was no hope of converting my "relationship" into a normal, loving father-son connection. This put a fine point on everything and told me any further emotional capital spent on him was wasted. As importantly, I knew it was time to leave his house. As has always been the case, my intuition (God at work in my wiring) told me what was real and to roll up my sleeves, get up, move forward, and get the fuck out.

It would have been easy to live bitter and resentful of how I grew up and stay stuck. I had seen that kind of pain live on in so many, tearing them apart from the inside out. I can't even fully explain my own drive to find a loving, rich, purposeful life beyond those tough years. My dad's harsh words were a valuable gift, but there had to be much at work than that. I am comfortable concluding the only thing that makes sense to me: That my higher power directly intervened to make sure my thick head would see how much good there can be in everything. I am happy that I processed my relationship with my father as exactly what it was—an unsalvageable energy sucking toxic relationship. It was painful to accept that I could not change my father's mind and still is at times, but immensely valuable that I saw it exactly for it was and not just another challenge level. His wholesale rejection of my love was what I needed. Thank you Dad. Thank you Universe. With less interference from this man, I could now focus fully on building a life for myself and working towards the vision I had experienced on my front lawn years earlier.

My time at Catonsville Community College (CCC) had proved that I could do well academically, something that going into it, I had legitimate worries about given my lackluster grades in high school. It wasn't that I was incapable, it was more that I was distracted with home life. Additionally, I didn't know how studying worked and didn't have a place to practice. I had been heavily involved in extracurricular activities at Lansdowne Senior but did very little to achieve my average grades. These activities were undertaken initially as approved reasons to escape my home and see my girlfriend. Later, I was fortunate that they also allowed me to have fun and make friends. Having spent most of my youth ducking bullies during the day and nights avoiding my parents, all while I tried to figure out where my next meal was coming from, the environment was not conducive to developing sound study habits and achieving academic excellence.

Both of my parents claimed they had done extremely well in high school and college while reminding me regularly that I was on my own after high school and that good grades were critical to the possibility of a better life. I understood and believed their warnings, but mostly I just heard that they were letting me know I was failing again in another aspect of my life and that, consistent with all of their messaging, they wouldn't be there to support me. They could not imagine what could cause me to do so poorly in school.

Sometime in the years just before high school graduation, my best friend and I changed our views on the importance of education. Knowing that we were going nowhere fast, we began to have many talks about the future and where we wanted to go in life. Up to that point, we hadn't done anything academically to support our lofty ambitions. We both realized we should have paid more attention in high school, and that if we wanted to leave Arbutus, it was time to get smart about our approach. With that, we each made a commitment to do our best at the community college.

By the time we stepped onto the CCC campus in the fall of 1985, we had repackaged our entire thinking, and, for the first time in my life, I was looking forward to focusing on my education and doing my very best with my classes. I was excited to learn, and excited to be excited about something so big in my life, which was a totally new view toward education.

Two years later, I would leave Catonsville with a 3.65 GPA. A community college was perfect for me—it was small enough that it was nonintimidating, but big enough to meet new people and see it as a place where I could start to become something. CCC had many names: Hopkins on the Hill, Cate State, UCLA (University of Catonsville, Left of Arbutus) to name a few. They were created to bring some levity to the supposed dregs of educational society that couldn't get into or afford better schools. I didn't mind the jokes because I was exactly where I was supposed to be. It may have felt like thirteenth and fourteenth grade, but for a boy that didn't even understand how to study and feared what the end results might reveal, I was in the clouds with optimism at my success. This was the big time for me.

Getting good grades at CCC was an important positive affirmation that told me I actually did have a brain that could focus and learn. I had significant undiagnosed attention deficit issues, but if I found a quiet spot to focus, I could achieve decent grades. Socially, I remained awkward, but I could tell that something was different. Unlike high school where ego plays a big role and popularity reigns, in junior college, it was clear I wasn't the only one whose priority was to work toward something better. These were people who either could not get into or could not pay for a large university, or who made the smart decision to save money on classes that would easily transfer and could be taken locally for much less cost. The students I associated with were like me, putting coursework first and fully committed to achieving their dreams. The academic environment at Catonsville Community College and community fed me and helped drive my ambition to do my best.

I had done well enough in community college to get a scholarship to cover two full years at the University of Baltimore. For a guy who had no money, a chance at free tuition at the University of Baltimore was enticing and ego feeding, since it was proof I had worked hard and that my results were good enough for a college to want me enough as a student to pay to have me attend! It is hard to explain the emotional impact that something as practical as a scholarship had on me. Of course, I was delighted to receive the gift, but more than that, it was another affirmation that showed me I had value and gave more proof of concept of my work ethic. That felt exceptionally rewarding and empowering.

I was not at a place where I could be selective with my higher education choices beyond community college, and this was the only opportunity at free money that had been offered to me. Either I was going to take this scholarship and go to school in Baltimore City, or I was going to go to the University of Maryland at College Park. The latter had accepted me but with no free money. Knowing that going to U of B meant staying and living with my father or living elsewhere and being stuck so geographically close to both parents and their emotional torture, I quickly chose U of M. Remembering the gift of clarity my father provided on his back deck also helped make that decision much easier.

Covering the entirety of my living and education expenses quickly signaled that a financial storm would remain indefinitely as part of my day to day struggle. Financial collapse was something I had already lived in fear of for some time, but I swallowed this additional level of financial anxiety because something was telling me that if I didn't go to Maryland and get out of his home right then, I might never leave. God again I think, was helping me along. If anyone was looking for proof of how bad things really were, they need to look no further than my decision to go to the University of Maryland. I chose to embrace a life of debt and financial struggle, rather than take the scholarship and stay in close proximity to them. With no job or savings, I began planning for my exit with cautious excitement.

With my expected departure, he exhibited no apparent sadness and there was no effort made to convince me to stay in a last ditch desperate effort to fix our relationship. He could easily determine on his own that my reason for leaving was our volatile relationship. After all, being penniless, why else would I forgo thousands in free money? And yet, even knowing I was leaving him, he still didn't care enough to build a bridge. Instead, his primary concern with my exit was the repayment of the large debt I owed in the form of reparations for my crimes. As I prepared to execute on my plan, he spent his energy making sure I knew the balance would forever remain open. He also made clear that he still expected regular visits to check his relationship reparations box while also insisting that I complete the long list of weekly chores that would remain posted. I should have been upset but given our history, his behavior was predictable. If I had any thoughts that leaving him forever might be the reason that he would work to improve our status, he succinctly let me know that this would never happen.

As the realization of achieving the dream of leaving home was unfolding, the gifts of decisiveness, direction, and hope began to feed the fire that was growing inside of me. While my self-esteem would need a lifetime to recover, scary but positive feelings of self-sufficiency and freedom grew stronger, and I began to allow myself to feel that there was more to me than my low self-image. I didn't know how to manage this positive energy that had come alive inside me. It was unfamiliar but I knew enough to know that what I was feeling was genuinely good and required more feeding.

Knowing there would be no easy way to leave his home without my father making a last concentrated effort to guilt trip me, I chose to avoid the interaction all together. I packed everything I owned into my 1971 VW bug, and, with two round trips, moved myself out while he was at work. It was the fall of 1987, and, taking one last glance, I said goodbye to his home forever. It is a door I have never regretted closing. The list of chores posted in the kitchen and the memories of all my stated shortcomings grew smaller in size and effect as the miles grew between the town I had called home my entire life and my new tiny "Knox Box" home I shared with three random upperclassmen in College Park.

It was my first real step out of the nest in a direction that would never lead me back to living at home. At twenty-two years old, I had a clearer understanding of what I had gone through as a child but didn't have a grasp of how that experience would impact my ability to operate freely in the real world. It's hard to describe my feelings upon landing in a small apartment with three engineering majors I didn't know. They were all seniors and on their way to important jobs waiting for them after graduation. I was a community college transfer student who was not quite a junior and, aside from a summer stint as a lacrosse coach at a Jewish summer camp, had never lived away from my parents.

When I first set foot on campus, I immediately sensed how big the world was, and this had the impact of making me feel even smaller than my ego already was and more vulnerable. But it wasn't all scary because I had a new start, and no one there had any idea of who I was or where I was from. Also, no one knew how "bad" of a person I was. It was an opportunity to build a life, and, despite my discomfort, I felt I was in the right place.

What I wasn't prepared for was how to find community when I was deeply lacking in social skills. I kept my focus on my studies and working, which were both good distractions. Since I was putting myself through school and the bills were piling up, education was priority, and getting through this would allow me to be away from Arbutus forever, and that was a powerful incentive.

I was able to get a small loan my first semester, which allowed me to breathe a bit as I set up a new life. Between my two jobs and slow tapping credit card debt, I was able to get by month to month. I never stopped being afraid of financial collapse, but I was seeing that I could make a life and bills were getting paid. I didn't exhale fully, but I allowed myself to be proud of my effort. This kept me working even harder but also put me under an immense amount of stress. Every atom in my body was committed to being successful. I would let nothing get in the way of me keeping my promise from my youth to make a better life for me and my future family. Independence, vision, willpower, raw drive...all gifts.

Of course, my father would remind me many times after my departure how badly I had hurt him with my sudden exit. It was another log on his giant eternal fire of pain. I heard him out, and with no solution to bring healing to his wounds, I threw his complaints on top of the long and dusty list of my crimes. Keeping my personal objectives front and center, while simultaneously learning how to ignore him and the other people I called family, I forged ahead. Even living away, he continued to work on my self-esteem by using our phone calls as a medium to air the usual list of grievances he had written down in advance of any possible contact. I knew I had been given great clarity, but I could not fully surrender the idea of a functional bridge someday being built between us. There was even a part of me that thought if I could land a college degree from a major university, then, for certain, I would finally earn his respect and love. That didn't work of course, supporting a lesson that I ironically learned in my college studies at the U of M—that creating impossible barriers for victims to overcome is the exact intent of the abusers.

From time to time, he would visit me, and despite working full time between my two jobs as a busboy and pari-mutuel (racetrack bet taker), he would be giddy with delight as he accepted my offer to pay for dinner at the local Sizzler steakhouse and buffet. I was proud to be able to do this, and. Despite adding the meal to my credit card debt load, I insisted on paying, wanting to steer clear of any additional debt being added to his tally. If I looked at it through the lens as the financial advisor I became years later, the interest he was charging was far greater than the twenty nine percent I was paying on my credit card. Still, it's hard to imagine what he was thinking by allowing me to pay.

By this point in my life, my mother was deeply depressed and drunk almost every time I saw her. She was immersed in her addiction and didn't care much if I came around.

While my father worked to entangle and control me from afar, the distance afforded me an opportunity to allow his grasp to loosen. In my coyness to step through my cell door to the daylight, I was experiencing true freedom, and in some ways it felt good. In other ways, it reminded me of the scary uncertain feeling that Morgan Freeman's character felt in the movie Shawshank Redemption as he finally leaves prison life. I wish I could say it was a *carpe diem* mindset and that I saw only beautiful upside to my new life. Instead, having spent years in fight-or-flight mode, I was suspicious and overly cautious. It would be a long time before I could dismantle the fear of my life unravelling and landing me in homelessness.

Along with fear of failure and the consequences that would come with that, I was processing how awful of a son I was thought to be, and searching for a remedy to be the good person I knew I could be. I was not healthy in my mind and didn't allow myself to believe I was a good man. I cannot blame this self-inflicted pain on my parents. After all, it is my responsibility to take ownership of my life, and blaming my struggles on them was and is an unproductive use of energy. However, while I had physically left them behind, years of abuse and the psychological manipulation had left an ugly stain that still had a strong impact on my life and my ability to assimilate into my new environment.

I didn't want to spend time with either of them, but I traveled back to see my parents primarily out of a self-administered combination of duty and guilt. The duty I felt was another example of the wiring I was built with. I think of the anger and frustration and the corresponding spike in heart rate and stress levels I felt every time I drove my car toward Baltimore. As I drove, my disposition was somewhere between distraught and psychotic. The turmoil that occupied a wide swath of my head space as I drove in the direction of Arbutus was being played out so actively in my mind, I often didn't realize the time had passed as I pulled up to the sidewalk to parallel park. On one hand, I could not get there slow enough. On the other hand, I couldn't wait to get there, fulfill my self-imposed obligation, and leave. I would become almost completely unhinged by the time I set foot on the steps going into their homes. In those moments, I was not only angry for what they had done to me, I was also angry because I was spending time and gas to go back to a place that represented the most painful years of my life to be with people that had hurt me so badly.

I could have done as many do: leave and never look back. Now I understand that my hope for family, ours and my own, was another gift. I was called by the Universe to be an agent of change for these people and in their own undeserving way, they still needed me. It may have seemed at first that God should have steered me out of that mess quickly and prevented me from wasting time and energy on these people, but there was much to learn still, and I think that is why I remained connected. Maybe the Universe's intention was for me to be there for them, but also to have the unsubtle, often disturbing reminders that it knew would be fuel to keep me on the right course.

I achieved my bachelor's degree in three years. I had hoped that one of the big consulting agencies would have interest in me after graduation. My grades were above average, but not anywhere near high enough to meet the minimum requirements of these coveted positions. It didn't stop me from trying, but I received nothing but rejection letters. As I wandered around the on-campus career center, it became obvious that my marketing and general business degree was fast tracking me to a sales position. However, there was a small glimmer of real hope for an esteemed position that turned out to be a disappointing tease.

After interviewing heavily, I was offered a position in bank management with a large regional bank based in Baltimore. I went through a rigorous multi-level interview process. There were many tests, people to meet, and scenario-based quizzes that were complex and difficult to game. I must have done well, because in my last interview, I was asked to come back and enjoy a lunch at their offices with some of the other leading candidates and a handful of executives from the bank. Our lunch was in a conference room high up in a Baltimore skyscraper. The walls were adorned with fancy wood trim and the food was outstanding for an Arbutus boy. The room had a bank of long, tall glass windows overlooking the harbor. It was the fanciest place I had ever been in.

Coming from a family of scarce resources, I had a habit of eating as much food as I could get in a sitting. They told me I could go back to the buffet as much as I wanted, which blew my mind. I took their encouragement to heart and unapologetically visited the food line several more times than any of my contemporaries. I never hesitated where free food was concerned. In hindsight, I must have looked a little silly and low class to my dining mates.

As I ate, I looked out over the city and harbor while enjoying a meal with these banking bigshots. I privately mused to myself, *This must be what "making it" means.* Clearly, only "successful" people would be able to get access to such luxury. I sat in my new Syms Store sixty-five-dollar suit purchased with my newly minted Syms credit card and feasted. I allowed myself to feel big-headed and prideful.

When the lunch was done, my hosts made the glorious announcement that the people at that table were the best of the best and would all be getting offers. This was immediately followed by more head swelling. I was so excited I thought I would burst. I couldn't wait to get to the parking garage so I could jump around like a maniac in early celebration.

True to their word, a week later I received an offer letter from the bank to join their executive bank management program. There was a salary, bonus potential, benefits, and upward opportunity. I was thrilled, as was my then-girlfriend, Ann-Marie, who would later become my wife. I was so excited to finally be able to get away from waiting tables and taking bets. I would now become a banker and make all of my dreams come true. The letter told me I would join the elite management class sixty days later. And there it was... All laid out in front of me—no more stinky restaurant clothes and late nights—my hard work had paid off and I would finally become something important—a banker!

With visions of my new career in mind, I came to realize I would need to purchase a vehicle for transportation. Up until that point, my Schwinn High Sierra mountain bike had become my primary source of transportation after I abandoned my broken down 1971 Beetle on the side of the road some months back. My bug had multiple issues, including no reverse gear, a spent clutch requiring me to park on hills so I could start the car by 'popping the clutch', and an oil leak so bad it required me to carry a case of oil in the back seat wherever I went. The leak was so bad that if I was planning to drive for a couple hours, I would have to feed it a half case of 10w30 or risk blowing the engine up. On the day that I turned the ignition key and the engine refused to catch while simultaneously filling the car with a thick, white smoke, I knew it was over. I was barely making enough to cover my living expenses, so there was no money or room on credit to pay for car repairs. And since asking my father for a loan was akin to volunteering for indentured servitude, I made the hard decision to remove the tags and all of my personal possessions and left the car on a street near College Park. I never saw the car again, and, fortunately, the police never tracked me down to cover the towing and impound costs.

After securing another credit card offered by the Schwinn dealership, I quickly grew accustomed to using a bicycle for any travels. My bike was dependable, didn't need gas or insurance, and I could handle all the maintenance myself, a skill I fondly called up from my youth. As a student with everything in close proximity and no great desire to go home, I now had a great excuse not to and no more expense of a car. Who would have thought that losing my car was such a major win? The Universe was once again guiding the way. But after being awarded the banker position, I knew I would need a vehicle to commute. I began to acquiesce to the idea that I deserved to have a nice car and something new. I was going to be making good money, so after sitting on the happy news of my new job for a week or so, Ann-Marie and I decided to go car shopping.

It didn't take me long to select what I wanted: a brand new four door Honda Accord. It was not too flashy, had a long reputation for being reliable, and would have enough room for the children we were talking about having. In the dealership, I picked out a new silver-gray model and ventured through the loan approval process. While I had low documented income because I worked for a restaurant and most of my income came in tips, they said my offer letter from the bank would be helpful. A day or two later, I was excited to get approved for my fancy new ride. My life seemed to be moving in the right direction. For a bit there, life seemed easy and fruitful, and I remember walking around virtually in a dream state. The struggle seemed to be coming to an end.

The day before I was supposed to pick up my new car, another letter came in the mail from my future new employer. The bank explained that due to some organizational changes, they had decided to cancel the executive bank management program. I called immediately to ask if this was more of a delay than an elimination of the program. Hearing that the program was being discontinued indefinitely, and that they had no plans to hire me in any capacity, I was crushed. Soon after, it was announced that the bank had been acquired, the likely reason the program was scratched.

Sadly, I contacted the dealership and let them know I was not going to be picking up my new ride. I have experienced plenty of disappointment in life, so I have a habit of never counting my blessings until those blessings are in my hands. But, admittedly, having to return suits and take a pass on the car I could no longer afford made it searingly difficult to get over the bad news quickly. Not being committed to these items financially yet was a gift. It would have been a nightmare to own a car I couldn't afford. The greatest gift of the whole experience was that a major bank had reviewed hundreds of resumes, interviewed dozens, and out of all those people, made the decision to choose me. Even though the program was scrapped and the prize unrealized, the gift of feeling that a group of people believed I was impressive enough to be hired to an elite program was a powerful positive affirmation.

Around the same time as the rejection, I had become very close to a fellow waiter at the Calvert House where I worked in College Park. Steve was an avid biker, and there was a lot I really enjoyed about our relationship. He was a rich and colorful character and was a sweet, generous man. Most importantly, Steve accepted me for who I was. This must have been challenging for him, given my insecurities and general inability to deal with social situations. At this stage in my life, I found that most people took me in small doses and found me to be just way too broken to have a long-term relationship with. As they say today, I was "extra." Looking back, I don't even know how Ann-Marie could deal with me. She had the patience of a saint.

As neither Steve nor I had a car, we ended up biking many miles together. He was lanky and over six feet tall, and I was shorter but solid muscle from the waist down. Despite that difference, we could pace well together on long rides. After a ride one day, Steve had the wild idea that we bicycle across the country, a trip that would take months and would mean quitting my jobs and leaving everything behind. Despite the risks, and that I would be coming back to no job or savings and lots of bills, I was immediately all in.

A short while later, I opened another credit card at the bike store so I could purchase a new Schwinn touring bicycle that was specially designed to carry heavy gear. We started biking more regularly in training for this trip, extending our distances so that long one-hundred-mile-plus days would not be a shock to our system. We both invested heavily in panniers and the necessary gear that would allow us to be self-sustainable on the road. For months, we built the hype with friends and family, as many wondered if we had lost our minds. While the risks were high for me, I felt exhilarated with the feeling of finally being able to see other parts of the country and to do something that would be a landmark achievement in my life. I had never gone on a spring break or any extended vacation. Everything had been about work and survival, and there was no option to miss work to do things like have fun and explore. I was suspicious of fun and adventure, but with this decision, that was no longer to be the case. This was going to radically change all of that. I don't know why my normal anxiety about failure did not take over as it always had. It seemed that the Universe wanted me to do this.

I may have been naïve, but I felt daily adrenaline rushes at every thought of seeing our great country and leaving behind the stress and constant grind. There was nothing in my life to compare to this bike trip, and I could not leave fast enough. I had gotten myself in the best shape of my young life and knew I was up for the challenge. With the exception of Ann-Marie, I was looking forward to leaving everything behind. I gave my notice at work and voiced hope that they would let me return to my waiter position after the trip. I was answered with well wishes and some healthy skepticism about what we were about to do. I heard quiet murmurs on and off that Steve would never leave College Park to do this. I didn't believe their words and didn't care what opinions they had; Steve and I had ridden thousands of miles together in training and matched up well. There would be no way he would back out, especially with all the investment in gear and the expensive plane ticket to fly out west. I didn't know how long I would feel this good, but the potential for pure, reckless freedom felt great, and I wasn't going to let anything, or anyone, take away from that.

Then, with no warning, Steve came to me a week before the trip and told me he no longer wanted to go. I don't remember exactly what his reasons were, but I remember being devastated. His delivery had a lot of words, but I would summarize them as he just didn't believe in himself. This was the guy who talked me into going and spending thousands on gear, training, and travel, all huge financial risks for me. This was shocking. I had experienced letdowns in my life, so I had been extra diligent about confirming his commitment from the start and intentionally checking in with him at many points along the way. On every occasion, he emphatically assured me he, too, was all in. I was in such disbelief that for a few minutes, I thought he was joking. It was such a one-hundred-and-eighty-degree turn, one that didn't sync up at all with everything I had been told.

I let him finish his explanations and after realizing there would be no changing his mind, I told him the only thing I could tell him: I was going to do it by myself. He was astonished at my response. Despite my training and our previous parallel confidences, he now seemed to be doubting my ability to complete the ride. Oddly, he proceeded to try to talk me out of it, explaining the dangers of travelling alone on a bicycle across the country. He wasn't wrong; it was the mid '90s, so there was no GPS, no cell phones, and no way to contact anyone if I were to get hurt or lost while biking in sometimes very remote areas. Still, none of his comments mattered to me. I had learned that I was built to do hard things alone, and this adventure, whether I liked it or not, now fell in that bucket. The big, beautiful difference between my tough history and the journey that lay ahead was I was intentionally choosing this extreme activity and going headfirst all in. There would be pain and suffering, but it would be *my choice*. This was exciting and a great example of one of the first times I ever leaned toward doing something just for me. I was unshakeable in my commitment. His words were disappointing and irritating but none of what I heard mattered. I quickly transitioned to the mindset that I was going on my own and nothing was going to stop me.

After Steve folded, previous supporters were falling like dominoes. I could see not many believed I could do it and doubted I would carry on with my plan. Even with all my training and only days earlier being all in himself, Steve, much too quickly, had an opinion that was starting to sound like my other co-workers. Now that it was just me, they were becoming more vocal about how foolish it was for me to even consider doing this on my own, especially without Steve. The previous quiet murmurs were now louder. Their words told me it wasn't just foolish but stupid and dangerous.

There was a lot of truth to what they were saying. After all, self-propelling myself alone over thousands of miles with over a hundred pounds of weight through steep mountain passes in barely inhabited areas was, in fact, quite dangerous. One bump from a logging truck while climbing the Cascades and I might not be found for years. That said, it seemed to me that Steve believed his decision to cancel would mean I would quickly follow his lead. I loved the man, but his misconception told me that he really didn't know me that well. I was pleased that I made the mental transition to my new circumstances so quickly and easily. I knew that what he really wanted to say—that I would fail—

was wrong, but there was no part of me that needed to prove anything to Steve or the others. I knocked out a couple more century runs on my own before my scheduled departure and knew I was ready. I spun up some Eagles on my Sony Walkman, and bore down on the pedals while dreaming of what the Rockies and the Great Plains would look like in person. Being alone was something I had lengthy experience and comfort with, and I knew I could depend on myself to achieve my goal.

Ann-Marie was my sole support. Only she and I believed I could do it. Using my credit card to buy my non-refundable, one-way plane ticket was my "don't look back" moment. After that purchase, I knew that, with or without Steve, I was going. I had weathered plenty on my own and worked harder in life than anyone I knew. By comparison, biking across the country should be a breeze, so much so that I thought of it as a vacation—all my missed spring breaks combined.

The night before my departure, I broke my bike down into a standard airline bicycle transport box. Later on that day, I packed my gear into Ann-Marie's car, and we shoved off for the airport. We shared a sad goodbye, and I boarded the plane for the second plane ride of my life. I was scared but excited as I waved to Ann-Marie through the little plane window. It was still a time that loved ones could come into the terminal to see you off from your jetway. I don't remember my exact thoughts as we pulled away from the airport and headed west. I was completely on my own, but because it was my choice and exactly what I wanted, I was secure in my decision.

After landing in Eugene, Oregon, I claimed my gear and carried everything to the street. My first error of the adventure had been exposed—that I would be legally able to bike on the roads leading out of the airport. I knew there were many roads that would not allow bikes but never gave much thought to exiting the airport. Fortunately, a woman I had sat next to on the plane noticed my predicament and offered me a ride away from the airport campus. Several miles away at a safe, biker-friendly location, she pulled over on the side of the road so I could unload my bicycle box and gear. As her old Toyota pick-up drove away, leaving me on the side of a well-travelled but legal for bikes logging road, I began to reassemble my bicycle and rack up my gear. With the sun setting quickly, I took my first pedal strokes in the great state of Oregon. I remember the smell of pine trees with every breath and beautiful scenery surrounding me. My soul was so excited I felt like I could burst; joy seemed to be radiating from me. The Cascade Mountains, the biggest mountains I had ever seen, rose up majestically in the distance. I knew my journey would place me at the base of those mountains in the next day or two, and I couldn't wait to take them on. I don't have the vocabulary (and this is one of the times I wish I did) to describe the feelings of happiness and freedom of being on the open road. Perhaps, the best way to write how I felt is simply to say I felt more alive and connected to everything than I had ever felt in my entire life. I allowed myself to enjoy all the sights and smells as I cruised comfortably by on my Schwinn Voyageur. I had no idea of where I would lay my head that night, but I smiled thinking of how it didn't matter to me.

All came together well. On my first leg, I bicycled about forty miles before night ate into my daylight. I had all the gear I needed to throw down camp anywhere but was not yet tracking on my Bikecentennial Maps (paper maps that showed exactly where bikers were allowed to travel, campgrounds, hotels, hospitals, bike shops, etc.). Bikecentennial was a company that plotted a series of recommended bike tours across the US. I had chosen their northern tour route. However, until I could cycle to a place where I could pick up my location on their maps, I was flying blind, patching together local road maps and asking about biker-safe routes from strangers as I pedaled along.

Knowing it was too dangerous to bicycle on logging roads at night, and that my stopping point was only about twenty miles before I could pick up on my map course, I chose a cheap motel to sleep on my first night. The cost of a hotel room was not in my thin budget, but it made sense to afford myself this "luxury" on night one. Having an actual bed, rather than throwing a tent up in complete darkness on the side of the road, felt right. The room was in need of serious refurbishment and appeared to be only partially cleaned. I could tell the bed had been well used after I laid my tired body on the springs, which sunk deeply in the middle. With a nice cross breeze and no air conditioning, I opened all the windows and took some time to inspect and check on my gear. Knowing I would push off early in the morning, I wanted no delays. It had been a day full of wonder and emotions, and my body was ready for rest. Feeling strong and confident, I quickly fell deeply asleep, as the bed seemed to wrap itself around me like a taco.

Sometime in the middle of the night, I was awoken by a scratching sound. When I looked up, there was a man staring at me through the screen of my open window, with his arms resting on my windowsill from the outside. He had the look of someone nonchalantly studying a zoo exhibit. I had no idea why he was there, but when he saw me wake up and we caught eyes, he walked casually away, seemingly unconcerned. After that, I was shaken up a bit and didn't sleep much for the remainder of the night. The man looked to be part of a motorcycle gang that had taken up residence hours after I had fallen asleep. I closed and locked the windows and slept only lightly for the rest of the evening.

With the exception of not having completed the trip, the entire adventure was a terrific experience. After climbing through multiple mountain ranges, various terrains, and cycling over two thousand miles, I dropped down off of the Rockies into Pueblo, Colorado.

At that point, I had no cash or credit left. With my cards maxed out and nutritional desperation setting in (you need a lot of calories to bike all day), I was pulling into towns and scoring meals by walking into fast-food restaurants and telling them I had just gone through their drive-through and items had been omitted from my order. This lying and stealing technique was a skill I had learned in my youth. It was wrong, but it really came in handy when I was hungry, and not once was I unsuccessful.

Eventually, I realized I would need more than hamburgers and fried chicken to get by if I was going to make it all the way home. I decided to bite down and take a five-hundred-dollar loan from my father. As always, taking anything from him came with a big price which would be paid when I returned, but I had no choice. He wired it to a Western Union promptly. His terms were that I pay interest and would spend time with him when I returned. I knew exactly what that meant, but with nowhere else to turn, I graciously took the funds. With the cash in my wallet and feeling a bit more secure, I headed from Pueblo east to the Kansas state line. Once I crossed the line, I sat down at a country market to enjoy a snack and a drink. It was a place that sold giant T-bone steaks with a giant plate of pasta for less than five dollars. I guess being in close proximity to so many cattle ranches made it possible to give such good prices. After I enjoyed the steak and pasta, I mounted and continued East.

Somewhere in the beauty of the Kansas great plains, I realized I had left my wallet and all of my remaining cash behind at the small country market. I pedaled furiously for hours to return to the store in hopes of finding my lost belongings. The cashier and food server remembered me but had not found my wallet. I couldn't have been more deflated. Knowing I had taken the loan from my father and now had lost it, and that another loan was out of the question, I had no choice but to turn my bike back toward Pueblo and call an end to the adventure. My father covered the hotel room for the night and the plane ticket to come home in a second loan, all of which I would eventually pay back on his terms. I was sad about the outcome, as I had every intention of biking all the way home and showing my doubters I could complete the virtually impossible. Instead, I went home having only gone about half the distance. Still, even coming up short, I believed I had done something truly great and that the experience had changed me in many positive ways. I was also happy about how little I cared about what people thought of my premature return.

Despite the trip being cut short, there were many highlights of the journey that made it worthwhile and life changing—real tried and true independence, beautiful wildlife, climbing and coming down the back side of the Cascades and the Rockies, camping in the woods of Oregon, bicycling in one-hundred-plus degree weather all day in Hells Canyon, Idaho, meeting a gay bean farmer who tried to seduce me, and feeling so alive and free that on most days I couldn't stop smiling. Most importantly, I had shown that I could thrive under extreme conditions out in the real world. I promised myself I would finish the trip one day, and, many years later, I did just that.

Upon returning home, with no money, bills stacking up, and no job, I found a job waiting tables in Alexandria, Virginia, at The Chart House. During the day, I took a job in Washington, DC, selling financial securities by phone in Georgetown near the canal. It was tough work cold calling strangers by phone, but I was good at it and was able to generate some income. A prior life of hearing and experiencing NO all the time had prepared me well for my new position. While others around me struggled under the weight of all day rejection, receiving a couple hundred failures every day in my new job did not dissuade me. I had success in winning new clients, but the money I made there was not enough to support me. As compensation was 100 percent commission, I had to keep waiting tables at night.

I also accepted an unpaid internship at The Wilderness Society in Washington, DC. This was a research position both for the non-profit and for me. I sought this out because some part of me wanted to go to law school and fight for environmental issues. Being in this great organization with so many environmentally focused lawyers seemed like the right place for me to learn what it was all about while doing some good for the world. The staff were incredibly unselfish and giving people. I learned much about the California Desert Tortoise and grazing issues and became a sort of expert on these topics. The position afforded me the opportunity to work with some top gun lawyers in the environmental lobbying space who were great resources for learning more about the career I was considering. The Society gave me plenty of positive affirmation that I was doing important work and doing it well, and seemed to appreciate my efforts. The appreciation later came in the form of a full-time job offer, which is something that doesn't come easily inside of a non-profit. However, when I realized how much law school would cost me and how little lawyers for good causes like protecting the environment get paid, I quickly realized this work was not for me. As much as the position might be personally rewarding, I could not follow a path leading me to a life of poverty. I had lived and was still living poor and did not aspire to continue in this way. Research completed, I knew I needed to pivot.

I left my securities job in Georgetown to join a much more reputable firm called Wheat First Butcher Singer. After several mergers, the company became First Union, then Wachovia, then Wells Fargo. The pressure of cold calling day in and day out was what I knowingly signed up for, but it was exhausting. I had no family or friends with money, so my only income came from complete strangers. I had done well for a cold calling Arbutus boy, and my clients appreciated my stock-picking skills and that they could count on me to make handsome returns. They also appreciated that I did not churn their accounts. As the position became financially unviable, my interest depleted, and I left shortly before the dot com stock market bust of 1999. This was good timing on my part.

Corporate foreign currency exchange became my next financial services job. I sought out this work because I wanted something that had a global scope. I had left Arbutus, seen a wide swath of the United States, and now wanted to know more about what lay across the oceans. I couldn't afford to travel there, but I thought I could learn a lot about these places by having a position with a global focus. My new salaried position allowed me to leave my waiter job forever. I have always held deep respect for my time as a waiter and those who make their living that way. Without that work, I would never have been able to afford college. Not only could I survive on tips, but the work paved the way for me to build a life. That said, it was nice not to have to work two jobs and smell like a restaurant every day.

Ann-Marie and I married in the mid-nineties and had three beautiful children, Connor, Kathryn, and Ryan. Ann-Marie was an elementary school teacher and great at her job. Along with my commercial currency trading job, I was beginning to do night work rehabbing residential properties with my best friend. It was a great way to get together, while catching up and chipping away at our American dream. They were long days, but we were able to score some nice checks, enough to get Ann-Marie out of teaching and allow her to be home with the kids. I was also able to pay down much of my debt.

Times with Mom and Dad were still tough during all of this. Dad continued to make me feel guilty about not solving for all of his grievances that he still held against me. Absurdly, he also added guilt about his minimal contact with my children. At one point, he had gotten to be too much, and to preserve my mental health, I opted not to talk with him for several years. I held guilt for all those years, but my family was too important to allow him to continue so directly and aggressively. I have no idea why a man who hated having his own children and was hardly involved with us would have such a strong desire to be close to my children, but I wasn't going to take the bait for many good reasons. It was the right decision, and admittedly, I enjoyed that time away from him.

My mother was degrading quickly. I had hoped that our beautiful babies would give her a reason to get sober, but as any addict will tell you, external factors are rarely the answer to finding long-term sobriety. She was an absentee grandparent and couldn't find a way to be an active part of their lives due to her inability to stay sober. While I understood that she was sick, it bothered me that she could not mentally and physically show up for her grandchildren. With her disease taking over, there would never be an opportunity for her to be close to them.

I never dealt with any of my early trauma directly with therapy or any other conventional treatment method. My coping mechanism was to work as hard as possible in my currency trading position and late night rehabs in an effort to guarantee the success and longevity of my family, all while trying to be the best father and husband I could be. Giving myself to my work was a great distraction from dealing with my past. Having "things" felt right, but seeing progress toward securing a future for my family felt much better. For that reason, keeping up with the physical possessions of my neighbors and peers never mattered much to me. The promise I'd made to myself many years earlier to break the cycle and be the father I didn't have was coming true.

Knowing I was heading in what I thought was the right direction, I tripled down on my work ethic. The unfortunate by-product of having such strong conviction about my direction was that I deeply suppressed everything that was inside. This avoidance manifested itself in the raw fear of everything unwinding and all five of us ending up in ruin. It wasn't just me anymore—there were four other people who depended on me. For that reason, I never even let myself get close to failure. I understood and recognized what failure looked like, and I made sure that everything I was doing was driving me and us forward. Ironically, the exact success I was driving toward would ultimately be the thing that unwound me.

I may have been a great provider with a deep love for my family, but I was an asshole to live with. Deep insecurities remained, and, at times, I sank into depression I could only address through isolation. Being alone was an old friend that provided fake comfort, but it kept me from drowning many times. Ann-Marie and the kids could not understand my behavior, but that time with myself was the only thing that could get me through the rough days.

Eventually, I couldn't get out of the hole I built for myself, and our marriage suffered badly. Like most supportive, collaborative spouses, Ann-Marie was not a person who appreciated being alone in a marriage. This must have been a form of torture for her because she was a social person and enjoyed making new friends and being out and doing things whenever possible. Even knowing I was coming up short on her hopes and dreams, she stood strongly by me as I tried to work through my issues in my completely dysfunctional way. While I continued to build the foundation for financial success and security for our family, and remained active with the kids, I failed our marriage and eventually we divorced.

I couldn't feel any worse for the pain I put her and the kids through. The only thing that got me out of bed in the morning in my new home, a one-bedroom apartment, was knowing that even with divorce, there were still four people who still depended on me to keep them safe and secure. Even not living with them, my obligation and commitment to their well-being remained. In walking out on Ann-Marie and the kids, I broke a lot of promises I never thought I'd break. However, making sure I was involved in my children's lives and being the best father and provider I could be (staying on mission), even divorced, were promises I have never broken.

There were a lot of lessons to be learned in all the time I was now spending alone. I know that had I dealt with my issues sooner, I would have probably been a better, more available husband, but I wasn't ready at that time. Instead, I chose to live in even more fear and isolation, building a moat around myself. On my island, I used the successes gained in my work setting as positive affirmation, fueling me to push myself even harder. It was a dangerous cycle that bred anxiety and loneliness, while leaving my mental health and happiness as a gaping, unattended blind spot. I could never let myself feel that I deserved to be better or happy, and had fear that addressing my demons would be a distraction that would take me off mission. It wouldn't be until after I was diagnosed with cancer that I would come to understand the high price I paid for suppressing the pain and suffering I had experienced. For all my newfound material success, I was a moron when it came to comprehending just how big of a role that unresolved trauma had on my life and how important it was to get right with myself, while learning and enjoying being present.

18

What Happened with Mom and Dad?

The Short Version

Mom picked up drinking more aggressively and became a recluse and later died alone in her bathroom. Dad continued his efforts throughout his life to saddle me with guilt while trying to manipulate me into accepting his narrative about how he viewed our relationship. He died of two slowly debilitating diseases, which he used as a platform to demand and want more from me. He never chose to make any significant effort to genuinely reconcile.

The Longer Version

In the late nineties, my mother's drinking and drugging became her full-time job. She could no longer go to work as a programmer for the state of Maryland, an agency where she had worked for decades. She had worked hard to make it to where she was and was well respected and much loved by her co-workers. Over several years, my mother became quite sickly and was living alone. John had moved out to live with his girlfriend and David had moved to California. Her care became my everyday worry. She was reclusive and refused to respond to messages and many times would not open her bedroom door after I'd been knocking for long periods of time. Despite literally carrying her into the emergency room to get sober, she never agreed to get any help. With all options for assistance off the table, it seemed clear she had a death wish.

Ironically, and thankfully, my father was involved in checking in on her. It was peculiar to me that he was checking in and communicating details of her status to me, but I was grateful because he saved me many trips. Living just a couple of miles away, it was easier for him but was not his obligation. I appreciated his efforts, especially given that I had two toddlers at home and a growing business that demanded much of my attention. I came many nights after work to make sure she was safe and alive. My usual process was to tuck her in and sleep on the couch until I knew she was sound asleep, and then drive home in the early morning hours.

I accept responsibility and am disappointed in myself for the coldness in how I handled things with her. I was angry and frustrated with her much of the time, and that was not helpful as her primary caregiver. This anger was likely harmful, but I had no idea at that time in my life how to be patient and compassionate toward her and wasn't yet mature enough to set aside negative feelings and be the unconditional support she desperately needed. I also didn't know how to accept that this was a mentally and physically sick woman who needed softness and understanding and who had long ago lost the ability to make good decisions for herself. I also had not yet forgiven her for all that she had done to me, so our history continued to simmer in the back of my mind.

Throughout my life, our connection was weak and distant, so trying to flip a switch to change that was impossible. I knew my brothers would be of no use in saving her, so it was on me, which, unsurprisingly, also contributed to my anger. My brothers thought nothing of taking whatever resources they could pry from her but, in her hour of need, had no time for her care. It was as if the well dried up and they moved to greener pastures. It was difficult to handle this alone, but I understand why they would be uninvolved. They may have lived with her, but as had always been the case, they were not close. They also likely had their own anger issues about how we had been raised. Along with that, both were wrestling with their own substance abuse issues. David was sometimes reliable, but he was focusing on being a drummer in a rock band and ignored my requests for assistance. I was on my own, feeling like I had just been pulled back into the world I'd worked so hard to escape from.

I was also resentful that I was finally carving out a life for myself and starting to notch some successes but now felt strongly compelled to come back to my hometown and reinsert myself into the drama and trauma.

As always, my personality would transform the minute I was heading in that direction. While my intention was to genuinely assist my mom, I was angry she consistently rejected the idea of getting help and annoyed because of the time I lost with my family. My regular check-in drives to Arbutus had become largely autonomous, with almost no thought going into the various turns that would land me at my destination. Not having to think about driving allowed me to focus my time out loud complaining about her and all the time I had to allocate to this mess. I had young babies at home and was working hard during the day, so giving my nights up to her wasn't something I received much satisfaction from. I was tortured knowing I was trying to do the right thing, while at the same time questioning the reasons I was involved at all. Meanwhile, my mental state was diminishing, and I was isolating at home; everyone was paying a price for my poor decisions.

Along with gratitude for his assistance, I also held anger that the man who had abandoned and manipulated her for most of her life was now involved in her care. I had worked to leave these people forever and now I was fully immersed back into the darkness and pain. I wish I would have known enough to be different toward her and am deeply regretful I did not handle this situation in a more loving, gentle way. I also wish I had practiced the power of forgiveness and compassion much earlier.

It never occurred to me to ignore her as my brothers had, but I am puzzled that I never even considered it. Why couldn't I just ignore the person who neglected and abused me? I think part of it was a last effort to win her favor, but now I know that the Universe demanded it. As maddening as it was to be her caregiver, I've learned that what God wants isn't always easy and comfortable. I was being tested once again and reminded that, no matter her sins, I must be there for this human only I could help. With so many good reasons to turn away from her, I can only believe the Universe wanted me to help this person who shared responsibility for the trauma I was still carrying around. This was another gift—the gift of values—knowing that we must protect and serve those who cannot do so for themselves. That said, I certainly didn't serve her with grace and true compassion.

There were times when I sensed she was dangerously close to death. Many times, she passed out in her bedroom behind a locked door and became unresponsive. With only a grunt or two from behind the door, I had no way to tell what her true condition was. For the times that she was alive but unable to effectively communicate in any way, I would have to kick in her bedroom door. One might think it gratifying to grant myself this much power when, as a child, we were never allowed to even enter her room. However, the truth is that as a grown adult, going into her room was frightening to me. It was like going behind the curtain of the great Oz.

Behind the door, I gained access to a scene of many empty bottles and terrible living conditions. Physically, she couldn't have been more gaunt, and, even though she was intoxicated and passed out, she was barely drawing breath. It is a testament to just how weak she was that she couldn't fight back. I gathered her frail, light body in my arms, placed her in my car, drove her to the hospital, and then carried her into the emergency room. While it was traumatic, the positive was that the event offered an opportunity for her to get sober, which meant another chance to potentially see that she had much to live for. Their process was to admit her to the hospital, then give her a space to provide intravenous care so they could speed hydration and nutrients to a body that was in desperate need of these things. After just a few hours, she began to sober up.

By this point in her addiction, she was never sober, so hearing clear words and even hearing her anger toward me for bringing her to the hospital was refreshing. Once her neurons started firing more actively and withdrawal started setting in, she wasn't pleased to be in the hospital, and immediately started thinking of ways to leave. The gifts of hearing a voice void of the effects of drugs and alcohol and the situation potentially providing another chance to take her life back gave me reason for optimism. In her irritated sobriety, as gently as I ever had, I spoke with her about the rehab facilities I had researched and reminded her as lovingly as I could that we all cared for her and wanted her to live a long time. With the DTs beginning to set it, I could see she was antsy to leave and go back to her cave. Increasingly irritated, she sarcastically acknowledged my pleas for her to get help, but my voice was a distant second to the loud convincing message of her disease. I hoped for the best, but no matter how I delivered my messages, even softly and sweetly, I could not get through to her.

She was at her absolute physical worst on our last visit to the hospital. I feared she would die if she didn't choose to get sober. After carrying her again into the emergency room, I checked her in at the front desk and was told we needed to wait in the normal waiting room. I excitedly explained that my mother was in terrible condition, with a low heart rate and shallow breaths, but this didn't seem to matter. Their best advice for faster care: "If this happens again and you are really concerned for her health, call 911, and have her come by ambulance." Minutes of waiting turned to several hours. My mother was becoming withdrawn and irate. Without the normal high levels of alcohol she physically relied on, her already deteriorated condition was sinking fast. I knew that if she did not receive addiction care soon, she would find a way to leave.

In a terrible turn of events, she suddenly fell out of her chair and began to convulse on the floor of the St. Agnes's emergency room. It was very scary, but I saw an opportunity to use this development as the reason they must have a doctor see her. I demanded the attention of the administrative staff while pointing to my mother. They seemed concerned and even a bit sympathetic, but incredulously, would still not admit her. There was a sea of patients waiting to be seen, some with serious injuries, and putting a drunk, even a convulsing one, in the front of the line still wasn't an option.

Anyone who has dealt with extreme addiction and the American hospital system knows that addicts and alcoholics are treated as the lowest-class citizens in hospitals. Between my mother and older brothers' addiction issues, I spent time in many hospitals, and the treatment was always relatively the same—cold, insensitive, and impersonal. When hospitals like St. Agnes see so many of these cases, even ones as bad as my mother's, admittance staff are naturally desensitized and sometimes dismissive. I understand why this is: Addiction is a national issue, and the hospitals and emergency rooms are overwhelmed with these hurting patients. They often see the same patients repeatedly and must deal with the frustration of knowing that other patients with different issues are having their care diluted and delayed because an addict must be seen.

Unfortunately for the waiting patients, my mother was my priority, and I could not allow her to lay on the floor while I casually waited for care. After several minutes of failed negotiations, I had no choice but to resort to threats. I pulled the legal card, explaining to the staff that if they did not admit my mother into the emergency ward now and something more serious happened to her, I would sue the hospital and staff. It was a bluff, but I must have been convincing, because, in less than ten minutes, she was gathered up and wheeled into one of the ER care units.

As had been the case before, after intravenous hydration and nutrient delivery, she became lucid again. It warmed my heart to see her communicating with me, albeit angrily. Knowing there would likely not be a next time, I pleaded for her to accept help and get into a program. She heard me out and seemed to indicate that this time she might consider it. "Considering" it was a giant move forward and a reason for measured optimism, but the word meant different things to each of us. I hid my feelings of excitement that she might finally get on the path to recovery, even knowing she was likely pacifying me. After refusing to leave right from the hospital to Sheppard Pratt, the recovery center, which I had been lobbying for, I took her home, but only after she agreed to talk further about the program. My thought was to give her a couple of days to process with hopes she might see it was her time to beat the disease.

Taking her home turned out to be a major mistake because, within less than twenty-four hours of returning, she used her newfound sobriety to order several cases of wine from the local liquor store and paid for them to deliver it to her front doorstep. I must give her credit for resourcefulness, because residential alcohol delivery was never done at that time. She was back to full-time drinking, and any thought of getting help was not only quickly forgotten but no longer allowable subject matter. This was overwhelmingly sad for me; she was at the end of the road, and there was nothing but darkness ahead.

Every recovering alcoholic I have met has communicated how important it is to get a person into a rehabilitation facility the moment the patient indicates they are ready. As had happened with Mom, most will change their mind if put back into their familiar surroundings, a lesson I learned the hard way. Hindsight is 20/20, and, as they predicted, she once again disappeared behind her door, and I was back to square one. All the effort and hope were lost, and I was back to being angry, sad, and now frightened. Death was not something I knew how to process, and it seemed more likely all the time.

The experience had taken a lot out of me, and my energy levels were running so low that I could feel myself sinking deeply into depression. I returned to being angry about investing so much time in someone who had invested so little time in me. Not only was I suffering with this process, but so were Ann-Marie and the kids. I should have thought less of myself and more of them. Things were getting worse all around; with me, with my family, and with my mother. I was spinning out of control.

On August 4, 2000, a Friday, I headed to Arbutus to check in on Mom. She had gone quiet again, having not returned my calls for over a day. This was usually my trigger to get to Baltimore to check on her. When I arrived, I was pleasantly surprised that she was downstairs sitting on the couch, watching television. I was always grateful and relieved for the times I didn't have to communicate through her door; it was such a humiliating, juvenile thing to do. While it was a positive that she was awake and not locked away, she was in bad physical shape. She had no appetite and looked weak and malnourished. She would not let me provide food, and forcing it on her was pointless. While these episodes were often frustrating and hard to witness, on this night she had a good attitude and was willing to talk more than usual. It was a fleeting sense of stability as her overall health was obviously on the decline. But it was nice to have a conversation about nothing important and not be in crisis mode.

After a rare bit of catching up on my children and the progress of Ann-Marie's pregnancy with Ryan, we decided to watch a movie. We never spent time together as a family hanging out, not even to watch a movie, so this was unusual but nice. It was sad that most of my time with her was focused on her care and attempting to convince her to get help. I know now that fixing an addict and pressuring them is about as wrong a thing as you can do when trying to offer support. In all my efforts to "help," I likely only did more damage. My negative disposition and outward-facing disappointment in her was likely only giving her more reason to drink and use drugs. Given our history and where I was in my head at the time, I doubt there was much I would have done differently. I simply didn't have the patience, capacity or education back then to offer loving and effective support. Hell, I didn't even know how to take care of myself as I sat drowning in my own issues. Knowing how far she had taken herself in her life against all odds, her refusal to try any form of help continued to feed my resentment and anger. She had given up on life, but there was no way I could give up on her. I wanted her to get better, but I also wanted to be with my family and execute on all the things I had planned for us. This idea of putting all this effort forward and trying to do all the right things, while hating it at the same time and achieving no progress, is a hard phenomenon to understand unless you have lived it. That said, on this evening, things seemed relatively calm, so I allowed myself an opportunity to exhale and cautiously appreciate our time together.

We decided to watch *Six Days, Seven Nights*, a movie with Harrison Ford and Anne Heche. It is not a great film, but we found some humor in the goofy story line and spent the time poking fun at it and sharing a few laughs. It was a gift to be able to giggle with her. For a couple hours, I felt like my mother was my friend. Her willingness to make small talk, crack jokes at a bad movie, and share a laugh were perfectly timed, highly unusual gifts from the Universe.

After the movie and the laughs were over, I checked again to see if she would allow me to get us dinner or if she needed anything else. She turned down my offer, and I began to gather myself for the ride home. With no crisis in front of me and a bit of a light feeling in my soul, I envisioned getting home early to Ann-Marie and the kids. In a slew of bad days, this one was turning out to be pretty good. My mom got up to say goodbye to me, and we hugged. With so little fat remaining on her body, my embrace felt as if I could snap her in two. We shared a gaze for a moment. I knew she was not well, but she seemed stable and was smiling. I kissed her and exited through our rear sliding glass doors to the single parking pad. We even exchanged the words, 'I love you.', a positive gesture that was relatively new to our relationship.

As I was just about to get in the car, I looked back at my mother waving to me through the open curtains of our rear glass slider. She looked happy, but then, with our eyes still locked, she suddenly fell backwards into the house. Her fall was not a careful descent to the floor. Rather, as I watched, the fall looked more like how a trusting parishioner falls when being healed by their pastor on the television—full weight with no attempt to protect herself from a certain hard landing. I immediately ran back into the house and found her lying on the floor conscious but slightly disoriented. I helped her to her feet and noticed she had a large gash on the back of her head. Surprisingly, there was very little blood for the size of the wound. When she had fallen, her head had made contact with a hexagon-shaped wooden end table. However, she did not want to go to the hospital and could not explain to me why she had fallen. I retrieved some first aid supplies and cleaned and covered the wound. Despite my family being excited for me to get home earlier than usual, I insisted I would stay overnight and began the process to help her get back up to her bedroom so she could lay down. I know now that someone with a probable concussion shouldn't have been put to sleep—another regret. She was weak, and I stayed closely behind her to eliminate any risk of her falling backward down the stairs. I told her I would stay for a while on the couch as I had done many times before. She insisted that she was fine as I equally insisted that I would not leave.

After returning her to her fiefdom, I listened to her shuffle around in her room from outside the door. The noises continued as I lay on the couch that was just beneath her room. I was confident she was actively in the process of getting her drunk on, but at least she was active and awake. Except for her odd fall by the door, all seemed relatively normal. I watched TV and it seemed that she had settled in to sleep. I was itching to go home and see my family. Our plans for the day had already been ruined and it was now late, but, if I went home, I could wake up in my own bed and see my family in the morning. With Mom asleep and seemingly stable, I decided it was time for me to leave. I journeyed up the stairs, knocked lightly, and told her I was leaving for the night. I got an immediate response with a boozy approval. With that, I gathered myself and headed out on the empty early morning roads toward our townhome in Crofton. Leaving was a mistake I regret heavily to this day.

Sometime in the early morning hours of August 5, 2000, I received a call from my father. His calling me in the early hours of the weekend was highly irregular, so I knew as soon as I heard his voice that something was wrong. His words were few: "You need to get here quickly." I pressed for more information. He essentially repeated the same words and hung up. My heart dropped, and I had trouble catching my breaths.

I kissed the kids and Ann-Marie goodbye and knew that whatever plans we had that day, I would not be a part of them. The roads were clear as I sped in the fast lane from 3 to 97 to 695 to Sulphur Spring Road to her home on Selford Road. My head was full of sad, terrible thoughts as I projected the worst onto the unknown. I knew she must be hurt and fought off the thought that she may have died. Hurt or dead, I was pounding on the steering wheel, already regretting that I had left her that night. My driving was erratic and reckless as I flashed high beams at anyone in my way. I was praying to a god I didn't believe in (at the time) that I would get there in time to help and protect her.

When I arrived at her home in Arbutus, there were several police cars out front of the little rowhome I had grown up in. I parked my Isuzu Trooper and sprinted from the sidewalk, up the two flights of stairs to a door guarded by a policeman. I told him who I was, but he wouldn't let me in the house. I insisted, but the officer physically restrained me from making it through the front door. After a few minutes, I was allowed into the kitchen area only. I don't remember who told me the terrible news that Saturday morning. It could have been anyone, but I think it may have been my father.

Even today, it is a traumatic thing for me to revisit the forty-eight hours around when she passed. My father had gone to check on her and could not get her to answer through her bedroom door or make any sounds that would indicate she was alive. He kicked her bedroom door in, and, when he moved into the bathroom, he found her lying there, soaking in a puddle of congealing blood. Apparently, he felt a weak pulse when he arrived, and then called 911. However, by the time the emergency services arrived, they could no longer find a pulse, and she was pronounced dead at the scene.

By the time I arrived, the police suspected that the cause of death may have been a homicide. This was understandably due to all the bleeding and the large wound on the back of her head where she had fallen. Also, whatever caused the wound was not something that could be connected to anything found in the bathroom, increasing the suspicion that a crime had been committed. I can't remember if I actually saw my mother lying in her own blood, or if I stitched together the details I learned after the fact to contrive the image of her lying dead on the floor of her tiny bathroom. Perhaps I don't want to remember seeing her in that condition. Given the detail that stays in my mind—her lying on the floor, back facing the tub, her head near the toilet, and the blood on the floor thick with dark reddish-colored syrup—I know I must have at least gotten a glance. It broke my heart then and now to think this is the place where she took her last breath.

While the police let me in the house for a short while, I was soon asked to wait outside but to stay close. I sat on the hill down by the sidewalk. Alone, I sat there and cried to myself. Sharon, my father's wife, moved toward me and tried to offer some kind words as I sat there. I didn't know her very well, and, since I had a volatile relationship with my father, my contact and interest in her was minimal and always guarded. I was aware enough to know that she was saying nice things to me, but I could focus on nothing else but the sadness and regret playing in my mind. I could not acknowledge or process the sounds leaving her mouth. My mind only desired to process how I had failed my mother in her greatest moment of need.

It would take many years and my father dying before I could find out just how sweet and kind Sharon is. Since his passing, we have loved having her in our lives. She is a loving, unselfish, and sweet human my father was lucky enough to call his wife.

Sometime after I had sat a long while on the front hillside of our yard contemplating all that had gone wrong, the medical examiner must have made the decision to remove her body from the home. Riding on a gurney in a black zipped-up bag, they wheeled her right past me, crossing Selford Road to their van parked on the opposite curb. Either not recognizing that I was family or not caring, the two workers responsible for the gurney and my mother's body decided to take a smoke break before putting her in the black vehicle. Perhaps God had a good reason for making me sit there in open daylight with a clear sight line to her bagged corpse for the five minutes that followed. Flicking their cigarette butts to the street, she was pushed into the van and the doors closed. The workers made no eye contact as they started the vehicle and drove her away. I watched the van for as long as I could see it. Eerily, it reminded me of when animal control services came to take my dead dog years earlier. Like these two guys, I could see that it was just a job, nothing more.

Once her body had cleared the house, the police asked me to come to the police station with them. As the last person who had seen her alive, they had questions for me. They drove me uncuffed in the back of the car to the station house off Wilkens Avenue. My father and Sharon followed close behind. My brain was so twisted and unhinged that I could not fully process that I was being driven to a police station to be questioned as a potential murder suspect.

I was led to the basement of the station house, where they sat me down and had me walk them through the events of the previous night. I gave them the play by play, including the awful dead weight fall that had happened to her. Once they felt comfortable I was telling the truth, my father drove me back to my car, and I quickly headed back to Crofton. I cried hard on that drive. I didn't have a functional relationship with my parents, but I had some self-pride that no matter what they had done, I would still be there for them. Until the very end, I had hopes they would think of me as a good son. For the many visits and encouragement to help get her clean, I had failed spectacularly. It's incredibly hard to think of how helpless and alone she must have felt as she drew her last breaths, knowing that no one would come to save her. All those nights, and the one that I chose to leave was the one that mattered most.

Ultimately, the medical examiner determined she had died because of a hemorrhaging blood vessel in her neck, and that her death had nothing to do with her fall. The specific cause of death was from esophageal varices, a common occurrence with alcoholics where a blood vessel bursts in the neck and the person bleeds out. Had I been there, the internet says there is a good chance medical help could have saved her. I try not to spend much time thinking about that, but I wish it had told me something different—like that death was instant and unavoidable. I know I should not blame myself for something that was likely to have happened anyhow given her terrible condition and unwillingness to get help. This point is accurate and not lost on me. While I don't blame myself for any part of her sickness and understand that healing starts with a person's own desire to get sober, I am upset that it happened on my watch. If I had been there and she'd landed in the hospital instead of a body bag, maybe this major medical issue would have been the singular event pointing her toward sobriety. The "what ifs" have played out in my mind for the many years following her death.

I considered formal therapy to help me come to terms with this experience and others. I believe that therapy is useful in many aspects of life, and that most could benefit from the help of a good therapist. However, I have learned that some things cannot be therapied away, and that I must accept that painful events, like my mother's passing, will always be a part of my makeup. Her death doesn't haunt me any longer. I know there were many factors in play over a long period of time, and none of her disease progression was my fault. By accepting the circumstances of her death, just as I accept the circumstances of my upbringing, I see the experiences as part of my makeup, but not as defining me. There are things I cannot change, and, rather than let them fester, I choose to learn from the experiences and use them to be a better husband, father, and human. It has been difficult to write about her death, but, as mentioned previously, doing so is a powerful form of therapy in itself.

My father passed away in 2012. He had been sick with two different diseases. One was a disease that had a painful effect on any cartilage found in his body. The other was a type of blood disease. It was frustrating for him because medicines that seemed to help one sickness would have the effect of worsening the other. This condition lasted for many years. He was in and out of hospitals and eventually died at home in hospice care.

As with my mother, I spent many hours commuting and spending time with him in the hospital or being guilted into sick visits at his home. As with my mother's care, I was bitter about giving him attention and thought of that time as being stolen from my own loving family and a thriving business. However, unlike my mother, I did not dive deep into his care or do any work to try to help him find a path towards his healing and had no desire to do so. I offered his wife Sharon assistance, but admittedly was happy she never took me up on it. I was the helpful son, but the reality was that I abhorred every minute I spent with him, and didn't do a great job hiding it. Fortunately, Sharon was an ace at managing his care, and her willingness to do so allowed me to exist on the periphery.

Perhaps I should have put myself all-in with my father's care, while forgetting all he had done and continued to do. Fortunately, the Universe did not call for me to do this. Unlike my mother, I did not feel compelled to help him and did not feel guilty about keeping my distance from him. I needed to apply the lessons from my experience with my mother, and one of those was that my mental health was important. I was kinder to him than I had been to my mother but kept a healthy distance as he headed to the finish line. Keeping that distance was necessary so I could minimize harm to myself and the people that loved me the most.

In my visits, I would often witness him yelling demands at Sharon and giving her condescending gestures. Even though I didn't know her well at the time, I knew enough to know she was working around the clock to care for him and was doing so in a sweet and gentle manner. No matter his condition, she was not deserving of this type of abuse. His cruel behavior toward her while she was waiting on him hand and foot says a lot about the man. He would sometimes pull back his insults with self-serving rationale, a behavior I had seen many times from him. His explanations for his actions had the familiar feeling of the manipulation he had been so effective at in my childhood. It made me grateful I was not his primary caregiver and sad she would take that kind of verbal abuse from him. In all that time, I never once saw her retaliate with anything other than patience, kindness, and love. How he landed her and why she stayed with him are both mysteries to me. She was his greatest gift. The gift to me was that she was taking blows that would've likely been mine had she not been in his life.

As with my mother, I wish circumstances would have allowed for me to be a bigger man about things when he was sick. I could have done a better job setting aside negative emotions so I could show love and compassion toward him. But that is easy to write when so many years have passed. However, unlike my mother, my regrets are limited. I did my best to be there as much as I could when he was sick, all while trying to keep a boundary that would prevent me from being pulled far into his world. I was still navigating the landmines of our history, and his behaviors in sickness were not much different than how he had always been. There was a benefit of the many years of abuse and neglect I received from him: That the negative history made it easier to keep a healthy distance and not engorge myself with guilt while watching his health deteriorate.

As his health descended to a place where I could see he was not going to live to be an old man, I was hopeful this degradation might be the catalyst for him to fight for a real relationship with the only son who ever cared enough to remain in his life. I fancied the thought that the unconditional love, respect, and acceptance I had hoped for my entire life from him might somehow be born out of this situation. I hoped my experience might be like what I saw in the movies, where a person close to death comes to terms with their mortality and the wrongs committed, and works with great purpose to right the wrongs.

Fortunately, I didn't invest too much hoping for a bright and sunny reconciliation because not only did he do nothing to improve our relationship, but he also chose to use the experience as license to further his "bad son" agenda. I was used to it and by then had largely forgiven him, making it easier to ignore his attacks. It seemed he would never change. Here I was thinking that he might finally see my worth and the evil of his ways. But instead, his expectation was clearly for *me* to work harder and right all the wrong *I had done* to him, rather than the other way around. Unfortunately for me, his narcissism didn't abate even under the worst conditions.

Luckily, I had good friends and a loving family and positive life experience in my own environment, so while sad, his behaviors had much less of an impact on me. Having my own children and knowing how hard I was working to be a good provider and father reinforced my belief that I could make lasting generational change. I was realizing my vision in real time, which was a powerful neutralizer of his last minute attempts to control me. My path in life as an adult made me see even more clearly how poorly he had handled his responsibilities and how acidic our interactions were. Still, it was challenging at times to field his complaints, especially when my great hope was for *him* to do the work. It was clear that even in bad health, atoning was not on the agenda. Having abused me as he did and then seeking apologies and reparative actions from me rather than sincerely making amends to me is the best example of gaslighting that I can think of.

Looking through the cancer lens I live in now, I am, thankfully, the guy facing death who wants to right as many wrongs as possible and lean toward being a better human in all my roles. Fortunately, I don't do this to be an offset to my father or as any type of reaction to anything he and I experienced. Rather, my desire to be my best form of humanness to the people I love comes naturally. I didn't need training or a revelation; direction came through instinct, through God. It is the same instinct that was gifted to me at birth. I knew I needed to retool, reorient, and choose to look at my life with a fresh perspective. I smile as I write this and know that what I dreamed about on my front lawn as I waited for mother to come home from work so many years ago was never lost in the shuffle of life. It was a gift to have that insight back then. And it is a gift to fully feel these moments, acknowledge that I have not been perfect, and accept happily still that I will never be like him. Clarity on all levels—as a son, a father and as a human—is a wonderful gift. By far, writing about this gift of understanding in relation to my father is one of the most important discoveries rewarded by writing this book. I think of it as a big part of the therapy I needed.

In a general, broad-stroke, "let's get this out of the way" kind of delivery, my father apologized to me several times for the things he did. He was never specific about what the apology was for, yet I accept that at least a shred of his apology was a legit and difficult effort for him, as would be the case for any textbook narcissist. He made certain not to go too far with his words. How the words landed gave me a sense that there was a "checking the box" mentality behind his actions, and that there was an ulterior motive.

While so unusual I would be moved to tears, I know his words were tactically delivered to solicit an apology from me. In some cases, he would literally ask me for apologies as soon as his own had left his mouth, so I didn't need to be a detective to understand he was giving something in hopes of a much bigger get. Having apologized, he also accompanied each attempt with strong verbiage that having delivered his apology, I was restricted from bringing up any of his crimes again or seeking a better understanding of what he had done and why. In short, the expectation was that, given the gift of his words, I must believe his effort was so grand that I must accept them and be happy with the expectation of no further discussion of his abusive history.

I believe he did have some level of regret for his actions and that his apology attempts were likely breakthroughs in his mind. As desperately as I wanted to hear them and to have a deeper relationship with him, there was never a time that an apology came without caveats. Every apology was either immediately or shortly after followed by something like, *"...But you knoooowwwww??...you did lots of bad things too, right? So maybe I could have been less hard on you, but it was deserved because of all of the things you did. Right? (don't you agree?)"* With these types of follow-up comments, there was always a pause as he waited for a bookended outsized apology that would also serve as the confirmation that he had been correct about everything all along.

Sometimes, I would concede and give him what he wanted, but it made my stomach sick when I did. On hearing my apology, he would get giddy and press further. He would go so far as to ask what I was apologizing for and then coach me on the areas where I should spend more time understanding what I had done wrong to him. If my repackaged explanation didn't satisfy his needs, he would strongly recommend that I go away, think on it more, and come back later so I could perform a higher quality more detailed apology. However, this was not a two way street. As a rule, I had to accept that his opaque general apologies were an offering of the highest value that I was lucky to have. He must have known at some level that his "apology" was a strategic tool—a Trojan Horse. Even in its general form, if the bait landed in the right space in my heart at the right time, he knew I would be seriously vulnerable to his influence and manipulation. That vulnerability could then be used to get what he really wanted from me—a from-my-soul head bowing detail packed apology that he could then catalog and reference in future conversations about my sins.

Of course, this dance of words and psychological abuse never led to any meaningful relational healing. I wish that I hadn't fallen for his traps because they brought so much tortuous anguish to me that I would be depressed for days. I felt both like a fool and a failure. I was a successful businessman and building a great life, but I remained so desperate for something real in our relationship that even as an adult, I would let my guard down for the opportunity to fix things. Eventually, I stopped biting but he never stopped trying. I was experiencing positive relationships in my life and real love, and because of how genuine and uplifting this was, I saw more clearly that his behaviors were truly dangerous to my well-being. In response to that, I built a deeper and wider moat and saw him as the sick man he was.

We made some minimal progress in the last several years of his life that was mostly the fruits of me forgiving him and the confidence of knowing he could do no more real harm to me. Keeping our engagements to a minimum, I could remain stable and avoid taking the bait of continued irritating and hurtful actions. Also, carefully choosing the circumstances for sharing space with him and limiting one-on-one time, virtually ended his opportunities to attack. This helped me build and present a more positive disposition overall, and greased the tracks for less-strained, albeit superficial interactions.

I would never have a real father-son relationship with him. At times, we were quite friendly, and, at those times, I enjoyed his sarcastic, wry sense of humor. We even went to a pool hall one time to hang out, something we had never done. We shot a couple games and enjoyed a couple beers, and like the movie watching moment with my mother, those couple hours seemed normal. It was one of the only times in my adult life that we had a father-son interaction where I wasn't under complete duress; however, I was always on guard. It was a good memory, but there were too few of these to make any difference.

I always knew a huge weight would be lifted off me when he died. It didn't feel good to feel this way, but most of our interactions brought pain and being in his presence usually made me anxious, angry, and generally neurotic. For days after visiting him, I was destabilized and would struggle to get back to level. Ann-Marie and my children suffered because of him as well because they had to deal with the fallout after I emotionally shut down from visits. I was sad when he passed but knew my self-flagellation was ending, as I seemed to quickly accept that I couldn't argue with a dead person. I was sad for him, as I would be for any human who had to endure such a slow, debilitating health decline. I was also sad when it became obvious there would be no path leading to the functional relationship I had hoped for. However, as the days and months passed after his death, I felt lighter, and, psychologically speaking, was truly much better off.

My father and mother were both dealt terrible cards coming into this world. We all handle what we are given in different ways. There could be a case made that with all they were exposed to in their youth, it was impossible for them to offer their offspring a more stable childhood. Taking it further, one might argue that the environment and parent package offered up to us was so immeasurably better than their own, that I should be grateful that we got it so good. Even today, I struggle at times with what my own expectations were for my parents. I ask myself, *Daniel, knowing that these two people grew up in terrible circumstances and that you received much better than what was dealt to them, how can you then think you were due better than was given?*

The answer doesn't come easily and creates a conundrum in my mind that I'm sure many with similar backgrounds have considered. Does the fact that things worked out very well for me mean that whatever experiences I had in my life, positive or negative, were delivered as a bundled package and have led me here to this fantastic place? This would mean that my parents' controversial contributions were as important as any other experiences I had in my life, and, as such, deserve some credit for my success. Believing this means that their parent package including the abuse were an integral part of making my life the great life it is today. Further, maybe they deserve credit for my use of the pain and suffering that came with their treatment as high octane motivation for achieving success in my life. Or is it more accurate for me to believe that God/the Universe worked around the issues of my home life, diligently showing me a path through the difficulties, giving me many gifts along the way, and that this direct involvement is the primary fuel for all my success? Or, lastly, is it the case that the summation of all of my experiences, luck, hard work, and determination were the combined drivers deserving of the bulk of the credit? I believe that what makes the most sense is that all of these options played a part in finding my path.

As I study my situation, I am left feeling the confusion that comes with being subjected to lengthy abuse. I wonder if my willingness to bring an abusive history into the forefront of this discussion as rationale for success is itself a manipulation from the grave. I suppose that any trauma experienced by any soul has the potential to have a positive influence on a life. For example, a person investing with Bernie Madoff loses all of his money but then becomes much more astute in his investing, leading to many years of secure and successful investing—a great outcome to a bad event. In a more complex example, I went through hell to arrive where I am today. I write a book about it and make a few dollars selling it. I then take that money and give it to organizations that help at-risk children, allowing some to benefit from my experience while potentially changing the course of their lives...a wonderful outcome that started from a horrible place. Does that mean I should give more credit to my abusers?

It appears that the question answers itself: Just because Bernie Madoff stole your money doesn't mean you are lovingly going to give credit to him for making you more wise about your future investment decisions. Most victims would have a visceral response to such a conclusion. As it sits now, in my lite approach to this hairy topic, I arrive at and accept that how events are digested and broadcast over the balance of our lives comes down to a personalized decision by each victim. In my case, despite the programming from my parents, which still has the lasting effect of pushing me toward guilt for writing negative words about them, I will give them credit for being the parties responsible for giving me life. However, I will not actively credit these people with any success *or failure* I have experienced in my life. Admittedly, this conclusion doesn't feel completely comfortable in my mind and I suspect will evolve over time.

It is dangerous to give evil deeds as much consideration as I have, because, in doing so, I put myself at risk for allowing manipulation from the grave and opening old wounds unnecessarily. However, the conclusion above keeps me above the fog and allows me to focus on what's of greatest importance; I must keep my childhood vision as a guiding tenet so that I do not carry the negative of my experiences into the next generation.

Beautiful reconciliations rarely happen as portrayed in the movies. Broken things often remain just that—forever broken. Remaining hopeful and open, and accepting that "broken" is all my relationship with my parents ever was, was an important step toward mental stability and independence. It was not conventional therapy that got me to a level place—it was believing as fact that the abuse was wrong and not my fault. My acceptance of this absolute truth allowed previously challenged healing to begin and take hold, while creating space to give myself some grace. I am truly just fine the way I am—even better than fine.

The thought process leading to my conclusion: *My parents did horrible things to me. My parents don't get credit for my successes. I give credit to God, the gifts of countless others I have met or not met, and the gifts I was given before I left the womb and all along the way. I have forgiven my parents. I worked hard to have relationships with them and show them love and support, and those efforts wholesale failed. I am confident in my accounting of the facts of my life, and, in reviewing those, I know there is no excuse good enough for the pain and struggle they caused me. Rather than live in pain and victimness, I choose to be Crutchless and use the experiences as fuel to build a reality* that has broken generations of dysfunction. I am at peace with all of this. I will not feel guilt for calling my parents what they were—abusers. I deserve to be my authentic, unapologetic self, free of the burden of the pain they caused. I deserve to heal and leave this all far behind. I am worthy.

This truth is an anchor in my life that has encouraged a deeper healing. It's a wonderful gift to get to this place and look at my history without hatred, blame or a need to reprocess the experiences. My perspective becomes (almost) that of a trained objective observer with no emotion or direct engagement. From there, I give myself permission to live a full, rich life and for healing to work. My relationships with my parents were "net negative," and it's OK for me to accept that conclusion and move on.

Knowing my life was not honored and cared for as it should have been, and that harm or death were options throughout, I am grateful to God for all the gifts that led me to remain alive and healthy. Through all I have seen and experienced, I have prospered despite any doubts or obstacles that challenged me along the way. I have embraced the totality of my life and know that all the roads, smooth and rough, led me to this wonderful life. None of what I hold dearly today could have happened without me being here on this planet. For that reason, I am grateful to my parents for bringing me into this world. It is satisfying to know I don't need to acknowledge their distant but discernible voices trying to convince me they deserve higher praise or that I am thinking of things wrong. Instead, I acknowledge their presence and allow myself to feel compassion for their own terrible life experiences and the pain they suffered. Their voices no longer have any power. Because of this, I am free to see things as they authentically were, rather than a narrative they demanded compliance with over decades. This transformation in thinking is a gift I can't express my gratitude enough for.

I know my thoughts regarding the immense relief that came when my parents passed are not unique. Ultimately, relief and freedom are exactly what I felt. I had built a good life, but it wasn't until after they were gone that I could let the wounds find healing. I don't believe I can completely heal from decades of their treatment. The experiences will always be a part of my makeup. However, with forgiveness and letting go, I have minimized these negative experiences to a place where it is part of me but does not own me anymore. In fact, it has shrunk so much that having survived and thrived feels a lot like something to be proud of. I also acknowledge that my experiences in total make me who I am. I have done some incredible things in my life so far, and I couldn't have done it without having gone through all of this. The memories, pain, and suffering have been reduced to what feels like a small marble I sense sometimes just under my left rib cage. I don't know why my mind goes to this spot on my body, but that seems to be where it wants to go, and so I allow myself to be OK with where and how it has chosen to exist within me. It is there but benign and will never do me harm again. I welcome its place inside me and don't set any expectations or dedicate any energy to making it smaller or trying to vanquish it. I am comfortable with its existence and don't have to "therapy" it away or take medicine to dull it. The marble can feel more active at times when memories arise, but it can never again take me to a dark place. The marble is a part of me the same way my leg, liver, or even the cancer that lives inside is a part of me. It does not stop me from loving deeply, laughing, or living fully. In fact, when I consider my marble, I see it with gratitude and respect.

Because of this repackaging, so much emotional bandwidth has opened for me. I have found deeper relationships with my family, insecurities are fading, and self-esteem is rising. Allowing myself to be self-aware and course correct without undue influence from my parents are all gifts that became available after their deaths. I wish I would have been strong enough to do this work much sooner. To do so would have been an act of self-love and self-respect. The Universe's assistance in helping me square away my history into the practical form of a marble is an incredibly helpful thing to me.

Additionally, while accepting that the marble will never leave me, I also know it will never define or control me. I am satisfied this is the best I could hope for in reconciling our relationships. My confident conclusion is yet another gift.

Lessons Learned from All of This

In 1984, a movie called *St. Elmo's Fire* was released and nicely set up the careers of some famous actors. The collective group of actors in this film were called the "Brat Pack," a play on the name of the older "Rat Pack" (Frank Sinatra, Dean Martin, Sammy Davis, Jr.) and included names like Demi Moore, Rob Lowe, and Judd Nelson. I was drawn to the movie multiple times because it told the story of young people going through the trials of life to become something more for themselves. While I enjoyed the movie, the self-titled song, "St. Elmo's Fire (Man in Motion)," written by John Parr, gave me a burst of needed confidence during a highly volatile period as I approached my senior year of high school. Lyrics like, "Play the game...you know you can't quit until you're done. Soldier on. Only you can do what must be done. You know in some ways, you're a lot like me. You're just a prisoner and you're trying to break free", offered a direct message of camaraderie and high-octane motivation. "I can make it. I know I can. You broke the boy in me, but you won't break the man" were more lines that made me want to burst with enthusiasm. I knew the Universe was, once again, giving me a lift. With leaving home in my sights, I knew God was using Parr's most famous work to give me more fuel for the journey, while telling me to keep my head up and stay the course. Thank you Mr. Parr. Undoubtedly, this song was a gift that empowered many.

To achieve therapeutic healing value for myself, my primary objective in writing this book, I knew that I needed to shine a light on the darkness

I had lived through. Despite the difficulty, which at times was immense, I knew that getting it out of my head would support my healing.

Getting bad experiences out of our heads is not a unique idea. Writers, poets, musicians, and artists of all types have long freed their pain through writing and other outlets of expression, knowing it is better to have their difficulties out in the open, rather than buried and festering deep inside. The lyrics of Nalick's song make some profound points, but what made it most impactful to me was that it was released in 2005, approximately two years after I started this writing project. Her words gave me the affirmation for why I even bothered to write this book. It has been challenging to sit down and write about my experiences. At times, I even hated it, walking away for months. However, there was never a time I didn't believe in the importance of this work to my well-being. Did writing this book clear the history from my mind like deleting an email? No, but I know I have achieved my therapeutic goal, and that, in doing so, my past is less heavy. Instead of forcing myself to watch reruns, my history is like a bad movie I know exists on DVD in my closet. I know it is there, but I have no desire to see it again.

The secondary objective was the hope that someone might read this and find something helpful, perhaps an opportunity to know they are not alone in their journey. Sadly, there are too many of us who grow up in broken, dysfunctional environments and, even with good therapy, still carry heavy loads. Many don't find answers that help them leave their pasts behind. Maybe this book will help in some way. It is a lofty objective, but, if by sharing my story and the lessons learned, someone finds some connection or comfort, then that makes the effort much more rewarding.

If you've made it this far, I hope you will read on. I am happy that years of writing copious notes, building thoughts into print, and freeing myself of some uncomfortable history are all behind me. What follows is the practical part of this writing journey, taking my life experience and relaying how I have used it to benefit me personally and professionally.

Lesson 1
It Has Never Served Me to Have a Victim Mentality

I've described some difficult conditions in my childhood and the struggle to survive them. One of the natural outcomes of that experience was feeling like a victim and allowing myself at times to be weighed down in self-pity and resentment. It was an expenditure of energy with no constructive purpose or value. As I have described, feeling sorry for myself has never yielded much benefit. My parents taught me there was no benefit to complaining or pouting; instead, this would only lead to more consequences. Also, culture at the time supported the "suck it up at all costs" mentality, and complaining about pain and suffering was not something a boy should do.

It wasn't until my teen years that I became comfortable discussing in a general manner how things were at home. I don't believe the reason for sharing was because I was bursting with a desire to let out my pain—it was more because I didn't have a choice. My friends witnessed oddities resulting from my family situation, and it was difficult, with their pressing, to just let those things go unexplained.

As a positive, I discovered that revealing some of my circumstances wasn't all bad. Seeing that my friend and girlfriend were willing to be patient and caring listeners was new to me and gave me some license to go further. Despite how difficult it must have been for my girlfriend to date someone so broken, she was always compassionate and helpful. Her positive energy about everything provided me reason to believe I could allow myself to accept help and comfort without consequence. I did so with the trepidation of a heavily abused dog being offered food from a stranger, but they never made me regret it.

Letting out some of my personal lived experience felt good, but, as I offered more, I began to realize my friends were starting to withdraw somewhat and avoiding these conversations. It hurt then, but, as I look back, it makes sense. These were not qualified counselors or therapists. These were kids in the prime of their young lives with a desire to live life to the fullest who were neither prepared nor qualified to be weighed down with my troubles. Like all kids, they listened initially with great interest in the way that everyone listens when they are about to hear a heavily guarded secret. After that, the law of diminishing returns kicked in—I was losing their support while at the same time feeling the familiar feelings of guilt and being a burden. My Debbie Downer downloads were negatively impacting our friendships. I witnessed first hand how support fatigue, a term I learned about in fighting cancer, is unavoidable over long periods. I did, thankfully, get a taste of what it felt like to be vulnerable, but clearly this unveiling also taught the lesson that self-pity and feeling special because I was a victim was not going to have true long-term benefits to me. At the same time, I learned that having a victim mentality was something people eventually get tired of, and that friendships become strained or lost when self-victimization is the primary theme. Pulling back was the new answer, because losing friends was too high a price to pay.

In my youth, I believed that my pain was unique and that no one could possibly be going through what I was going through. I could have made a case to live a life of self-pity and expect that others should honor that identity with heavy doses of sympathy and hand holding. Fortunately, one gift my parents shared, but didn't realize was a gift, was when they taught me that self-pity would only yield more serious negative results coming in the form of more abuse. This direct connection trained me that self-pity had the opposite effect I was looking for. It was obviously not the preferred way to learn, but this disguised gift might have been one of their greatest. If they had instead been parents who felt remorse after an abuse event and coddled me in response to my self-pity, I suspect it could have had a major impact on who I would later become. If giving me a positive response to their abuse had been their behavior, I might have grown up believing that craving sympathy and living as a victim were the only things that could get me attention.

Of course, there were some periods of self-pity, but I kept that mostly in my head. With no one hearing all that was going on in my head, it was not difficult to conclude that all minutes allocated to this activity were wasted minutes with only a negative return on investment. Being a victim was a short acting drug and a forward progress repellant that directly worked against all of the plans and dreams I had for myself. However, deep within my island, something else was taking place within my psyche. With some wins happening, I was seeing that taking the path of self-reliance and applying my proven work ethic was making me feel genuinely good inside.

Feeling good, even just from time to time, was a powerful cornerstone of success. It had a compounding effect, and while difficulties persisted, a second more positive narrative was building: I could choose to use my life circumstances to feed a determination to leave and to do better. It started slowly at first, but then it fused into my identity, an identity that believed in possibilities and overcoming tall mountains. As I graduated to adulthood and headed off to college, something else happened that made me grow even stronger—I learned that the world was a much bigger place than Arbutus, Maryland.

When I went to community college, I met all types of people but did not quickly make new friends, as I was still too focused on my own path to put my head up and realize that some form of struggle is a part of everyone's life. I didn't upload many new data points, because I hung out with the same friends from high school while focusing on school and work. I could not see or wasn't ready to accept that my situation was not all that unique. As home struggles became less acute, my eyes eventually opened to my new environment, and I was given the opportunity to see that the world was big and many people attending Catonsville Community College were just like me. They were consciously choosing not to be victims and were fully committed to making positive change in their lives.

At community college and then later at the University of Maryland, the extent and depth of the issues that people shared with me provided another important piece of information. The trauma and other difficulties I had experienced were not even all that unusual. Struggle is real and shows up in many forms. I also noticed that the struggle is relative to each individual. Even things that I would not count as serious through my lens of life, I could see the issues were very serious—as serious as any problem that I had—to the person sharing their experience.

As an example, I had many heartfelt conversations with someone who had become accustomed to living a life where his parents met all his needs and desires. However, when the family experienced a major financial collapse, almost overnight the fancy car, the paid-up tuition, and the coverage of all expenses, including spring break trips, disappeared overnight. The formerly wealthy student was abruptly forced to turn in his Maserati and find a job and support himself. It was not lost on me how terrible this was for him to experience after having a lifetime of luxury and unlimited financial support. I had my own experiences, but I had never had everything and then lost it all. The intriguing part was that I was able to recognize that his suffering and pain were as authentic and real as any I had experienced. This humbled me and showed me that pain, struggle, and trauma come in many forms, and how it is experienced is very real to the people who are impacted. In this and other examples, I witnessed firsthand the resilience and a determination to lick their wounds and find a new life course. These other living and breathing examples of fortitude and determination were a solid confirmation that my thinking was right and that living in victim-ness would only hold me back.

For the story-tellers that could not make the adjustment to their new circumstances, it was especially difficult to watch. In these cases, the impacted individual allowed their lives to fall apart and spent their time complaining and seeking pity much longer than was beneficial to them. As in the positive cases where I received positive affirmation of my mindset, these different examples also had a positive effect on me: It was proof that living a life based on self-victimization is not helpful and could make things even worse.

We must move through our trials, learn the lessons, and do the work. Also, healthy friendships and romantic relationships can't be built and sustained with one or both parties living a life centered on their problems and victim identity. If one party to a relationship has no such negative history but thrives on being a support system to the other party in the pair, they become the enabler. Enabling just keeps the problems and complaining alive, and it is no surprise when both are dragged down in the muck. This knowledge didn't make my problems any less impactful, but it taught me that any energy invested in stewing on my history or current circumstances would have little, if any, positive yield. Presenting as a victim constantly leads to lost friendships, and my presentation to the world became the summation of my struggles and not much more. While living as a victim may have garnered some attention, sympathy and compassion in the short run, it always slowed me down or moved me backwards.

Preferring instead to be Crutchless and purposely avoiding a weak, victimhood-based persona was the correct and only move for me. That decision paved the way for deeper healthier relationships in my life and clearer focus which accelerated my momentum toward achieving a long list of proud successes. It didn't happen easily or overnight, but more minutes toward goal creation and realization, and less toward complaining and self-pity led to me being much happier and more fulfilled. It also paved the way toward what I believe will be positive generational change.

The benefits of foregoing a victim mentality has shown up in numerous places in my life. One such place is my current battle with cancer. Here are two scenarios displaying how a victim-centric patient might see a cancer diagnosis vs. someone who moves quickly through self-pity and wants to overcome the obstacle and use whatever tools they have to influence the outcome. I live in the Scenario 2 bucket, but early on flirted briefly with Scenario 1.

Scenario 1. Mindset: *Embrace My Victimness!* I receive a stage four cancer diagnosis. Multiple teams of doctors say there is no effective care. The only offer is to take a class of drugs that has a 10 percent or less chance of having a positive impact, and, in those cases, the benefit is usually short-term. I put my faith completely in the hands of doctors and roll the dice that I am one of the ten who gets a favorable result. I consider myself in this scenario to be a victim of a terrible disease and wear it well. As I passively sit by wishing for the best, I wallow in self-pity and fear, burdening my family and friends. This is allowable in my mind because I am powerless over the disease and thriving on sympathy is an acceptable behavior under these terrible circumstances. Being a victim is also justified because I had a tough life and don't deserve this after what

I have already gone through. I give complete control to the doctors and believe that I have little or no responsibility to my own healing beyond heeding their words and recommendations. After all, as a victim-centric human, feeling sorry for myself is a full-time job and should consume all of my energy. I ignore common sense and all the gifts around me that suggest answers might lie beyond these recommendations. I find that victimhood is my place in life and accept that I am powerless to change my circumstances. I die one year later, sad I didn't have more days to tell others just how much I have suffered in life.

Scenario 2. Mindset: *I have fielded the punch that came with receiving the diagnosis. After a brief period of wallowing, I recalibrate and embrace the task ahead. I respect that God has well equipped me from the beginning with tools I can use to help solve this problem. I am expected by the Universe to combine these tools with knowledge (life experience + education), instinct, and work ethic to earn a favorable outcome.* I acknowledge the doctors telling me of my limited conventional choices and accept their expertise as a data point. Refusing to be a victim of any kind, a position I believe is an insult to my higher power, I begin reading vigorously on non-conventional treatments that compliment chemotherapy and can potentially mount a powerful attack against the disease. I build a second team of experts to support my healing, accepting that reading is not enough and trusting that God doesn't put all answers with just one set of experts. After careful consideration, I make a plan and implement a myriad of healing mechanisms I believe plot the best course toward healing. My family sees I am in control of my health and are relieved to know I will never put my fate in anyone else's hands completely. I know I am honoring all that I am and have been, regardless of the outcome. I will not live as a victim. I will use this as an opportunity to heal my mind and body while living the richest life I am able. I die four years later knowing I made my best effort and lived fully. I have no regrets, no matter the outcome.

I think that it would almost have been impossible for me to live my experience without having moments where I leaned into pity and victimness. I suspect that most people would do the same. My point in writing that being a victim never had a long-term positive impact for me is not to say that being a victim for a short while is unhealthy or even unavoidable. Rather, it is more to explain that even with conditions where I could get an endless audience of sympathizers, spending energy focused on my negative experience never moved me towards the long list of positive things that have occurred in my life.

Lesson 2
Music Is a Powerful Gift

Music being called a gift likely comes as no surprise given how, early on in the book, I describe how music has been so important in my life, and specific musical references can be found throughout. How it saved me should also be clear: I was nudged to listen with great interest to the artists and their works for ways to help myself. Without it, I am certain I would have landed somewhere different. Perhaps, reaching for the healing power of music in my prison was similar to how a literal prisoner would reach for the Bible and connect with the prison chaplain to survive his incarceration. Music guided me when I was directionless, voiceless, and hurting. This concept is not new, as many have written about the power of music to heal and transform. In fact, live music is often brought into hospitals to aid in the healing process. The songs are gifts but looking deeper, the writers and musicians that composed the songs and circulated them to the world are also gifts. The combination of everything that went into each song as well as the many methods to deliver that music, was immensely therapeutic. Also equally powerful was the conclusion I made that to write the powerful messages I was hearing meant that someone understood me and that I was not alone. Wherever one of these songs and many many others found me, it was an opportunity to drop into group therapy.

When there was no one there to help in my darkest moments, God allowed music to help me gain perspective from the gifts of strangers. Our wiring to share our gifts so the world might benefit from them is so wonderfully undeniable. I praise all the artists from Kanye to Willie who have guided me in the worst of storms. The Universe desired that they share their gifts with the world, and, in doing so, they collectively served as my therapists and spirit guides, moving me forward and through in my life. Without that exposure and consciously recognizing the value I received, I am certain I would not be here today.

As an afterthought, perhaps the more important message is that different people respond differently to different stimuli. For me, music was a powerful friend. I didn't realize in real time that the gift of my wiring was pushing me to listen to these songs and find comfort and direction. To others it may be cooking, mindfulness, walks in nature, animal contact, a long drive, or exercise that gets them through the troubled times. I think the key is to be aware enough to recognize what helps us at a deep level, and use it for that purpose. My sincere belief is that these things, whether we consciously know it or not, are provided for that reason. With life experience and a more open mind, I see how the Universe wanted this for me.

Lesson 3
My Averageness is a Superpower.

While growing up in the '70s and '80s, I felt bombarded by external messages driving me to be my best and to make my own fate. It wasn't just that my parents were letting me know frequently that if I didn't work hard, my future would be bleak. Their messages were convincing but weren't the only broadcast in my orbit. American culture at that time was pushing that the American Dream could be accomplished with intention, a strong work ethic, and a consistent commitment to overcoming obstacles in all weather. This was something I could get behind and thought of the messages as facts. If I wanted to create the circumstances that would allow me and my family to avoid the worst parts of what generations of Wellingtons had experienced, I would have to follow these themes while steering clear of a victim-centric mentality. Based on early vision and all that was growing inside of me, I felt strongly that if I accepted my lot in life and did not attempt to make significant improvement, I would be hurting myself and generations of Wellingtons to come. Honoring my vision from my youth, I had a responsibility to make change for all the Wellingtons, present and future. I believe God was with me and insisted I embrace the messaging, listen to my vision, and work toward this improved outcome no matter the struggle.

Entering the career phase of my life, I couldn't help but notice that another widely dispersed message in America was that it was important I work to be the very best at everything I did. I also perceived the message as telling me I was not good enough if I was in seventh, eighteenth or ninetieth place. Heck, based on what I think I was hearing, being this low in the rankings was hardly even worth an acknowledgement. I had already fully accepted that hard work would be required, so I was OK with that part. However, based on seeing who I was through a realistic lens, attempting to be the best at anything was likely not in the cards for me. My work ethic had led to great achievements, but if I looked at my peers and their achievements, I could easily say that how I was performing would land me at a solid average ranking.

However, I knew my results were meteoric compared to where I started, and, fortunately, also realized early on that in my view and in *my world*, I was accomplishing great things. With that, I learned that being average was not a weakness for me. Comparing the impressive results I had achieved to the circumstances I had elevated from and not to my peers, I accepted that my slow and steady forward-moving turtle mentality was powerful. More than that, what I was doing and how I did it was working. Sure, I wanted to go faster and wanted *more* like the hare, but it was a resounding gift that I didn't waste time worrying about my level of accomplishment and how fast I got there. I realized that when I did try to keep up with the best, I was only stealing the joy of achieving my accomplishments while making me feel small. I didn't need to be the fastest or best at anything to feel proud of my success. Being remarkably average was my always dependable superpower, and that on its own was always something to be proud of.

I realized there are significant advantages to being average and that I could be OK without sitting on the top of everything. Being average as an advantage is not something most people hear every day. In fact, some may read this and think this is nonsensical and that being proud of being average is silly. Whatever the opposing view might be, there was no discounting what was right in front of me: that being less than the "best" was landing me in great places.

To say that I am average does not mean I haven't achieved great things. In fact, to come from where I came from and successfully achieve a productive life with a loving family is itself a massive accomplishment. From there, creating a global business with over a billion in annual sales and then selling it wasn't too shabby, either. Being average just means I get things done at the fastest rate I am able to and never make my primary driver to be the best at everything. There are applications in business where I feel like I can excel, and, in those cases, when I give it my all, I might, in fact, be the best. For example, I adored selling and winning business, and in my company, I was the best at this function within our walls. Also, I was deeply devoted to the customer experience, even though we were never officially measured. By what I knew of our competition, I believe that we landed at a place that was best in class.

Having comfort in my mediocrity, I could then move to a place where I realized that being me might have worthwhile practical advantages that fell beyond simple comparisons of results. In general terms, because most people are "average" (falling in the middle of things), I realized that since I do so well living in the middle, I am plugged into what *most* people think at all times. Relying on this principle has been a key driver to my success in business. By having a clear understanding of what I personally would want in a business relationship and never surrendering or allowing those expectations to erode, I can project those beliefs onto my prospect and client base, build processes and systems to support those beliefs, and achieve maximum satisfaction and loyalty. I didn't need to be the next Elon Musk or Bill Gates. Millions of people were just like me, and all I had to do is be who I was and put myself in front of them.

All average people have uniqueness, of course, but We The Average are powerful in that we have the greatest numbers and have the power to move the needle more than any other subsegment of the population. We don't realize it because the above average wants us to believe that The Average must be led and told what to do. In large part, as the worker ants, we accept our lot in life and maybe even believe we are destined to bow our heads and be of service to "the best," but it doesn't have to be that way. Striving to be the best at something when this is clearly an unrealistic objective is the wrong way to think about goal achievement and not a necessarily good use of my energy. Having enough humility to accept my averageness led to a place where I could see that being average could work handsomely to my benefit. Being secure in this thinking also made my life a lot easier.

In business, I anchored our mission in simple strategy and tactics to achieve great success. Unyielding attention to the customer experience is always tied first to the Golden Rule: treat others as I expect to be treated. My expectations for how I wanted to be treated were very high, so I knew that building around that was going to serve the needs of millions. Other themes, including under-promising while over-delivering, quick and effective failing and recovery, efficient and evolving processes, always improving, authenticity, dependability, owning mistakes, personal interaction, never forgetting in my words and actions that clients are the ones who truly pay the bills, and that nothing is perfect, are all examples of thinking of what most people would appreciate. None of these elements required a genius level IQ or even a slightly above average intellect; rather, they were all simple, uncomplicated concepts the bulk of the people on the planet can appreciate. All proved instrumental to my success in building a business.

None of these ideas will land me a multi-million dollar book deal because they are boring and usual. There has never been any fancy buzzwords or meaningless word soup intended to wow clients by sounding super sophisticated and floating above my audience. I was not above anyone. I was truly in word and heart *with them*. Because I could bank on the average-minded human thinking like me and being attracted to these themes, and because those numbers of people are by far the greatest on the planet, I never had a problem winning and retaining business.

Unrelenting business values wrapped in consistent execution have always resulted in predictable and lasting success for me.

I have accepted and benefited from being average. I don't have to be the best, and, in fact, what is "best" is always being redefined and is about as achievable as trying to set my sights on becoming perfect. It only matters that I am happy, living within my values, and working toward achieving that which I think is important. I recognize I am part of a huge group that sometimes struggles with whether we have done enough in life, have enough stuff, are good enough, are respected enough, are wanted enough, but I am not alone and I don't need to be anything more than what I am. Accepting this, while not feeling inadequate, is a great gift.

Accepting averageness also means I recognize that I am not a titan of genius ideas and will never be a featured TED talker. But in understanding this about myself, I can be more compassionate to myself while having deep connection and conviction about just how important We The Average are. When I deal with a guy scooping my ice cream and see he is obviously in a bad mood and perhaps not attending to me as I would like, I practice seeing him through the eyes of my averageness and assess the situation from there. Seeing through this lens allows me to be more accepting. *This guy is like me back in the day. He likely has a lot going on in his life...financial struggles, possible relationship issues, bad roommates, life moving slowly, hates his job.* I accept he cannot be perfect in everything, and, in my averageness, I know he is allowed to have a bad day, even a bad month. I accept this because as an average person, I have been there, and the bulk of the world—the world of the average—has too.

This subject of embracing our averageness has so much more depth to it than can be explored here, but dialing into the power of averageness can help solve challenges in almost any setting. I never have to look too far or too deep for the answers. I am average and therefore think like most people, so given this, I can start with a simple question to problem solve... *What would I do?*

Of course, not everyone in this massive group would agree with what I would do (we're flexible that way), but I can be confident that however I would handle a situation of any type is probably going to lead me in the right direction. Exploring the answer to this question taps into my life experience as being an average soul and nicely matches up with the sage advice that we should treat people as we would want to be treated. Politics, marriage, friendships, and careers are all areas where an average person who is confident and secure in his averageness can problem solve with a high degree of effectiveness. Those who walk the earth proudly as average are the true drivers of everything, and, despite averageness often being interpreted as meaning inferior, accepting that we know what most people want is, indeed, a superpower. WE are the ones who make the world spin. WE have the greatest numbers. WE are the most powerful. WE lead ourselves just fine and are not meant to be led by the handful of people that our culture tells us need to be in place to run our lives. It is OK to let others be our leaders as someone has to do that job. But gauging their success as leaders should be based purely on their actions and results in representing us—the masses. This is too frequently not the case.

If you count yourself as average, then welcome to the wonderful, bountiful land of Average-topia. Congratulations to you for being confident enough to not only accept who you are but also recognize how much power you have. You know what most people think. You know what most customers want. You understand what most bosses want. You know how most relationships will thrive. You get what it's like to scratch and claw to make it in life, and see that as a strength not a weakness. You know who you are and you make no excuses for it. We are the most reliable, most relatable, most authentic people on the planet. This little nugget of personal discovery is not coming from an "expert"; it's coming from just an average guy who is somewhat self-aware and, based on the numbers, is likely a whole lot like you! Thanks again, God for giving me the self-awareness to not get stuck in an ego driven social construct. I just keep using what you gave me and good things keep coming.

Lesson 4
Netting Things Out Has Changed My Life

One of the most frustrating things about low self-esteem and a constant need for affirmation from others is that I tended to remain engaged with people, places, and things that were obviously hurting me for long periods of time. With no active role models, I didn't have the necessary skill set or mental prowess to remove or mitigate these harmful elements in a timely manner, and sometimes not at all. Often, I would just allow the element to exist like a festering wound I ignored and pretended wasn't hurting me. My relationship with my parents is a good example, but this behavior pattern wasn't just reserved for managing through the tumultuous relationships with my mother and father; the dysfunction extended to many other aspects of my life. Because I felt no love or respect for myself, and only outside influences were responsible for whatever my mental disposition might be from day to day, I was addicted to harvesting every fragment of affirmation I could find. It didn't matter how small or tangential—the perceived gift of a thimble's worth of positive reinforcement was so rewarding to my fragile ego that I could not allow myself to pass on any chance to try. Mom and Dad's pattern of regularly signaling how worthless I was, while at the same time giving me just enough encouragement (using that word liberally) to keep me coming back, inhibited my ability to make good decisions about many things, not just relationships. As broken as it was, this model was all I knew, and so that was my approach to everything. The ROE (Return on energy/effort) was embarrassingly low, but that didn't register with me.

When I became an adult and more removed from my family, I began to find some fragments of self-confidence. The more this positive quality grew, the more it became evident how badly these things were hurting me. The gift of positive, healthy relationships only added to my security and self-awareness. In a healthier environment, I was seeing that I no longer had to intentionally subject myself to hazing in hopes of getting something good in my life. I still had worry that dependable, loving connections would fall apart at any time, but I could not reject that I was seeing how wonderful life could be in mutually giving relationships. Unselfish love and friendship made me see that the engagement I had with Mom and Dad and with other harmful relationships was only hurting me and pulling me back toward something I had spent my entire life trying to leave behind—low self-worth and feelings of not being good enough. Oddly, I was still allowing space in my life for elements that were hurting me, while simultaneously positive relationships were feeding me strength and security. The effect was that the positive was being muted by the negative, and I was doing nothing about it. However, I was fortunate that the juxtaposition between broken relationships and the newer positive healthy relationships made me realize how ill-equipped I was at proactively addressing things that hurt me.

Old habits die hard, and so I allowed them to continue, essentially allowing space for old harms to continue to do what they always had. Realizing I was doing the same acts over and over again with the result being the same lousy feelings, it became obvious that I needed something simple and easy to understand to make me want to change these behaviors. I could no longer allow relationships and habits that were fed by low self-esteem to be carried on in perpetuity. Particularly, I needed an easy process for an average person to eliminate things and people in my life that were hurting me. Enter the simple T-chart and the netting process.

The T-chart I first learned about in high school has many years later been a great tool to help me make business decisions. It is simple and easy to process for my average intellect, while providing a compelling visual. It forces me first to take the emotion out of a decision and to look carefully at the benefits and disadvantages of any problem I am studying in a business setting. Fortunately, it takes almost no effort to complete, and the answer to the dilemma is usually obvious in just minutes. Having success with this tool in a professional setting made me wonder if using the tool for personal purposes would be equally beneficial. As a visual thinker, I knew most of the benefit for me was in literally seeing the undeniable result right before my eyes.

The idea was triggered by another episode with my mother where I made the decision to leave my family waiting at home so I could instead check in on her. I can't blame her for my choice as she likely didn't want me there, and I certainly knew there was very little chance that much positive would come of this visit. Yet, as always, I still made the nail-biting journey to Arbutus to honor my self-imposed obligation to care for her. As when I was a child, on this occasion I was reduced, once again, to knocking on her bedroom door for a long time to get her attention. Similar to many of my visits, she did not come out of her room or even open the door. We exchanged a few words through the fiber board in between long delays, and then I waited around downstairs while I seethed at the thought of the lost time with my own family. Ultimately, I left having never actually seen her in person.

In my anger on the drive home, I was thinking about how I was intentionally exposing myself to this pain, with full knowledge of what the probable outcome would be. I could only blame myself for the outcome but was asking myself why I kept coming back for more. The T-chart then popped into the forefront of my mind, another unexpected gift. It struck me that if I wrote down all the positives alongside all the negatives about my relationship with her and my father, the visual outcome might be so overwhelmingly negative that I would have no choice but to see the results and push myself to change course. This was an exercise I was comfortable with in business and had no good reason why I shouldn't use it in my personal life.

The results were of course overwhelmingly net-negative, but I still chose to ignore them. With a twisted sense of loyalty, despite the pain and stress they caused me, at that point I remained committed to remaining involved in their lives. However, the value and simplicity of using the T-chart as a tool stayed with me, and I knew it could be handy elsewhere in my personal life. Even if, in seeing the obvious results, I was still unwilling to break from my parents, there was nothing to prevent me from using this simple tool to reduce or eliminate other nagging pain points in my life. I didn't need long books on how to find happiness and navigate my life, of which I had read many. I just needed something that would take less than five minutes to complete, with the results pointing to where I needed to go. Bottom line, if I see a long list of positives and a short list of negatives, my result is "net-positive." If the result is the opposite, then it is "net-negative." It's that easy.

When I began to T-chart my problem areas, the results were sometimes so convincing that it made my decision obvious, another great gift. Seeing such a compelling visual result was exactly what I had hoped. The undeniability of the true outcome allowed me to set aside the emotional baggage I had always connected to these issues. Previously, I might have always known that what I was allowing was hurting me, but after the emotional part fueled by decades of self-harming behavior weighed in, I would land at crippling indecision. The T-chart (netting) analysis result provides the opportunity to set aside these deep, emotional roadblocks and keep separate and silent the outside influences that might impact how the chart is completed. In these cases, the tool is especially effective and was desperately needed by me. In an environment free of duress or acute emotional pain, I arrive at the answer that best serves me. It was my cure for analysis paralysis.

Armed with rising self-esteem and my repurposed tool, I knew it was time to allow myself to begin the process of eliminating items that were muting the good I was seeing in life. It was finally time to lighten the load, and this was just the tool to do it. I deserved to be free of this pain, and it was time to do something about it. With practice, I grew comfortable that the results were true and reliable. From there, I could see what the right decision was, and if ready, could take the steps to begin what must be done.

The easiest place to start was the cases where I knew I would be brave enough to execute on change, which usually meant that challenges from outside forces were minimal or did not exist, or where I could simply wall them off with ease (like blocking a phone number). With little or no resistance challenging me, it might not seem like a good example of being brave, but in my case, where I often allowed cancerous-like elements to stay embedded in my life indefinitely, the word fits. Starting with easy targets was a great way to get the reps in and to experience first-hand the benefits of those decisions.

The best and easiest targets for change were those designated by grossly lopsided net-negative results. Blocking calls and all electronic contact with a distant, unstable, alcoholic friend who insisted on inserting stress and difficulty upon me was a great example of acting on a net-negative element. It was wonderful to feel peace and freedom rush into the space this person was no longer filling. All of that good feeling came from a simple chart and a few clicks on my phone. The emotions that come with decisively stamping out misery are energetic and empowering; it made me want to tackle more of my demons.

Another somewhat strange example was when I began to make decisions to cease contact with people who clearly wanted nothing to do with me despite me truly wanting that person in my life. In these cases, the analysis hurt to see, but the results were overwhelmingly net-negative. It was difficult to accept that I had failed in my efforts to retain the relationship, but the answer was the answer: My pursuit of the relationship was hurting me much more than it was benefiting. In these cases, I felt some loss when I executed on the results, but the outcome was worth it. My self-confidence was growing with the control I was taking of my life.

Ironically, in cases where the person didn't want a relationship with me but where I persisted with best efforts to salvage it, the person I released from my life didn't know or feel my decision and likely could care less. They might even be happy I finally "got the memo". While the process is freeing in nature, a lack of concern by the other person, evidenced by little or no effort to reconnect or investigate my disconnection, was undeniable proof I should have done it much sooner. Just think of all the time and energy I could have diverted to people that really wanted my attention. More importantly, my previous stubborn commitment to staying engaged was proof of false narratives supporting one-sided obligations I invented inside my head. Inside of the new freed up bandwidth came more happiness and peace, and more time to pursue other interests or invest more heavily in the net-positive influences in my life.

Knocking out the easy things was exactly what I needed to start to see the dysfunction of my ways and to get proof of concept of the effectiveness of this simple analysis tool. I was seeing that where I had thought I had to be like the bull forever mindlessly chasing the matador's red cape, this construct was another myth created by only myself. As elementary as a T-chart and netting is, the introduction of this analysis process to assist me with taking ownership of my behaviors and creating lasting accumulative change was a grand gift. It allowed me to shift away from self-harming behavior and build confidence at the same time.

One example of an overwhelming net-negative and potentially easy target to correct was attending the funerals of people I didn't know. I abhorred these events and hated that I would give myself this pain when I had no connection to the deceased. Funerals are infrequent, but my attendance at these events has consistently triggered great stress and anxiety. I believe the origins of my pain came from the experience of my father forcing me to spend time studying my grandmother's corpse and the circumstances around my mother's passing. After a quick analysis using this tool, I quickly realized that the experience was net-negative. Previously, I would force myself to attend these events, ignoring the real struggle that was happening in my mind. The disappointment I believed would come from Jo if I missed a funeral, like many net-negative cases where my narrative is inaccurate or flat out wrong, turned out to be a myth created in my head; another destructive behavior leftover from my early years. Seeing that it meant essentially nothing to her to miss these moments was more proof that I was self-harming for no real reason. For funerals today, I attend those where JoAnn needs me. These funerals are net-positive because I want to support her in her time of need and doing so is a high value net positive for me.

There are many examples in my life that could show how this simple netting analysis has worked and resulted in an immediate positive benefit in my life. I use the netting approach with events (i.e., an annual party I have never wanted to attend), physical items (i.e., a fancy car I have no use for) and places (i.e., visiting my father's grave) by completing an honest assessment of the emotions and the practical net value for these things in my life. With practice, I have become committed and grounded enough to recognize how these elements impact me and that they need review. I subject the issue to analysis, accept the results, and move to monitor, mitigate or eliminate the problem. I am essentially forcing myself to make positive changes and allowing myself to consciously put myself first, something that took most of my life to figure out.

More on using a netting rationale for relationships...

Using the netting process for dealing with the more deeply interconnected relationships in my life has been more challenging as evidenced by my failure to carve out my parents from my life despite clear and consistent net-negative results. As described above, less involved relationships can be discontinued sometimes without the person even knowing or caring that I have made the decision to end the relationship. However, dealing with net-negative relationships that are deep and entangled bring the most discomfort and come with the greatest risk. The primary risks are that I am not fully prepared to deal with the multiple layers of guilt that often come with the decision or that when I execute on my decision to be done with the relationship, the other party responds by ratcheting up their effort to keep me in their orbit.

A good example of people making an effort to keep me in their life despite my desire for a clean exit came from those in my life who have made it a habit to use me for resources in the forms of time, emotional capital and money. I am guilty of enabling in these cases, but I allowed it to continue due to a false sense of obligation. If the party on the other side were to conduct a similar analysis of our relationship, their T-chart netting result might curiously look like the exact opposite of my result. Essentially, their result would tell them that they must keep Daniel in their lives. In those cases, the other person certainly feels the loss resulting from my decision and their reaction would be opposite mine. They would double down on their efforts and apply pressure or guilt to reinstitute that which has served them so well. The pushback campaign can lead me to feelings of self-doubt, which at times make me rethink my decision. However, decisions made to address long-term dysfunctional relationships are not made easily and, unfortunately, came only after years of me having endured great discomfort with little or no return value. In those moments, I remind myself of why the relationship qualified for the analysis and the years of pain it caused. Unless the other party makes overt genuine changes that would swing the chart to be net-positive for me, I must make the changes that serve me best, and stand by my decision.

Because of why and when these relationships were born, some of them formed early in my childhood when I was at my dysfunctional peak, the other party cannot or does not want to change. With the foundation of the relationship anchored in my enabling behavior—my willingness to take nothing and give everything—they are of course quite satisfied with the way things are. In these cases, my ending or quietly demanding different behavior from the other party, sends the signal that they are the ones that need to change if they want to save the relationship. Unsurprisingly, under the new conditions, the relationship often ends, and the other side moves on to greener pastures. The bottom-line realization is that I am not worthy of a saving effort to that person unless I remain in my old form. Happily, this only proves how valuable and accurate the results were and how important this tool is to my well-being. After some time has passed, when I run an analysis of the fallout from my decision through the same process, I see that discomfort or some sadness exists for me, but the positives that have come from the decision far outweigh the small itch I might have to resume the relationship. I wish I had done this so many years earlier. Thank you Universe.

Addressing relationships that previously had a true positive value but that, present day. no longer serve me (I'm proud I am now confident enough to say that a relationship should serve me!) are difficult to end, especially when they are rooted in a positive, loving, and supportive history, but that has unfortunately evolved to be unhealthy. The chart makes me see that despite years of fond memories; the relationship has been net-negative for a long time. These situations find a place in the middle of things for me. The findings of the analysis are obvious, but for several reasons I may decide to park the issue and observe further.

During the observation period, I might address my concerns directly with the person, reduce my interaction, and await their response. I might also choose to allow the relationship to exist in its current state and monitor without any discussion. It may seem like I am not committed to change for these cases, but that is not the case. Putting it on the table as an issue, performing the analysis, and receiving glaringly negative results is still a form of proactive action. Also, some relationships deserve more time to process and some grace to allow for change. After analysis, I move my understanding of the relationship from the autonomous "just take it as it is" mentality and move it to a more realistic current day view; that this relationship is hurtful in ways and challenging my quality of life, which, ultimately, could mean I need to end it. Once on my radar, I make certain I am viewing the relationship accurately and objectively and decide what amount of time and what changes I need to see to make the relationship worth continuing to me. If I set the clock at six months, and if at six months, nothing has changed, it is time for phasing out that relationship and ending my suffering. In these cases, I am thankful for the great times, acknowledge that nothing, including relationships, stays the same, and move on.

In cases where a conversation happens and we agree that the relationship must change to equally meet both our needs, I must be committed to that change and stand ready to make a tough decision if things stay the same. At that point, words are not enough; actions must follow. I remain attentive and make sure the relationship is how I need it to be. If the desired result occurs, then the relationship begins again in its new form. If nothing or not enough change occurs within a reasonable time, then the relationship flickers out, and I am now free to invest my time and energy elsewhere.

Some reading this might scratch their heads and consider all these words to be common sense to them. These are people that perform this process naturally, almost subconsciously, without much agony or purposeful effort. I admire that quality and wish that is how my brain worked as I guess it would have made my life much better. The great news is that with practice, some decisions are beginning to happen without a deep dive, signaling that I am folding this healthy process into my natural cognitive abilities. In essence, I am changing who I am and how I do things. This has been a beautiful and unexpected outcome.

For most of my life, I chose to continue subjecting myself to relationships and other life-sucking issues that were dysfunctional and destructive. I did this while completely ignoring the cost to my mental health. It was nothing more than self-destructive behavior patterns learned at an early age and allowed to continue into my adulthood. Embracing this simple process to help make important decisions that enhance my quality of life was an important step toward giving myself some true love and self-respect. With this process, I could no longer ignore, deny, emotionalize, or rationalize these issues away. I also learned that I had no obligation to keep bad things in my life simply because I had programmed myself to do so, or because the social narrative says I must. If a person, place, or thing makes me feel poorly for a long enough time, flagging that item and being committed to no longer ignoring the problem has been empowering, perhaps even life-saving. My confidence has soared, and the benefits are numerous and healing. Whether in my head or on the back of a napkin, 'checking the net' comes naturally now. I no longer willingly accept anything that takes from my quality of life.

For all of those years, I had accepted and, in some cases, even welcomed elements into my orbit that brought me pain. Essentially, I had built my own prison. Through this simple process, I am tearing down the walls and it feels great. My life is my life and owning it means I need to be active not passive in how I manage everything in it. I now see myself as worthy enough to intentionally route pain and stress out of my life. No one is going to make the hard decisions for me, and I must remember I am allowed to invite and dismiss what and who I want to share my life with. Netting does work, and the only requirement is a willingness to be proactive and honest with myself and be prepared to act. The wiring was always there; I just didn't choose to access it. Thank you, God, for helping me realize the power of intentionality.

Lesson 5
God Owes Me Nothing

I mentioned in these pages that I had embarked on a religious self-education journey in my early forties. I did this because I was developing a slow-growing belief there might be a higher power at work; however, I didn't have a practical way to frame this notion in my mind. I thought a review of the world's most popular religions might help me with this. The effort yielded a broad understanding of how each works and while it didn't provide the definitive answers I hoped might be revealed, the exercise was worthwhile. I learned much, but the big takeaway was that faith in a higher power can be anything I want or need it to be and is a very personal intimate thing. I build my thinking out more in the appendix section of this book.

I also decided that for my purposes, it was OK to believe in a non-denominational God and its influence on everything, while giving myself permission to ignore the various scripture, rules and regulations that typical modern-day religions offer. It felt good to come away with this understanding and have it come after making considerable effort to be objective. I am grateful I took that time because now I had an entry level theological education and felt I could make an informed decision about how to frame *my* God. Pairing all of my thoughts on why there must be a higher power while choosing not to get lost in the rules and scripture, I arrived at what was most important to me: God exists. That decision has helped me in ways I never imagined.

I don't understand the full complexity of such an immense power and its influence, but I sit comfortably knowing there is more at work than just a ball of dirt spinning at breakneck speed around the sun. The change in mindset was groundbreaking as I now confidently accept that a higher power must be involved. It was very freeing to not have to process my thoughts through a Christian filter or feel any guilt in how I arrived at a God-only focus point. To get to this perspective feels uncorrupted, pure, and organic. As a practical person venturing into the spiritual arena, getting to God in this way was exactly what I needed to make it stick. Coming to this peaceful yet firm conclusion was another great gift, perhaps the most important gift of all.

After I received my cancer diagnosis in 2019, I started a new deep-dive research project on how to cure myself of a rare cancer that has no effective conventional treatment. I was accustomed to doing the necessary work to overcome obstacles, so it was no shock to my system that I needed to create my own course toward healing. What I didn't realize is that the self-healing world offers an endless number of perspectives, many of them conflict with each other. And with each of those perspectives comes many subtopics, which themselves can be vast in the amounts of information to review. I was venturing into a subject matter I had no understanding of and that is so wide, I am frequently lost or confused about direction. I like certainty and absolute terms, and I had to accept that my current journey toward physical healing will have none of that. I am reduced to trusting my gut with what I think I know and, in some cases, rolling the dice—accepting the unknown and being hopeful that what I am doing doesn't hurt me, or worse. I am very optimistic in my direction on most days but also have come to accept that the answers might not come in time for me to heal. But in this research, wonderful new gifts have revealed themselves. These included the gifts of mindfulness, self-awareness, and the ability to be grounded and present. These were all things I had little or no experience with prior to my diagnosis.

Radical Remissions, the book I wrote about early on, had been my first read on my self-healing journey. I couldn't have been more blessed that this was my first resource in a sea of cancer-fighting resources I have studied. Dr. Kelly Turner does an excellent job of succinctly putting together the nine commonalities (which later became ten in her follow-up book, *Radical Hope*) of cancer patients who have experienced unexplained cancer remissions. It is easy to read and I'm certain that, like me, most came away after reading it with a good deal of hope. What is very interesting is that of the nine factors detailed within the pages, most had nothing to do with science or medicine. Instead, people were finding healing by leaning into their spirituality, quality of life, and self-awareness. I started with the hope that there would be silver bullets of healing detailed in the pages but soon realized this was not going to be the case. However, after reading through it a couple times and realizing how absent spirituality, stress reduction, and self-care were in my life, I was immensely grateful for the lessons on mindfulness and how, for some, spirituality can be an important bridge to healing physically.

I also accepted that there would be no certain path to my physical healing. Their stories were not based on science, but there was no refuting they had experienced unexplained remissions. I became very optimistic that something outside of science had played a role. With an acceptance of God as an anchor, I allowed myself to believe in the possibility of faith and self-awareness as true and functional components of my healing. This was a significant mind shift for me. While I believed in God, I hadn't yet come to an understanding about God's involvement in healing the body.

Given that the case studies were coming from my new peer group, those with Stage IV cancer, I was reading with great personal interest as each explained their reasons for healing. I knew I could never know for certain how God will influence my situation directly, but I realized my version of spirituality could be beneficial to my day-to-day practical life while providing space for answers to present themselves. I accepted that, even if moving toward spirituality didn't physically heal me, if it could help me reduce stress and have a higher quality of life, then this was still a way God was helping me.

Many had mentioned meditation as a tool for finding a pathway to spirituality. I downloaded a meditation app and began a simple mindfulness practice. The proof was immediately evident and only improved with more focus and commitment. My practice has paved the way for much greater spirituality and presentness. The cancer remains, but the life I live is so much better. Of course, I want to live much longer, but this discovery has led to so much peace that I couldn't be more grateful for having learned this.

My hope is that in taking these steps, I am signaling to my psyche and physical self that I want to live a long and happy life. While connecting with God and building self-awareness, and at the same time netting out and actioning on that which hurts me, I am discarding stress and creating ideal conditions for my body to heal. I want all that I am doing to collectively be a loud voice screaming out to my body not just to work harder to fight, but also that I am worthy of living longer. Physical healing has not been achieved yet, but many wonderful things have happened along the way that make me realize that the Universe is working hard to drop all kinds of gifts down upon me.

So much has happened to make my life better that it is hard not to be bowled over in gratitude at how impactful my mindfulness practice has been in my life. It is helping me cure my cancer, but, as importantly, the healing process has begun to address the trauma I have discussed in these pages. For starters, where I spent an embarrassing amount of time reviewing, processing, and reliving past negative events, I have finally trained myself to understand that the past is truly the past, and that processing these things repeatedly only hurts me. There is literally nothing I can do about my past experiences except to learn from them and move on. To spend any more time on this than the time it takes to comprehend the lessons is a waste of time and valuable energy. What got me to this beautiful place? Cancer and the Universe. Perhaps God knew that the only way I would slow down and see the real beauty in life is to allow a deadly disease to show me the way.

Unfortunately, I had another problematic co-existing habit: When I wasn't fighting past or present battles, I was breathing life into future fantasy problems. I write that they are fantasy issues because these issues were those I was stressing over *before* they were even a reality. Because of my fear that my world could fall apart at any time, I invested serious time—a terrible investment—in these projected problems. In the therapeutic world, they call this catastrophizing. I felt an innate need to look ahead at what I thought could be an obstacle and begin planning to overcome it if it should appear. This works great in business, but pouring emotion into possible personal issues stole volumes of time and peace from me. How my mind managed these non-issues, and the energy that was expended to do so, was a bigger problem than any of the actual problems. Much of this was triggered by a childhood filled with dangerous circumstances. Decades of believing my world could fail at any moment forced me to build out an advanced warning radar ensuring I was always prepared for the worst. The unfortunate side effect was difficult to leave behind because it was ingrained in everything I was.

Meditation and mindfulness had great rewards, but the journey was challenging. As one might imagine, between the past and the future worry mongering, there wasn't much left of me to be present. Due to this and my drive toward spirituality, I accepted I had a real problem with plugging into what was happening in the here and now. Finally knowing the importance of reducing stress in my life as another tool for physical healing and living better, I was willing to acknowledge that this dysfunctional behavior was harmful and realized it was time to make changes. I knew that letting go and being *here* right now was an important component for healing, but my practical brain was screaming that I would fail if I didn't keep up with this self-torture. In its initial reveal, the experience of being in this strange place of "now" felt like fear and confusion. The idea of being present in the moment was so foreign to me that I didn't know what to do with it, and enjoying it wasn't what naturally came to me. *Fear* is the right word here because I had such a worry about letting anything slip, that telling myself it was OK to just sit with myself and enjoy the quiet seemed like a high-risk activity. I understand how dysfunctional this reads, but it was who I was.

The inner turmoil I was feeling in my early meditation sessions not only told me just how foreign "relaxing" was to me but also provided clarity regarding how important this work was to my psychological healing and the bridge to the physical healing that I had yet to build. I had been told many times in my life that I did not know how to "chill." I knew they were right to some degree, but I didn't think my life permitted this luxury. Now, with eyes physically closed to the sound of earthy downregulating recordings, I was experiencing the irrefutable evidence of just how much stress had ruled everything in my life. I found a version of myself that felt balanced, available, and happy. I wanted more...much more. I allowed myself to receive the gift of the most important self-care pivot of my life, while simultaneously accepting that I was worthy of this beautiful experience and have allowed the benefits to slip into other parts of my life.

Acknowledging that stress will always be a part of me and accepting that the struggle is normal and not "me," but just a function of me, has paved the way for my body to lower certain harmful biochemicals associated with stress. Those lower stress hormones have left me in a more grounded state, vastly improving my life, and that has, in turn, improved my chances of physically healing. I continue to go deeper in my practice and have a sense that the ultimate answer to my complete healing lies somewhere in this work, which I know the Universe is guiding me on.

This is all transformative and positive, but what does any of this have to do with God not owing me anything? To get to that part, I must fast forward from what has been a discussion on the value of mindfulness to a practical understanding of what impact it has had on my life. To do this, I need to provide an understanding of my mindset prior to cancer and prior to mindfulness.

As a kid, I took the trauma I experienced, pressed it down deep, and became a person obsessed with finding a better life and future for my family. Unfortunately, I did not know how to achieve this in a healthy, balanced way. Hard work and determination while swimming in a sea of troubles was a better mindset than caving into a victim mentality, but it wasn't a fun journey. While I was successfully earning that which I sought, I was hardened and broken inside. I was paying a price for ignoring the pain, but I was not aware of just how high the price was. For all the times that I read and agreed with the quote, "It's not the destination, it's the journey," I never adopted it. The promise to make change for myself and those that depend on me was paramount. My thinking was that any pain I was experiencing would be dealt with, if I wanted to deal with it at all, but only *after* I crossed the imaginary ever extending finish line in my mind. Admittedly, not considering myself worthy of help played a role, but surviving and following my vision were the most important themes of my life, and the little wins along the way were the primary affirmations that kept me driving forward. *My therapy* was to get wins and prove to myself that I could make something from nothing. This fed me emotionally and literally fed me by keeping food on the table.

However, just months after committing myself to my mindfulness journey, I was beginning to see I had been living my whole life in a constant state of fight or flight, and really had no idea of how to be present and at peace for any meaningful amount of time. Living in the moment was a fanciful idea that I aspired to reach in some far away future, but it wasn't meant for people like me as a way of living day to day. Learning I didn't have to be fretting over my past so frequently or preparing for future battles was not just uplifting, but also truly enjoyable! So much so, I couldn't believe I had ignored the value of peace and relaxation for most of my life.

Getting better at going deeper in my meditations allowed me to set aside the thoughts that were crippling my ability to enjoy life. In those moments, I discovered what peace and groundedness feels like. Most critically, in this space, I see in real time all the gifts being offered to me daily. I also see all those gifts that had been offered in my past that I had failed to recognize, but that had played a large part in all the successes on my journey. Many of those gifts have been mentioned in the pages of this book. Most of these gifts I regrettably didn't realize had been a part of my life until decades later. However, in a grounded state, I am full with gratitude and can see through a clearer and accurate lens that a higher force has been working in my favor all along.

I don't think of God as an entity existing to grant wishes, but I discovered something even more valuable to me. My mind had finally gone quiet enough to see how God had been playing a role in my life from the very beginning. In this state, I see with laser focus all that has been gifted. I recognize the gift of being human and possessing a body that is so intricately designed and functional at levels that even modern-day medicine can't fully explain. Then came the gift of troubled times that taught me many lessons that helped me get to where I am today. God was also responsible for allowing me to have the experience to do great things on my own. Rather than collapse because of my circumstances, with the support of the Universe, I embraced difficult times as the motivation needed to push myself. Instead of a reliance on victimness, the Universe kept me focused on my lifelong mission to lift me and future generations out of the Wellington cycle. Being obsessed with generational change was not conducive to an easy-going life, but at the same time, not wallowing in self-pity while life passed me by was also a gift. The more self-aware I become, the more gifts I realize I have taken for granted. Any doubts of a higher power have vanished. More practically speaking, my brain was previously too preoccupied with my history and an unpredictable future that I could not be "here" enough to see what I know now to be the truth—that God has showered me with gifts, and none has been greater than the knowing that my higher power is always there.

There is such a deep involvement by a higher power that I no longer dismiss them as random happenings. I've listed some below as examples, but the list is obviously much longer.

- Blackberries in a Baltimore City rental. Even as a toddler, these treats helped close the summer hunger gaps. I don't know how a patch of blackberries landed there, or how it survived with no care.

- Claudette, an upperclassman who saved me from a group of middle-school girls beating the stuffing out of me. She did this with complete unselfishness and with no fanfare or need for the deep gratitude I felt—an angel sent directly to help me.

- Mrs. Hickman, an English teacher (and therapist, unbeknownst to her), who helped me learn how to be free with my pen in expressing myself, allowing me a means to expel ugly energy while providing a tool to help weather my life.

- The Honorable *Sensei* Najib Amin (he's not a judge or elected official, but he is deserving of this prefix), an eighth *dan* karate instructor who was my most significant role model as a youngster. He showed me loyalty, discipline, direction, and the value of hard work.

- Finding friends that accepted me even with all my insecurities and dysfunction. It couldn't have been easy to be my friend with how I was living in and out of my head. I am deeply grateful for their influence and friendship.

- Ann-Marie, a great human who tolerated and loved me in such a broken condition, loved me unconditionally, and blessed me with three wonderful children.

- JoAnn, the best wife and friend I could ask for, who gave me two additional children and showed me what uninhibited spirituality and deep enveloping love looks like in practice.

- My five wonderful children, Connor, Kathryn, Ryan, Josie and Geaton. Each one is a beautiful mystery who has brought so much joy, purpose, and love to my life. There will never be a greater thing that I will do than being their father.

- Being blessed with a vision in my youth that provided the clarity for a lifelong mission; an unyielding compass that allowed me to set a course for a better life for my family, present and future.

- Living Crutchless-ly and not as a victim.

- Dr. Tomek Wyczesany, a chemist from Australia (originally from Poland) who became a mindfulness guru. From across the globe, he has been my mentor, guide, and friend on this beautiful self-aware journey.

- The soothing and healing sound of snow falling on snow on the quietest of winter nights.

- My brother John, protector and hero.

- "Ullabetta"—laugh often, live well. A gift from my eight-year-old daughter who taught me that living presently and happily is a choice.

- Cancer. Without cancer, I would have missed out on so much good in my life. The disease has not only positively impacted my life but has also created the opportunity for long-term, beautiful change. Without cancer, I suspect I never would have arrived at the clarity I have regarding my higher power.

I realize that despite having complete confidence in my God, I am only at the tip of the iceberg with how many gifts have been offered and accepted by me and how they have helped form this wonderful life I have.

Praying means different things to different people. I pray to find solitude and quiet time with God and to offer gratitude but never do so hoping for a special request to be granted. I consider myself to have been given all the gifts that I deserve and more. Those gifts started arriving the moment I was conceived. With the knowledge of all that has been created for me to have this life and how blessed I have been, it almost seems like it would be an insult to ask for anything more from God. Without ever asking or desiring credit, God keeps working in its quiet but purposeful way to make my life better all the time. Whatever happens, good or bad, is not the fault of my higher power—it's just life's normal course, which is still all part of a plan that is filled with innumerable gifts.

I know the generosity showering over me leaves me with full confidence that I am already living the gifts all around me with each breath and that with that profound gratitude, my only humble offering is that I know God owes me nothing. But having received so much, what else am I responsible for?

For the answer to this, I turn to instinct and experience. I believe that what the Universe expects or wants for itself is essentially nothing. It is eternally unselfish. However, I can't just accept all that I have enjoyed and benefited from and stop there. Based on my intuition, I believe the answer for me is simple. I am responsible for doing my best, despite any circumstances, to explore all the gifts God granted to me since before I was born and all along the road of life. In doing so, I can make the world a better place by sharing these gifts the way that so many have shared and continue to share with me.

Also, I feel strongly that God expects me to honor, love, and support those I had a part in bringing into this world. I also believe that the Universe expects that we will continue to learn through all the days of our lives so we can be better individually and as a species. Clearly, the great religions of the world got it right: Living a life of service to others, honorable interactions, a focus on commonalities not differences, concern for beings of all types, and support of family and friends are all ways to show our gratitude. These and other baseline positive human attributes are what makes the world a better place. I believe God would want that.

Bringing children into this world deserves more attention as I believe that how we treat our offspring is important to showing respect to God for the gift of children in our lives. Despite the environment I was born into, I was still granted the beautiful gift of life, and wonderful things have happened. And now, I have been given the gift of being part of creating life for five human beings. None of my history matters. I believe out of appreciation for these beautiful gifts, I have an absolute unrelenting responsibility to love, provide for, protect, and teach my children how to be good humans. I don't get a pass because I had a difficult upbringing. In my opinion, to bring my children into this world and not make best efforts would be a slap to the face of God. That might seem strong, but I can't imagine a world where I have accepted so many gifts and then choose to use my past for why I have failed my family or failed to make the most out of my life. For my purposes, it feels like my most important work and the most impactful way to give back.

Having accepted a higher power later in life while recognizing its guiding generous presence throughout, I am in a deep state of gratitude and respect. While I am incapable of fully understanding its great impact on my life, I know the gifts offered up to me have far outweighed the struggle, and it is massively net-positive in my life. With that mindset, I know I am owed nothing and search out ways to give back so that I honor these gifts, and honor God.

Important Case Study: Ullabetta as Proof of Interventional Gifts and God's Involvement, Brought to Me (and You) by an Eight-Year-Old

After my cancer diagnosis but before I had developed a working mindfulness practice, I was still dealing with issues much the way I always had. I was hyper-focused on running worst-case future scenarios through my mind and re-visiting past issues in supposed need of resolution. Both activities were using up much of my emotional capital and time. Living a life with the primary intent being to avoid failure might have kept me from being homeless, but it was a life heavy on mission and light on spontaneity and joy. I seemed to believe joy and peace were for the weak. Not fully bought into the idea that I could have good things, I needed something or someone to help me see all the endless subroutines I was processing night and day in my head and help me discover how good life can be just by letting go and seeing what happens.

In June 2020, almost a year after my diagnosis, I was just beginning to form a mindfulness practice. At times, I felt true moments of relaxation and lucid clarity where so much fuzziness had existed. I have had many teachers in my life but none that were successful in teaching me how to enjoy life and be grounded. This was not for lack of trying or me being disinterested. In fact, the concept of enjoying life held great interest for me, so much so that years earlier I had performed another personal study on the wonderful topic of *Happiness*. I learned so much, but the problem was that I was still all about the destination and not the journey, so I could not allow myself to adopt their wisdom. Meditation opened that door for me and made me crave more from it. However, meditation did not have enough impact on my everyday handling of things. In very much the same hammer and chisel work ethic I had used on every other perceived or actual problem in my life, I was deeply engaged in processing the terrible scenarios that are a real part of what I am facing. I was worrying intensely about dying and worse, dying slowly and being a massive burden to my wife and family.

Thankfully, my eight-year-old daughter, Josie, stepped in to teach me how to live my best life no matter the obstacles in my path. I think of her involvement as a direct intervention by the Universe because of how she was acting and what was directly delivered (gifted) to me in the process. It was so much more advanced than what an eight-year-old could normally offer. I can brag that Josie is incredibly intuitive and intelligent, which is true, but her involvement was far beyond that.

On a June night in 2020, I was tucking my six-year-old son, Geaton, and eight-year-old Josie into bed. I was not in a good frame of mind, as I was processing some recent medical results. Distracted, I was half-heartedly going through our normal nighttime process, a time I normally used to tap into the highlights of their day. My second stop was to Josie's room. After she and I caught up on the day, I headed downstairs with the intention of sulking on the couch and doing anything to avoid any more thoughts of my situation. As I had used so many times before, the plan was to call up my old friend "isolation" and use it to help me catastrophize the results.

Bent on giving myself to depression, as I was heading down the steps from their rooms, I heard Josie laughing. It was not unusual for her to be restless in bed and find ways to burn off energy so she could fall asleep. Sometimes, I would see a light come on or hear her moving about, but laughing out loud by herself was not something I had ever heard before. Still stuck in the muck of my brain, I yelled up a reminder from the bottom of the stairs that it was time for her to sleep. A few more minutes passed, and I could hear her laughing again, this time more loudly. I poked my head up the staircase directly below her bedroom and, more sternly this time, reminded her it was time for rest. A few minutes later Josie's laughing persisted, so, in a slightly irritated state, I climbed the stairs to see what the commotion was about.

When I arrived in her room, her little body was slightly propped up on her down pillow and she continued to laugh heartily, even as I stood there right in front of her. Urging her to stop laughing and to go to sleep had no effect. Even knowing I had come to her room for the specific purpose of getting her to settle down, she was literally laughing in my face. This was extraordinary behavior for her.

As I stood there considering my next move and listening to her beautiful laughter, I could not help but feel myself softened from the inside. Yet, I had a pressing date with isolation, so, in keeping with my bad habit, I continued to gently encourage her to stop so I could return to my perch downstairs. However, feeling a small lightness in my heart, I was beginning to be curious about what all this laughter was about.

Seeing that my efforts were in vain and that her laughter was only growing makes me smile today just thinking about the moment. I eventually asked her why she could not stop herself from laughing. My query came with no answer and only fueled a deeper, louder laugh from her, which, in turn, made *me* begin to laugh. In my giggling, I kept pressing, but at this point she could not stop herself enough to even speak. Another one of the gifts from the Universe I hadn't acknowledged before in my life was the power of laughter and how it can become contagious, soothing, and healing. It's as if the soul knows how wonderful it is to smile and feel joy, and the natural byproduct is that we can temporarily forget the negative and allow room for true happiness. What was happening in her room was a good example of this. Before long, the joy of laughter overwhelmed both of us, and, still with no reason for why it all began, we fell into a rare belly laugh. During all this great fun, I realized I couldn't even remember when I had laughed so hard.

Through our laughter, I eventually pressed her to offer up some idea of what the catalyst was for this remarkable moment. Barely able to get the words out, Josie finally said, "I invented a word." Of course, I asked what the word was, and this only triggered us to laugh even more. Minutes later, she said, "It's *Ullabetta!*"

I was in tears with my laughter as we both sat giggling at the foot of her bed. Barely able to speak at this point, I asked her what the word meant. She told me she didn't know, which made us laugh even more. Eventually, we wound down with smiles plastered on our faces as we discussed the moment. My face had not used the muscles needed for deep laughter in so long, and I actually felt soreness around my eyes and mouth from the experience. She had a thought that she might have invented the word as a name for a new type of needlepoint stitch, but she wasn't certain, and it wasn't important. What was most important to me was that I had noticed how I had changed, more like transformed, in those minutes with her. I suggested that given the extent of our laughter, maybe *Ullabetta* meant we should laugh often. We agreed this would be the meaning from then on. With us both breathing normally but still feeling waves of happiness, even euphoria, I tucked her in, and a short while later, returned to the couch. I felt like I was floating down the steps with joy.

The event was so incredibly unique and brought so much unplanned happiness to me in a moment where I was determined to sit in my sadness, but the story for me could not stop there. I processed the event with great interest in the minutes and days that followed. What was offered to me were amazing lessons on intentionality, true happiness and living my best life. I realized that Ullabetta was so much more to me than an odd one-off anomaly. In that moment, the marriage of my mindfulness work and practical life became joined. I could no longer ignore that feeling good didn't have to be reserved for the short moments I was meditating, I could potentially work to feel good in everything I was doing. I feel strongly that the event and the message I received came directly from a joint partnership between Josie and the Universe. Quite effectively, what had been shown to me was proof of concept that a force greater than myself not only wanted something much better and useful for me, but that this message had far-reaching implications on everything in my life from that day forward. Also, the massive positive physical impact that I felt for weeks was a direct example of how simply allowing for joy and happiness can be an important part of building the bridge to healing my cancer.

When I returned to my spot on the couch, I neither sat in purposeful isolation nor even turned on the television. I felt light and energized, and my soul was basking in the joy the moment had offered. It was impossible for me not to see how my mindset was wildly opposite of where I was before I ventured up those stairs. I'm certain the laughter had a biochemical effect, which might be how a physician would explain the positive physical change I felt throughout. However, I believe there was something much deeper than body chemistry to consider. Aside from our time being transformative in an immediate sense, Josie had managed to teach me a lesson about the joy of present-ness and the importance of being purposeful in what I choose to focus my headspace on. All of this wisdom came from an eight-year-old child! I had lived decades prior to this event, and, in all that time, I had never allowed myself the opportunity to purposely choose happiness and present-ness in the moment. It was Josie's unwillingness to cave in to my demands that showed me how fantastic life can be when I have the intention to be happy right now. I never thought that I would be someone that would ever type out the words, *happiness is a choice*, but truly it is.

Without ever conveying a thought while outright ignoring my unengaged attitude as I tucked her in, she challenged me in the strongest way possible. The message received from her and God was that I had a right to be sad and worried but concentrating only on those emotions offered no positive return. I was influenced by her to make a conscious choice. A battle was playing out right in front of me—I could maintain my disposition and continue to process and immerse myself in the worst, or I could look into the eyes of this beautiful child, hear her laughter and how it softened me to the core, and make the conscious choice to let go and be there with her in those moments. The Universe couldn't have sent this message in any better manner or had it be any better timed. It is as if God knew that a lifetime of blindness to the gifts around and a focus only on crisis would prevent me from seeing and hearing something I desperately needed. In knowing this, it decided to bring the sublime message through the actions of an innocent, precious soul it knew I respected and loved dearly. I could either be depressed and focused on something I have very little power to change, or I could hear the message and live in the much better alternative of spending time with a happy, laughing eight-year-old girl. As easy of a choice as this should have been, I still fought it initially, but the Universe persisted. I believe that God knew that I needed to hear this communication and knew just how to get me to listen. I also know that the lesson is an important part of my psychological and physical healing.

Choosing happiness is something I had read a lot about prior to the Ullabetta moment, but, true to my history, I had never acted on it. It would be useful information I might apply one day, but only *after* I achieved all my planned success. I understood the concept and believed it to be valid but foolishly believed that to do something so squishy as purposefully choosing happiness was something that would hold me back in life, *not help me!* I considered the pursuit of happiness to be a wonderful ambition that one day I might be lucky enough to consider. Wow, how wrong I was. In the beautiful fallout that followed, I can see how wonderful things are when I choose to ignore what I can't control and lean into the positive. It also highlighted how little I have done to give myself a break and reward myself.

The gift of Ullabetta continues to work in my life in important ways. Since that powerful moment, I practice frequently how to intentionally choose happiness and joy rather than pain and suffering. I also humbly accept that this has been a choice all along, but one that I didn't realize was available, or perhaps I had grown so dependent on the false rewards of catastrophizing that I couldn't see that it had always been a choice. Due to that moment with Josie, I know that living a life of joy and optimism is something I must spend the rest of my life working toward.

Understanding the profound importance and with a strong desire to keep practicing how to live a more positive life, I added to the definition and decided that the word should not only mean to laugh often but also to live well. I did this because the more I thought of the idea of laughing often (more literally, being positive and optimistic), the more I realized it is quite difficult to laugh often if I am not living well. I check in with my Ullabetta status several times a day and have built out the definition further to give me more specifics on direction as I live my life. It seems that even with such a beautiful, organically created message, my practical mind cannot help but build out a system to support and integrate Ullabetta into my life.

In the wake of the experience, I am proud of where Ullabetta has landed on my spiritual, psychological, and practical landscapes. The event and the word that hatched from it were just so strangely impactful to me that it almost seems like the experiences I have read about how people process out of body experiences or messages from non-earthly sources. In these situations, the person impacted often deeply connects with the moment and what follows is permanent life change and a deeper self-awareness. This was not an out of body experience, of course, but the event was so critically important in my life that I can't think of it as anything else other than a message from God. I *know* that I am supposed to take action on this information and incorporate Ullabetta into my life. Knowing this (not thinking or believing, but knowing), and subsequently creating a structure to continue this important work is a purposeful collaboration between the hammer-and-chisel Daniel and the newfound version of Daniel that is open and willing to see all the opportunity for happiness around me. It also shows respect and gratitude to Josie and God for this wonderful gift that means so much to me.

The definition of "laughing often" has evolved. Framed under Ullabetta, laugh(ing) often does not mean to me that I need to seek out belly laughs like that special night in every corner of my life. Of course, more belly laughs would be great but seeking that out as an objective isn't realistic and not really the point. What laughing often means to me in a broader, more conceptual way is that I should purposely be in touch with my day-to-day thinking in as real time as I can be and always make best efforts to point myself toward purposely positive experiences in my life. It is the mindfulness/self-awareness piece of the transformation. My check-in function is to be purposefully attentive to what I am engaging with in my life: Am I consciously choosing to tune into interactions that bring about joy, gratitude, happiness, friendship, authenticity, vulnerability, support, calm, peace, and, of course, laughter? Conversely, am I noticing in real time the situations that have the opposite impact on me, and am I turning away from them when I am able? My process is likely common sense to those where happiness comes easily. However, given my long history and addiction to leaning into crises, and knowing that this message was purposely meant as guidance for me to permanently change course, I feel called to be very intentional about keeping this beautiful initiative on my front burner.

Later, I realized that simply turning toward positive interactions was a great start, but that alone was not going to be enough to ensure lasting change. The practice of "laughing often," as I describe just above, is great, but I couldn't do that with any kind of consistency unless I also "live(d) well." The idea of living well is too broad to have any real meaning, but I knew from the moment I added this what it meant to me. It's important to note that the definition intentionally does *not* read "live adventurously," "live fantastically," or "live like you are dying." I needed something that was grounded and where a grandiose manner of living was not only *not* required, but also not the point.

"Live well," as part of the *Ullabetta* definition and check-in process, is the practical piece. It means I am consciously assessing the events, people, places, and things I am interacting with. If my assessment tells me that any of these things are triggering pain or discomfort, and that it has been repetitive and looks to be something that has predictable long-term exposure with probable downside to my well-being, then I make a mental note and become more curious about why. If I cannot effect immediate change on that which I have identified as harmful to me (clearly net-negative), then I know that with no change, an about face from that element is in my near future. I also challenge myself on important baseline check-ins like my physical health and psychological well-being, diet, and my value system. This process addresses the fact that finding ways to laugh more (being more positive, loving, and optimistic) is much easier and has a higher chance of lasting success if how I am living is creating fertile ground for joy and happiness to occur more easily.

Running my life through my *"Ullabetta, Laugh Often, Live Well"* filter and using that process to check in with myself is creating new life-serving habits that have laid the important infrastructure needed to make lasting change. I couldn't be more grateful to Josie and the Universe for this beautiful gift.

Sitting on my couch that day in June after Josie intervened on my behalf changed my life forever. There is the undeniable power of the word *Ullabetta* and the spiritual circumstances for how and why I think it was born, and that could be the end of the story. However, as important as the moment was the nuts-and-bolts proof of the struggle between positive thinking and the darkness that had lived within me for so long, and the little girl who was insistent on teaching me that my whole life could change for the better if I allowed myself to just laugh more and live in the now. Yes, messages and gifts are truly coming all the time from many sources. I am compelled to remember that to hear and see all that is being offered to me, I must allow myself to be available and open.

It took me a long time to write this section. The moment was so powerful to me that I worried that I would not adequately convey the event or the long-term impact it has had on my life. As I re-read my words, I feel like the message is there, but I know I will never fully be able to share the full meaning of its impact on me. However, I do hope that the story might help others. And as important, I hope it is a great example of how gifts are all around us and can come from the most unexpected places.

Josie and I enjoying the woods on a fall day. Nature is where I have always felt most at peace. Being with her fully in the moment, dreaming, talking and laughing—a pure Ullabetta moment.

Epilogue

I am happy to be at the end of this long project. It didn't take so long to write just because I'm a slow writer. It is true that I will never be the person who can sit down and write a book in a few months' time. However, the primary reason this has taken decades is because I've been writing here and there as my life ran its normal, busy course. I must remind myself that starting multiple businesses, two marriages, solving for cancer, being an active father to five children, and the myriad of other things I have been involved in do take up a lot of time and are adequate excuses for not finishing much sooner. There were months when not even a page was written, when my busy life had many supposedly important priorities.

Additionally, there were periods of time that I hated coming to my computer to do this work because writing this book, while liberating at times, was also tantamount to reliving my past. Old, scabbed over, but not fully healed trauma wounds, were seeing daylight again, and this was painful. Writing of my past was giving permission for my history to have a loud voice again, which dredged up a lot of bad memories and emotions. It's hard to dig up old bones; however, one of the biggest drivers of this effort was to attempt to free myself from significant baggage, and so I continued. Taking so long to write it only prolonged the discomfort, but it was what the Universe wanted. There were moments where I questioned if it even made any sense to continue and at what cost, but I kept coming back, thinking that it would mean something important to me and maybe others in the end. There were days I thought I should delete the project, but I am happy I never did. I think God sensed there would be the ultimate gift of healing and pushed me to continue.

I look at how much time has passed and how events have come and gone. I consider the years of notes of thoughts and experiences, and the emails written to myself or Post-its lying about my desk, and the uncounted hours of ideas and deep introspection that would never make it into this book. There is so much more there, some of it much worse than what is found in these pages, but what I captured is adequate to satisfy my intentions. I think of how far I've come in this time and realize that had I finished the book in a year, or say even ten years, the tone and I believe much of the message would have been significantly different. Even though the introduction of the book written many years ago might sound as if I was in a casual state of mind, I know today the truth is more that in those moments, my feelings of calm were rare, and that much of who I was then was still very much broken and lost. What a great journey it has been.

Knowing this, I still wanted to keep the introduction as it was, because it reflects the flow of my life and how I have changed. I am happily a different person today than when I started this book. For starters, it wasn't until recently that I discovered how to be present. With respect to a God, twenty years ago, a higher power seemed unlikely to me, but I would have been willing to discuss it, albeit with great skepticism. Ten years ago, I had evolved to a place where I knew I believed in a higher power but never connected the dots or felt gratitude and respect for the many gifts in my life. Today, I know God is omnipotent and an integral part of everything I do. I am living proof that people really can change in time for the better. I smile today knowing that *Crutchless* was completed when God wanted it to be done. Perhaps the Universe understood long ago that I needed to process ideas and my past when writing this book and that it would take a long time to do so.

If I apply the netting concept to the writing of this book, I think that the complete results are still to be revealed. While on the journey, there were many net-negative periods when I literally scowled at the keyboard when I sat down. However, as I got closer to the finish line, I had an elevated sense that even if no one reads this, completing it was still the right move for me. I can write resolutely that the project is emphatically net-positive. I know now that this was an important life mission for me, and its completion is an important part of healing both my mind and body. Does writing *Crutchless* fit inside of my Ullabetta model for intentionally living my best life (laugh often, live well)? Absolutely. Pain does still exist in my Ullabetta world, and I still must do hard things to put me on track to getting to the good of things. Using the book as an example, getting out all the muck from inside is part of *Living Well* to me. It meant that to have a better life, I was willing to undergo the pain and the work it took to finish this project, believing at most points that it will ultimately make my life better in ways I don't fully understand yet.

Not too long ago, I was driving down the road with my two youngest children, Geaton and Josie. It was a spring day and as usual, we were jamming out to some loud music with the windows wide open in my Toyota Highlander. The song that we were singing was "1, 2, 3, 4, 5, 6" by Fitz and The Tantrums, released in 2019. As I always do, I was reading the lyrics from my car phone stand as we sang loudly to the world flying by. The song talks about hard work, having a vision for your life, the lows and highs of life, choosing paths, doing it on your own, and achieving great results. Relatability would be an understatement. It was as if this song, like many others before it, was written for me to hear and process the message. The young people who co-wrote the song definitely know a thing or two about being Crutchless and that bad happenings don't have to stop us from having a great life. The experience in total—the kids' voices, hearing their laughter, the snappy tune, the relatable lyrics, the spring breeze—lifted me with joy and made me smile deep down into my soul. The artists' subtle reminder that we must be in control of our lives and all that we allow into it was a perfect affirmation of a lifelong, successful mission. It was a pure *Ullabetta* moment as we laughed and lived well bustling down the country road. As in that simple everyday moment, it was another example proving that there is always an opportunity to live my life more fully.

I dropped the kids at their elementary school drop-off line, then waited in traffic to get back out onto the main road. The song ended, the sun came out, and, with joy in my heart and a smile across my face, I played the song again and drank in the wise, poppy words of affirmation. I felt like these artists, and I had something in common as I wondered what they had overcome in their lives while thanking them for sharing their therapeutic wisdom in just three minutes and thirty-one seconds. They ask in the song if I can feel the vibe. You can bet I did. The song gave me more proof of how great it is to be present and to appreciate my connection to everything, while understanding that struggle of one kind or another is universal to all.

As I close out, I am reminded of a quote by Hermann Hesse that I had read somewhere; a perfect summation of my experience.

"God does not send us despair in order to kill us, he sends it in order to awaken us to new life." —Hermann Hesse, German/Swiss Poet and Nobel Prize winner

I have much to be thankful for in my life. Learning that God has been guiding and teaching me from the very beginning has been humbling and life changing to my core. Perhaps the greatest lesson was that living a Crutchless life, while using all the gifts that have been granted along the way, has blessed me with family, love and boundless opportunity. From this point, I hope to continue my learning and healing journey, while helping others. It is the least I can do for all that has been given to me.

Acknowledgements

Thank you...

To all who have shared their gifts inadvertently or directly. Your impact has been significant, and I am forever grateful.

To Megan for your help in editing this book. Your expertise has made this project much better.

To *The Average* for giving me the space where I feel most at home and empowered. I am proud to say that being here with you is the only place I will ever fit in. We Are The People.

To Angie, Christos, Alexis and Demi for allowing me to have some of Jeff's precious time. His impact was and is profound, and I am blessed to have called him my friend.

To cancer for creating the opportunity for me to be quiet and listen, showing me a path toward living a much more rewarding and engaged life in the right now.

To Genie, Christine, Sandy and Jen for reading Crutchless in its early forms. Your feedback was invaluable.

To Tomek for your friendship, encouragement and showing me just how far I can go.

To my *Forum*, Matty, Khaled, Ross, Jon and Burt. Your wisdom and friendship for all these years are a treasure.

To Josie for the gift of Ullabetta on one not so random June night. You have permanently changed how I live my life, and I will always be grateful.

To JoAnn, for being my best friend and supporting me tirelessly on this project. There is zero chance I could have completed it without your love and unfailing devotion.

Thank you to my beautiful family for your support. You are the fuel reminding me to give the best of myself for all of us and those that will come after us.

To God, for all the gifts given and all those that are yet to be revealed.

Appendix

How God Fits in These Pages

My view of religion is unconventional, and, while I have shared my views freely in these pages, I had no desire to influence or change anyone's opinions on the existence or influence of a higher power, nor would I ever want to offend anyone that might think differently. In my youth, whenever someone started talking about God, I would almost instantly start plotting my escape from the conversation. If you feel similar today, I can relate, as I travelled through most of my young life with no belief or faith in anything beyond the physical realm.

However, my path in life has unexpectedly led me to a place where I have no choice now but to believe. Coming to this understanding was a tremendously positive personal evolution fed by life experiences, observations, struggle, pain, love, and even *facts*. I can no longer refute God's presence in everything, though, I admit, my thoughts on this higher power will not fit neatly into any current dogma.

While some might be pleased that my view of spirituality is fluid and not bound by any limitations, others might be disappointed that I have not chosen to constrain my understanding of God to a set of rules, thought patterns, or scripture, or that I do not connect my beliefs to any specific religious doctrine. However, I believe my personal understanding of a higher power does align with the general value systems of most of the great religions of the world. For clarification purposes, I view the words *God, Source, Higher Power,* and *Universe* as being interchangeable.

When I began to write this book years ago, the thought of including any discussion about religion or a higher power was not on my mind. Back then, I would have best described my spirituality as cynical, albeit with a hope for something more. This hopefulness was anchored more in the fear of what comes after death than in anything relating to the desire for the help of any supposed God in my life. It's interesting how wrong I was for so many years, but that part of my journey would take time and experience to come to a comfortable understanding about my belief in my higher power.

There are several reasons for this change of thinking and for why this subject is important to this book. Having built and sold an internationally focused business, gone through a divorce then remarried, and had five beautiful children along the way, I tended to be very busy. In my mind, slowing down to even consider the *possibility* of a higher power and what value that power might bring to me represented time poorly spent. I viewed God as something unnecessary in my life. If "it" did exist, I didn't think it had any concern for me. As such, the topic could only be a time waster, a circuitous pondering that could never lead to any answers because there could be no absolute proof, and I was a man with no time to waste.

In my world, if I wasn't scratching and clawing to make something of myself, I felt my time was not being used well. I wrongly thought that spirituality was for people who needed to be led and for those who needed to find hope beyond the lives they were living.

I also had thoughts that God was for those with easy lives, easy enough that they had time on their hands for soft topics like giving gratitude to a God while their lives went swimmingly well. Based on that false premise, I determined that God must not be for me. And since I lived constantly in fight-or-flight mode with no obvious evidence of God working in my life, I spent my time where it would get the most return: surviving.

I realize now my opinion was wrong on so many levels. I simply had no understanding then of what it meant to have faith, and I am still learning today, in my own personal way. What I did know was I was living 24/7—yes, even in my sleep—with the intense fear that catastrophic failure was right around the corner. My fears included failing in business, failing as a father, and, generally, failing as a human being. My daily disposition was, "one wrong move, and I could be on the street." Truth be told, I wasn't far away from that fate on many occasions. As such, my drive was always focused on accumulating and building a mountain of wealth and material things.

I didn't seek out wealth and "stuff" because I was caught up with equaling or surpassing the accomplishments of my peers. Rather, my purpose for accumulation was the idea that, if I could only get my pile high enough, I could eliminate the possibility of ending up homeless and alone. This idea was materialistic, but, as you have come to understand my life better in these pages, you might see how this warped thought process made perfect sense throughout much of my life.

It took too many years, but I know now that while money kept me off the street, the little mountain I successfully built never reduced my fear and anxiety much. I cannot say my fear was all bad, as it drove me to be a success in business and a consistent provider for my family. However, after spending so much mental capital in a worrying-and-working state, there wasn't time left over to consider "impractical" ideas like spirituality or how stress was affecting my well-being.

Whatever effort I expended in those days *needed* to be spent keeping my fears at bay. If whatever I was doing wasn't targeted to keep the bills paid and moving forward, then it had no place in my life. I was so twisted that even exercising and relaxing made me feel guilty. I constantly told myself that if I felt good—if I did something to serve myself—then surely something else in my life was on the verge of breaking. Had I found some hope of a higher power and how to apply that in my life, spirituality may have been exactly what I needed to begin to understand my past and dispel much of my fear. Faith could have played a positive role, but I was not ready for that. I suspect it also would have helped me to be even more successful on both a professional and personal level.

While I was working and building a life and fending off fear as best I could, I still made time to read and to observe the world around me. From engines to ecosystems, I've always been interested in how things work. Religion, particularly as an enterprise, fascinated me. I recognized that billions of people were following various organized religions, and I believed there had to be good reasons for this fact, even if I did not subscribe to their views. If such a huge number of people were finding safe harbor and community, both of which I desperately needed in my own life by practicing their religions, there had to be, at a minimum, something worthwhile there to better understand.

So with the idea of gaining some general education in organized religion, I added some research time to my plate, and I learned a great deal in the process. My greatest finding might have been the discovery that, while there are elements that make each of the world's great religions distinctly different from the others, there are important similarities, too. At the same time, I also found myself struggling with a conundrum: If each religion believed their view of God was right as a stand-alone entity, then this also meant that the billions of people who believed in other religions had it wrong.

Herd mentality often contributes extensively to how we make many of our decisions. From my own professional experience, I knew this phenomenon was prolific in the financial field. If well-regarded analysts recommend a stock, claiming that it will go from $20 to $100 in a year, many of their followers will respond by investing a chunk of their life savings into the stock, perhaps with visions of an early retirement. Do big numbers of followers alone make the recommendations correct? Sometimes they can in a self-fulfilling prophecy kind of way, but we need look no further than the dot-com bubble of 2000, where many well respected analysts were banging the table to buy dot-com tech stocks all the way up to meteoric unjustifiable heights, only to see most of those recommendations crash to the point that they were worth only a fraction of that value in almost no time.

With religion, I recognized that the great number of believers across many generations is a proxy proof of its underpinnings. This confidence machine, carried forward across the ages, further fuels the beliefs of its newer members, who, in turn, carry it further, right up until the present day. Certainly, among the billions of followers, there must be some that step back and question the tenets of their particular faith, but many simply follow the herd. Curiously, this occurs even as billions of others are following another deeply established religion with hundreds of years of its own history and set of beliefs.

I'm not a herd-mentality person, and I don't ever think that because a room full of people think differently than me, I must be wrong. It's not that I'm an icon of free thinking. Instead, because I had so many years of life in which my voice was the *only* guide I had, I grew to trust it. Diving deeper, I was intrigued to process the idea that if Christianity, Hinduism, and Islam—each with over a billion believers—all claim that their version of a higher power is correct, and, for the sake of argument, if only one *is* in fact right, then billions of people are following religions that have it wrong.

I decided to set aside the debate of which religion had it right or wrong, and, instead, focused on the more basic idea of a general faith in a higher power. Why, I wanted to know, did literally billions of people have such strong faith convictions? And, more importantly, could faith do anything for me, particularly in regard to my lifelong battles with fear and anxiety, and my growing need to find something more in my life than just arduously climbing professional ladders and squirreling away nuts for my family's future?

Before long, I found myself reading a small stack of books on various religions and still more books by thinkers who took positions for and against those religions. I wanted to find the best in religion and determine if there was a place for me. I even took the time to read the Old Testament cover to cover. All of this material held my interest, but I found nothing that convinced me to buy into one specific religion over the others. I did, however, find significant positives in each, which was encouraging.

At the same time, the rules and regulations around worship were a turn-off for me. How could a religion preach about an awesome God, tout the amazing miracles this God supposedly makes happen in every moment of every day, and then try to convince me that this same God demands my worship in very specific, canned ways, and that I follow a set of rules that supposedly came from that God itself? That was confusing for my still-too-practical mind.

I also failed to grasp how providing affirmation through prayer or other actions to a higher power could be something that any version of God I could envision would want or need. To me, such a want or need seemed distinctly human. Even with framing my thinking using material from the Catholic sermons of my youth, I could not acclimate to the notion that all the great that God supposedly does was somehow supported, and possibly even fueled, by these very human lists of tasks to perform. Nor could I bite off the idea I was less worthy of God's attention and love if I did not perform these things.

More questions came to mind: *Does God have a need for positive reinforcement? Does God go away if we don't offer up enough positive affirmation?*

While I realize that deeply knowledgeable religious scholars and committed followers have their own answers to each of my questions, I ultimately concluded that the rules and regulations of organized worship represent guidance from man and *not* from God itself. In accepting that mankind is imperfect in many ways, it was hard for me to trust what man has committed to the pages of scripture as absolute *truth*, especially with thousands of years of interpretations and many translations. Having determined that some, or perhaps all, of the organized religions have elements that cannot be proven as completely accurate left me content to feel compelled not choosing *any* of them for my personal and practical application. Yet, in all of my research, I found it to be a positive that nothing yet had convinced me that there was no God.

OK, then, if I was not going to choose any organized religion, where did that leave me in my quest for betterment through faith? Despite centuries of religious-based violence, something else that was very positive stood out for me while performing this deep dive. Even though the various faiths don't always seem to practice what they literally preach, all of the great religions seemed to share the core values of peace, harmony, love, and acceptance. This was something I could get behind, and it allowed me to happily conclude that if a person can walk into a church, temple, synagogue, or mosque and find something to believe in, and that belief improves their lives and the lives of those around them, then that alone was proof enough for me to see and accept the benefit of a religious platform. These values are safe and beneficial to mankind, and if they are not contorted in some way as to poison the good that they bring, then I could see why these principles and sense of community would unify and fulfill so many.

Beyond that, it remains a big leap for me to believe that everything said under any roof of worship is a complete truth, or that the organization has any special access to God. Thousands of years of well-documented religious-sponsored atrocities proves that religious leaders often lose their connection to God along the way. Or, even worse, that their God, if it in fact was giving the orders as they had proclaimed in centuries past, is cruel.

More questions kept coming to my mind: *Did God evolve in its thoughts over millenium, to become more modern and less of a tyrant? If God instructed early religious leaders to commit horrific acts, has it now changed its mind?* I realize that thinkers and scholars with far more education and nuanced thinking than me have long pondered these and other important questions, and have answered them to their own satisfaction, but there remains for me a Grand Canyon-sized chasm between the greatness of what I think God must be and the humanized teachings across all faiths supporting worship of God. I struggled to accept the idea that the guidance from these religions comes from God itself. Still, I wasn't ready to completely dismiss in totality the value of religion and knew I needed to spend some more time on what it had to offer. I still sought to know whether I could "reach" God, and be reached, without the discomfort I was feeling about organized religion.

Finally, I had a personal breakthrough, one that I think the discovery of was precisely the thing that was making my whole deep dive so difficult to process. Cue the heavenly chorus in the background... My aha moment came after I realized the source of my blockage—that *religion* had become a catch-all word that had evolved to be an umbrella term bundling three distinct "faiths" within any organized worship group. Breaking down this everyday simple word used everywhere was the key to gaining clarity.

I realized that the *first faith* is faith in scripture, which I define as a belief in the documented stories and written history of each religion. These scriptures can teach great lessons and are fascinating on some levels, but, to me, did not alone represent proof itself of God's existence. Further, nothing I read seemed to be something I *must* believe to have God in my life.

Rules and regulations represent the *second faith* of any religion, and I believe these to be the only components to which the word *religion* should apply. I see these rules and regulations simply as the "how-tos" of worshipping God and living a life while adhering to those rules. Structure is needed in any organization so this is not concerning, but again I found that for my own needs, it didn't seem like something that is required to connect with my higher power.

The *third faith* that lives inside of the "religion bundle" is the one that I have concluded to be of the greatest importance to me. In fact, I believe it is the *only* one that matters. The third faith is the faith in God itself. To my way of thinking, when scripture and rules and regulations are bolted onto faith in God itself, it seems I am being offered an all-or-nothing proposition, and that simply was too much for me to passively swallow.

Partitioning off the first two "faiths" brought me tremendous relief in my quest. I knew then that God could be all or nothing of what I had learned. But, in truth, none of that needed to matter. What was most salient was only what I believed God was to me.

Playing out my life as a case study, my personal experience with the Catholic religion had been that if I wanted to be a member, then I was strongly encouraged to accept the scripture, the rules and regulations, and faith in God as a bundle. It felt a bit like choosing a cable provider, where I might not want channels like Showtime or HBO, but if I wanted cable, I had to take the whole package. It remains a mindbender to me to think that, in addition to making the big leap to accept God, I was not believing properly unless I accepted their brand's full package.

I understand that many modern Catholic priests would say I don't really have to believe *everything* I read or hear in the Catholic teachings to be a member of the faith in good standing. However, as a literalist, this pick-and-choose flexibility leads to even more confusion and a bit of frustration on my part. What good is modern-day religion if it lays out all the rules to living and serving God, but then sidebars that I only "kinda sorta" have to believe what I am hearing and reading?

Even if I allow for the evolution of religion over thousands of years, which has occurred to accommodate changing cultural and societal beliefs and tolerances, it weakens for me the credibility of the religion itself. If God is setting the rules and has done so for *eternity*, am I really supposed to interpret that even small changes, such as women no longer having to wear the required head coverings in the Catholic masses I attended in the 1960s, represent an order that came right from the boss itself? My mind processes this idea as follows:

Many ages ago, God gave a message through its most esteemed leaders that it was critically important that women wear head coverings to be accepted by God and respected by the men around them. Then, later, and coincidentally just about the time that mankind was thinking the mandate seemed dated, in an astonishing act of synchronicity, God sent a message to the leaders of the Church that the head coverings no longer were a requirement. A beautiful and convenient coincidence!

Did this change come directly from the deity itself or was this a leadership initiative from within the religion? If it was God, then why would it bother with something so mundane as head coverings, while at the same time being in the business of managing all other goings on in the universe...in *all* the universes? If it was the leadership and not God that changed the rules, how did that leadership justify breaking with God's word given directly to their predecessors ages ago? If head coverings were so important thousands of years ago, why not now? Did God change its mind? I wrestled with these questions the way a faithful child wrestles with trying to understand how Santa Claus packs a single sleigh with gifts for all the children of the world and delivers them around the globe in just one night by coming down the chimney.

While I perhaps am sharing too much of the mental calisthenics I went through, I do so because they led me to yet another firm conclusion. To me, the inconsistencies in conviction and regular changes in what God supposedly wants, clearly are more compatible with the imperfect human condition than that of the God I was beginning to envision. I mean, if God was so interested in head coverings and had made his will known to the earthly powers-that-be, why didn't it step up and issue some important changes to the Catholic Church, condemning the well-known generations of wrongdoing within the organization? Are we really to believe that God weighed in on head coverings but took a pass on the harm priests were committing on innocents? To me, that was proof enough that humans were running the "rules and regulations" department, not God.

And while I dive down the rabbit hole, I cannot ignore my thoughts on scripture. My understanding is that scripture represents what a relatively small group of men wrote down millenium ago, and that, over time, these sacred truths have been translated from various ancient languages into modern languages, and then further into today's languages. While such translations would have been necessary, it is difficult for me to believe they would have been completed accurately and without bias. These conversions were all completed by humans, some with personal or tribal agendas in mind, so it seems likely the end product would be impacted, perhaps heavily. Given that I have a low threshold for blind faith of any sort, I determined I could not place much confidence in the scripture component of the "three faiths" I define here, even as I can easily accept that there are many positive, worthwhile messages and life lessons to be found in those words.

Scripture is heavily linked to the "rules and regulations" part of faith, so how are we supposed to live our day-to-day lives in a religion that is found there? As discussed above, since scripture was likely affected by the humans who committed the ideas to print, then that means that rules and regs were also at risk of being influenced. So, here again, I was faced with another major leap of faith worthy of careful consideration. Did these people get the rules and regulations right? Of course, they would have had cultural and personal biases, and I certainly accept that as part of the human condition, but, to me, the extent to which God accepts human bias seems important. If the Church got it right so long ago, and there was great confidence at that time that the rules and regulations came directly from the word of God, then how can the rules of how we should live our lives keep changing over time, seemingly to be more in step with the here and now? Again, this felt too human for me. As a salesman by trade, I could not help but see these changes as a form of "marketing flexibility", possibly designed to keep bodies in the seats.

So, while I can't fully buy into these first two "faiths" (scripture and rules/regulations), I still had to come to terms with the most important and most difficult of the faiths to swallow, namely, whether or not there is a higher power at all. In my opinion, after my study, I concluded that a belief in God is the only one of these "faiths" that truly matters. The other two faiths have been tucked conveniently and perhaps strategically into an all-or-nothing construct that seems to suggest that if I want God in my life, then I must take the entire package. I understand the practical necessity of this "bundling," because without it, there would be nothing left but a pure, absolute faith in God, and there would be no need for organized religions as we understand them today.

The idea of being forced to accept the cable-like "bundle of services" frustrates me academically, because I have struggled a great deal simply to get to a place where I believe there *is* a higher power. While I am certain that reaching this point of true belief has improved my life greatly, I still feel excluded from mainstream belief systems because I do not subscribe to the full bundle. So be it. My belief in God is what matters most to me, and as a doubting Thomas, this was the most challenging of the three faiths to accept. Having travelled a long and windy road to get here, I don't see the need to believe in these other "faiths" I have described. This feels right for my needs.

I do not apply any judgment to those that consider these "three faiths" as an important package deal under the umbrella of their own religion. To each their own. If a person can find structure, community, peace, and faith through the world's modern religious structures, then I respect that and genuinely see its importance to the world.

To simplify my own thinking on what I believe is the important difference between God and religion, I crafted an analogy to help keep my head right. It is as follows: Religion is to God what Google is to the internet. Google, my favorite search engine, is a portal to get to where I really want to go, which is to gain access to the massive, virtually infinite library of information on the internet. Organized religion, like Google, is a portal, but it is a portal to God. Both Google and "religion" want as much attention and loyalty as possible, but both are tools, and not the final destination.

When we use a portal to the internet, it dresses up its face by using artificial intelligence (AI) to run advertisements and media pieces it knows you might find interesting. This is done to keep us coming back and hopefully buying things that we see there. Religion does similar things to dress itself up, from coffee and donut hour, to great activities for the kids, to upgraded changes in the processes and procedures; all are designed to retain parishioners and enhance community.

My point in comparing Google with organized religion is not to make light of organized religion in any way. I simply do not believe that if I want God in my life, that I have to access it through a portal (religion) to get to it. The truth is that religion, with its rules and regulations and ancient scripture, has nothing to do with knowing God for me. While I cannot get to the internet without some type of portal, I see no such limiting restrictions in how I gain access to and believe in my God. When I process my faith in this way, I arrive at a place that is comfortable and acceptable. Once I confidently concluded that I did not need to draw a hard connection between what modern culture thinks of as "religion" and God, I had license to explore *my* higher power without any thought limitations, and that has made all the difference for me.

With my academic-like study sorting my thoughts, what I have yet to explain is how a small-town guy like me came to accept that a higher power exists and why that is important. That takes me back to the stories found in these pages, the one in which I was living a life centered around surviving the environment I was born into, building a business, providing for my family, and managing existing crises while attempting to avoid future crises. All of that represented more than a full-time job, but I embraced it willingly. I knew that if I wanted to achieve extraordinary results, I would have to put in extraordinary effort of the practical type. I have no regrets about how I spent my time, and, in fact, I have done just about everything that I ever set out to do.

Still, living my life in this manner created a self-imposed blindness to worthwhile topics like God. Many would say the opportunity to explore a higher power is always an option, regardless of how "busy" I might have been, and they would be right of course. However, I would not have understood that notion back then. My only priorities at the time focused on realizing my vision for a better life for my family and celebrating the wins that slowly emerged out of that singular focus. I spent my life doing practical, terrestrial tasks that were built around *my* priorities, and I could not allow or didn't have the time to believe God had anything to do with me gaining these wins.

However, life has a way of bringing truth to the surface—even for someone as thick-headed as me. I would never have guessed that receiving a Stage IV cancer diagnosis, one with no effective conventional treatment, would be the *gift* that would change my life for the better and provide an opportunity to see just how God had been working in my life all along.

Prior to my diagnosis, I had finally become comfortable with concluding that God must exist. It was the only answer I had for the wonder that can be found in everything in all places. While not exactly a provable thesis, my conclusion was based on all that I had read and seen and my life experience. But it was the moments I found in deep meditation that led me to complete faith that God was with me then as it had been through all the days of my life. This deep faith leaves me comfortable with the idea that I might not physically heal. However, given that the space that opened because of my practice has shown me what a beautiful present life can be right now, I believe that another great gift has been granted to me.

I now appreciate this force that wants nothing from me but gives everything. I now know what it means to have faith in that which I cannot prove. Years ago, intellectual curiosity paved the way to a baseline education on God and religion. Cancer created the reason to find healing in my mind and body. Meditation was the tool that led me to complete faith in God. It's really that simple.

God wanted me to have this gift. I fought unconditional faith, and it took getting a disease to finally see just how blessed I am and to willingly accept God's constant presence in my life. Did I "find religion" as the saying goes? No. Instead, what was revealed to me was something much better, an opportunity to explore how deeply my higher power has touched my life and how God is actively at work all around me.

Throughout these pages, I have shared moments that I consider personal proof of *my* God. While I have reached the conclusion that God's existence is undeniable, it does not matter to me for readers to believe. Such is the beauty of a higher power—we can all discover our own uninhibited path toward God or none at all.

Our home on Wilkens Avenue, where it all started.

Letters to Mom and Dad

I often wondered what I would say to my parents today if I had the opportunity. I had many thoughts, but I thought these short letters summed them up well.

Dear Dad,
I know your parents made your life a living hell and that much of the negative that carried forward to me was almost impossible to prevent. You deserved so much better than you got in your young, hard life. I have complained, but I know I got much better than you ever did. I started to forgive you a long time ago for the pain you caused. Fortunately, this created some space and allowed me to genuinely enjoy some moments with you in the few years before you passed. Because of that, I was able to enjoy your dry sense of humor and our intellectual banter without our dark history inhibiting my ability to appreciate the moments. I agree with the experts: forgiveness is a gift to the giver, more so than to the receiver.
Thank you for all of the things you showed me: fixing cars, camping, Assateague Island and its wild ponies, shooting stars, pomegranates, Bing cherries, the joy of a passing freight train, and Willie Nelson's "Blue Eyes Crying in the Rain." Beyond the tangible, you showed me that a person born to nothing and parents with no interest in raising children could somehow

find a way to build a life. Thank you for bringing Sharon into our lives, a well-kept, wonderful secret I only came to know after you passed.

Despite the history, I wonder if more time would have opened more doors for us. It would have given forgiveness more time to marinate, and this could have led to a stronger father-son bond, a dream I held for most of my life. Maybe you would have had a chance to see the person I have become and how I adore and find deep purpose in being a father and provider to my family. Maybe I would have let you in more and you would have had a fairer opportunity to see me as who I really am, rather than what you thought I was. Maybe we'd laugh, knowing there was a better chance of us spontaneously sprouting a pair of wings than digging through and solving the muck of our past (you would have appreciated the levity).

But, seriously, Dad, I am sorry that so much pent-up anger and anxiety played a role in us not having much of a relationship. I'm not sure I could have changed anything, but I know that if I had the maturity and perspective back then that I have now, I would have tried harder, been more open-minded and more compassionate. Through it all, I loved you. I hope that you knew that.

Danny

Dear Mom,

I know your dreams for your life did not go as you planned. I know you loved Dad and I think he loved you at some point, but what I witnessed was his control and manipulation of you for all the days you were connected to him, including long after the divorce. He wanted out and easily went about living his life without us. But with so much of his ridicule and meddling in your life, despite working so hard, you could never truly find independence and freedom. Still a mystery to this day, you withstood his meddling and unwillingness to grant you peace with grace and patience. My guess is you mistakenly thought his involvement, albeit mostly condescending and dangerous, was at least some broken form of companionship. Maybe you kept him in your life hoping for his return, and so you accepted his behavior in the hope you might experience the life he promised you.

You were quiet and never articulated your feelings. I didn't miss what I never experienced, but I still wish I had gotten to know you better. When I was older, your attachment to Dad saddened me, because I knew he would never allow you to have your own life, and I know you always wanted and deserved a much better life for yourself. Your commitment to him also prevented you from protecting us from his abuse. This is terribly sad and dysfunctional, but perhaps you accepted it because fighting him might have meant risking the loss of him forever.

I forgive you for the pain you caused. Unfortunately, in the last years of your life, you were overcome with sickness. I could have (I should have) used that time better to work toward a deeper relationship, but I was focused on caregiving and did not give enough time to practicing forgiveness and real-time compassion. Regrettably, I had so much anger and resentment, I could not get to a place where that was possible. I had much to learn about the value of forgiveness, and I suspect that would have been immensely helpful to us.

The day you died was the most gut-wrenching day of my life. Dying alone in your bathroom and then carried out like a sack of trash is not how any soul should go. I was both infuriated and devastated when the workers left you on the gurney out in the street while they smoked. Directly addressing their insensitivity was the last thing I would ever do for you, which is sad. Watching you drive away knowing you were zipped up in a black plastic bag inside the county coroner van left me in sadness and a dark emptiness.

The night before you passed, we spontaneously decided to watch *Six Days, Seven Nights*, a not-great movie with Harrison Ford and Anne Heche as the leads. We laughed and made fun of the movie, and I was so happy we could do something normal together and be uncharacteristically silly. I can't remember the last time we had seen a movie together or if we ever had as adults. Feeling comfortable with the moment, in an unusual move, I tucked you in and left for the night. I could never have guessed this would be the night you would leave this world. I feel so guilty I wasn't there and know I could have saved you. Deciding to leave was the biggest regret of my life. I wonder if you knew all along how close you were and if that is why you were OK with me leaving you that night. Maybe it was because you never wanted anyone to fuss over you or were simply ready to go. Whatever the case, I wish I could have said goodbye. There was so much to say.

I am grateful for the rare times you showed affection to me, not in words but in the simple brushing aside of my bangs or a kind glance when I was low. I loved and still miss the jelly ring cookies and cranberry walnut bread you made every year at Christmas. I remember clearly in third grade how we made a log cabin diorama out of corrugated cardboard together. You did the bulk of the work, and the ideas were all yours, but doing this showed me that you loved me. The work was far beyond the skills of an eight-year-old, but I was proud as hell to have the best-looking project in the class. I don't remember how it was graded, or if Mrs. Huff ever found issue with your obvious assistance, but there is no way she didn't notice. It was a rare time that all the other kids were envious of me, which was a great feeling. I will also never forget how you aggressively defended me to the juvenile judge when I was arrested for stealing, and how thankful I was that you never told Dad.

I am sorry I was so insensitive when you were in the throes of alcoholism, a sickness I now know could in no way be overcome with my neat-sounding motivational quips and frustrated pushes for you to get help. I did the best I could to help save you, but, looking back, I know my issues with our history did not foster a safe, healing space for you. Showing patience, love, and understanding would have been so much more useful than working hard to solve your problem. I learned this too late.

I wish we could have had more time together. Looking through the lens I look through today, I know I could have found ways to build a richer bond. You were smart, driven, and funny at times, and I liked those parts about you. If I would have forgiven you sooner and been more compassionate, I would have been a much better son to you. I regret missing that opportunity immensely. We both deserved that.

Thank you for the slow dance in the living room to Anne Murray's song, "Could I Have This Dance". I loved hearing you sing along and hold me close. It felt so safe and connected. I will always miss and love you. I hope that you knew that.

Danny

As a successful entrepreneur, loving husband, father of five, and lifelong learner, Daniel Wellington combines practical wisdom with spiritual insight. His journey has been marked by resilience in the face of adversity, a deep appreciation for the unseen and previously underappreciated guidance of a higher power, and a commitment to living life with joy and purpose. Inspired by music, the American Dream, love of family, and an unwillingness to live as a victim, he hopes that the reader will find relatability, useful takeaways and community. Through *Crutchless*, Daniel shares his journey of mindfulness, gratitude, and spiritual awakening, inviting readers to embrace the gifts surrounding them, choose happiness deliberately, and live fully in every moment, no matter the obstacles.

This is the story of Daniel's life, from the worst to the best, and all the gifts that came with it. For inquiries or comments, email Daniel at djwellingtoncrutchless@gmail.com.

www.ingramcontent.com/pod-product-compliance
Lightning Source LLC
Chambersburg PA
CBHW021914180426
43198CB00035B/467